Women and Ageing

This edited collection considers the ways older women's life narratives redefine culturally imposed conceptions of what it means to grow older. Drawing on research from age studies as well as social and cultural gerontology, the contributors explore the subjective accounts and diverse voices of older women. In doing so, they examine the tensions between older women's social identities versus their individual narratives.

In their chapters, the contributors acknowledge, explore and contextualise women's experiences of growing older, thus counterbalancing the often one-sided, negative representations of ageing perpetuated by dominant cultural discourse. They focus on diverse forms of life writing including memoirs and (auto)biography, digital and visual forms of life narrative as well as autoethnographic accounts. As the chapters in this collection demonstrate, life writing by and about older women often necessitates opening out literary forms and modes of critique, searching for narrative and performative strategies, and creating spaces in which to inscribe subjective experiences. Relationships, intergenerational connections, and visual and material cues are often integral to these analyses, which assert the richness of older women's life narratives.

The chapters in this book were originally published as a special issue of *Life Writing*.

Margaret O'Neill researches in twentieth-century and contemporary Irish literature, culture and society. She is a postdoctoral researcher at the Irish Centre for Social Gerontology and the Huston School of Film and Digital Media, National University of Ireland, Galway. With Michaela Schrage-Früh she is co-founder of the Women and Ageing Research Network.

Michaela Schrage-Früh is a Lecturer in German at the National University of Ireland, Galway. She has published widely on Irish, British and German poetry and fiction, and is the author of two monographs. With Margaret O'Neill she is co-founder of the Women and Ageing Research Network.

Women and Ageing

Private Meaning, Social Lives

Edited by
Margaret O'Neill and Michaela Schrage-Früh

LONDON AND NEW YORK

First published 2021
by Routledge
2 Park Square, Milton Park, Abingdon, Oxon, OX14 4RN

and by Routledge
52 Vanderbilt Avenue, New York, NY 10017

Routledge is an imprint of the Taylor & Francis Group, an informa business

British Library Cataloguing-in-Publication Data
A catalogue record for this book is available from the British Library

ISBN13: 9780367562175

Typeset in Minion Pro
by codeMantra

Publisher's Note
The publisher accepts responsibility for any inconsistencies that may have arisen during the conversion of this book from journal articles to book chapters, namely the inclusion of journal terminology.

Disclaimer
Every effort has been made to contact copyright holders for their permission to reprint material in this book. The publishers would be grateful to hear from any copyright holder who is not here acknowledged and will undertake to rectify any errors or omissions in future editions of this book.

Contents

Citation Information

The chapters in this book were originally published in *Life Writing*, volume 16, issue 1 (December 2018). When citing this material, please use the original page numbering for each article, as follows:

Introduction
Women and Ageing: Private Meaning, Social Lives
Margaret O'Neill and Michaela Schrage-Früh
Life Writing, volume 16, issue 1 (December 2018) pp. 1–8

Chapter 1
Contemplation as Resistance to Ageism, and its Historical Context: Mexican Writers Carmen Boullosa, Guadalupe Nettel, and María Rivera
Emily Hind
Life Writing, volume 16, issue 1 (December 2018) pp. 11–24

Chapter 2
Ageing, Creativity, and Memory: The Evolution of Erica Jong's Literary Career
Ieva Stončikaitė
Life Writing, volume 16, issue 1 (December 2018) pp. 25–36

Chapter 3
From Girl to Grotesque: Exploring the Intersection of Ageing, Illness, and Agency in Auto/biographical Narratives About Seventies Icon Farrah Fawcett
Lucinda Rasmussen
Life Writing, volume 16, issue 1 (December 2018) pp. 37–50

Chapter 4
"A View from Old Age": Women's Lives as Narrated Through Objects
Leonie Hannan, Gemma Carney, Paula Devine and Gemma Hodge
Life Writing, volume 16, issue 1 (December 2018) pp. 51–67

Chapter 5
Reading Film with Age Through Collaborative Autoethnography: Old Age and Care, Encounters with Amour *(Haneke, 2012),* Chronic *(Franco, 2015) and* A Woman's Tale *(Cox, 1991)*
Rita Ferris-Taylor, Jane Grant, Hannah Grist, Ros Jennings, Rina Rosselson and Sylvia Wiseman
Life Writing, volume 16, issue 1 (December 2018) pp. 69–95

Chapter 6

Grace and Grit: The Politics, Poetics and Performance of Ageing as a Woman
Ann Webster-Wright
Life Writing, volume 16, issue 1 (December 2018) pp. 97–111

Chapter 7

Writing Life and Death Online: "I'm Not Sure How Many More Days I'll Have on the Computer"
Cathy Fowley
Life Writing, volume 16, issue 1 (December 2018) pp. 115–126

Chapter 8

Now that I'm Old: Life Writing, Women and Ageing
Elisabeth Hanscombe
Life Writing, volume 16, issue 1 (December 2018) pp. 127–138

Contributors

Gemma Carney is a social gerontologist and lecturer in Social Policy at Queen's University Belfast, UK. She is a member of the editorial board of Ageing & Society and a member of the Executive Committee of the British Society of Gerontology.

Paula Devine is coordinator of the ARK Ageing programme and Director of ARK at Queen's University Belfast, UK. She is also a member of the Executive Committee of the British Society of Gerontology.

Rita Ferris-Taylor has an MSc in Human Communication and a keen interest in all forms of communication, spoken, signed, and film. She is semi-retired and teaches massage and yoga to differently abled people and is an active member of the University of the Third Age in Brent.

Cathy Fowley holds a PhD in internet research. She is co-founder and director of Silver Thread Ltd., a social innovation enterprise whose mission is to engage older people in writing stories from their lives, in communities and nursing homes, and to publish these stories.

Jane Grant was born in New York and came to London in 1965 to study film and stayed. She was an ambulance driver/attendant before qualifying as a midwife. She worked as a lecturer and researcher but liked being with women in labour best.

Hannah Grist is co-Director of the Centre for Women, Ageing and Media (WAM), and works at the University of Bristol, UK. Her research interests lie in ageing studies, media and cultural studies, and qualitative methodologies.

Leonie Hannan is a social and cultural historian of early modern England and Ireland. She is a Research Fellow at Queen's University, Belfast, UK, in the School of History, Anthropology, Philosophy and Politics.

Elisabeth Hanscombe is a psychologist and writer who completed her doctorate in 2011 on the topic "Life writing and the desire for revenge." She has published a number of short stories, book chapters, and essays in the areas of autobiography, psychoanalysis, testimony, trauma and creative nonfiction in psychotherapy journals and magazines throughout Australia and in the United States.

Emily Hind is an associate professor with the University of Florida, where she received a University of Florida Term Professorship for distinguished record of research and scholarship, 2016–2019.

Gemma Hodge is an artist and educator based in Waterford, Ireland. She has worked as a community artist for several years in London and has exhibited widely in the UK, Ireland, Australia and Cyprus.

Ros Jennings is Director of the Centre for Women, Ageing and Media (WAM), and Professor of Ageing, Culture and Media at the University of Gloucestershire, UK.

Margaret O'Neill researches in twentieth-century and contemporary Irish literature, culture and society. She is a postdoctoral researcher at the Irish Centre for Social Gerontology and the Huston School of Film and Digital Media, National University of Ireland, Galway.

Lucinda Rasmussen is a lecturer with the Department of English and Film Studies at the University of Alberta. Her research focuses on the representation and dissemination of narratives by and about women in literature and mass media.

Rina Rosselson was born in 1935 and acquired a passion for cinema in her teens. After obtaining an MA in Film and Televisions Studies at the age of 63, she has since facilitated the Older Women in Film Group of the University of the Third Age in Brent and presented films about old people through the Ealing Oldies Network.

Michaela Schrage-Früh is a Lecturer in German at the National University of Ireland, Galway. She has published widely on Irish, British and German poetry and fiction, and is the author of two monographs.

Ieva Stončikaitė has co-taught as assistant lecturer at the Department of English and Linguistics at the University of Lleida, and is a member of the research group Grup Dedal-Lit.

Ann Webster-Wright has an academic background in health and education. In semi-retirement, she is an honorary research fellow at Griffith University and the University of Queensland, Australia.

Sylvia Wiseman was born in 1932 and holds a BA Hons, a Diploma in Social Work, and a Masters in the Sociology of Law. After working as a medical social worker and founding Brent Carers Centre, Sylvia retired in 2000 and travelled with her husband. After her husband passed away in 2007, Sylvia joined the University of the Third Age in Brent, chaired the committee for five years and remains an active member.

Women and Ageing: Private Meaning, Social Lives*

Margaret O'Neill and Michaela Schrage-Früh

As Penelope Lively puts it in her memoir *Ammonites and Leaping Fish: A Life in Time*: 'One of the few advantages of age is that you can report on it with a certain authority; you are a native now, and know what goes on here' (2013, 3). Lively is part of a growing number of women writers and artists who are not only productive in their later years but who provide valuable accounts—both fictional and autobiographical—of their own ageing. They follow in the footsteps of writers such as Simone de Beauvoir (1970), Susan Sontag (1972), Germaine Greer (1992), Betty Friedan (1993), Lynne Segal (2013) and Ashton Applewhite (2016), motivated to write about their ageing by their need to bridge the gap between the lived experiences of growing older and the dominant cultural narrative of 'old age' as a negative thing to be avoided and disguised.[1] This negotiation is especially pertinent with regard to women, who, to this day, face 'a double standard of ageing' (Sontag 1972, 31) and for whom 'aging casts its shadow earlier than for men' (Woodward 1999, xiii). In view of the limited positive role models for ageing women, the desire to communicate one's own authoritative report from the unknown territory of old age is shared by older women from all walks of life and there is an increasing need to have their diverse voices heard and acknowledged. Therefore, the focus of this special issue is on the ways older women's life narrative redefines culturally imposed conceptions of what it means to get older. Drawing on research from cultural gerontology and critical age studies, the authors acknowledge, explore and contextualise women's experiences of getting older, thus counterbalancing the mainly one-sided, negative representations of ageing as perpetuated by dominant cultural discourse. In doing so, they focus on diverse forms of life writing including memoirs and (auto)biography, digital and visual forms of life narrative as well as autoethnographic accounts.

With the focus on older women's life writing in this issue we endeavour to address an appeal by Germaine Greer to generate spaces wherein a woman 'could give an account of her own strategy for coping with old age' (2017, 325). Attending to the rich catalogue of women who are active in writing about their own and other women's older age in memoir and fiction, Greer, in her afterword to our collection *Ageing Women in Literature and Visual Culture: Reflections, Refractions, Reimaginings*, notes that the volume considers 'ageing women as depicted in literature and visual culture' but not 'older women who are active in literature and visual culture'. As she states,

> Yet I, who am seventy-eight, have been invited to write an afterword to the volume. In a true spirit of aged cantankerousness, then, I propose to remind readers that aged women themselves have been explicit and eloquent in memoir and in fiction about their condition. In far too many cases, though their works have been successful in their time, they are now forgotten (2017, 323).

The collection Greer refers to engages with symbolic aspects of women and ageing in literature and visual culture, and the power these constructions exert over public and private conceptions of older age. It stems from a project which began as an interdisciplinary conference on

*We have chosen to spell 'ageing' with an 'e' in this issue but 'aging' is equally acceptable and we have retained this spelling where used in the criticism and references.

'Women and Ageing: New Cultural and Critical Perspectives', organised by us and Cathy McGlynn at the University of Limerick, Ireland, in 2015.[2] Following Greer's call, this special issue of *Life Writing* shifts the focus from cultural representations to the subjective experiences and diverse voices of older women, exploring the tensions between their private meaning versus their social lives.

Margaret M. Gullette (1997) has shown that the dominant cultural narrative about ageing tends to be a one-sided, linear 'decline narrative', which associates older age mainly with the loss of cognitive and physical abilities. This master narrative of decline has been particularly debilitating for women, whose value in western consumer societies is often conflated with their youthful appearance so that their '[s]igns of age are read as failure' (Twigg 2004, 61). Older women's bodies are thus rendered both 'invisible and hypervisible' (Woodward 1999, xvi), either overlooked or reduced to their visible signs of ageing. In contrast, life writing provides older women with the opportunity to counterweight such negative associations and bring their own voices to bear on the cultural narrative of ageing, thus rendering this narrative more complex, subjective and diverse. A realisation central to this type of cultural and personal work is that identity formation and personal growth continue well into deep old age. In this regard, Gullette's concept of 'critical age autobiography' (1997, 220) insists that it is possible to challenge dominant cultural narratives and stereotypes about ageing by countering and complementing them with our own individual stories. This concept is further explored by Ruth E. Ray, who notes that '[a] mark of individual growth is the deliberateness with which one writes about one's self, moving beyond positions in which one has been "storied" by others to positions in which one reflects, reconsiders, modifies, rewrites, and "restories" oneself' (2000, 28). In restorying themselves, older women are empowered to resist 'the cultural forces that attempt to story our lives, especially in terms of age, throughout the life course' (2000, 30).

The first three articles collected in this special issue focus on how such cultural forces have impacted on and have been resisted by literary writers and celebrities in diverse cultural contexts. While Emily Hind looks at the ways in which Mexican women writers and artists have succumbed to or resisted ageism in the course of their careers, Ieva Stončikaitė's article retraces and analyses the trajectory of one iconic North American writer, Erica Jong, whose literary explorations of gender and age stereotypes have inspired generations of readers. Lucinda Rasmussen's article juxtaposes this journey of artistic development with the toll that is taken on the female celebrity who seeks to remain visible in public life as she ages. Specifically, this article explores intersections of ageing, illness and agency in auto/biographical narratives about seventies icon Farrah Fawcett. All three articles remain attuned to the personal and artistic exaction that derives from inscribing the self within a social order that celebrates youthful femininity and frustrates feminist art, while they emphasise the cultural power of restorying one's own life.

The first article included here, "Contemplation as Resistance to Ageism, and Its Historical Context: Mexican Writers Carmen Boullosa, Guadalupe Nettel, and María Rivera" by Emily Hind, historicises issues of women, ageing and life writing. Her initial question is, 'What was it like to be a "death's head" in a time when nearly no one identified the problem as such?' Hind refers here to Gullette's claim that ageing is culturally associated with narratives of decline to the degree that ageing women become 'deaths'-heads' (Gullette 2017, 14). In exploring this question, Hind contextualises autobiographical essays by Mexican writers Carmen Boullosa, Guadalupe Nettel and María Rivera, reading their narratives alongside a selection of earlier Mexican women artists who also faced issues of ageing, namely Nellie Campobello (1900), Frida Kahlo (1907), Griselda Álvarez (1913), Elena Garro (1916), Clementina Díaz y de Ovando (1916), and Guadalupe Amor (1918). Consulting the archives on the Centro

Mexicano de Escritores (Mexican Center for Writers, 1951–2006), Hind illuminates the ageism exerted on such women, and their methods of counteracting ageist pressures. For example, she attends to 'creative age mathematics' as a 'habit among celebrities from the last century', and dying one's hair, a strategy employed by Clementina Díaz y de Ovando, as practices adopted by women to veil their age in the public eye. And yet, such attempts to pass as younger effectively undermine a breadth of accomplishments only achieved with age. Thus, Hind considers how, ultimately, 'lying downward about age leads to feminism devoid of experienced feminists'. In the works of recent writers, she finds methods which sidestep this conundrum, as Nettel, Boullosa and Rivera elude the embedded narrative structures of age as decline, eschewing linear stories, incorporating sexuality-related moments, and emphasising process rather than pathology. Rivera, for example, 'suggests that ageism can be overcome in part by exiting the narrative arc of autopathology in favor of release in meditation'. Therefore, Hind points to the critical importance of recognising historical and cultural contexts while also searching for new ways of articulating the self, with mindful contemplation of the present moment arising as one such outlet.

Anne Wyatt-Brown asserts that '[o]nly by combining research with novels and memoirs can we begin to comprehend the varieties of ageing experience in our time' (2010, 57). Ieva Stončikaitė's article "Ageing, Creativity, and Memory: The Evolution of Erica Jong's Literary Career" takes its cue from this insight as she retraces the celebrated writer's trajectory from her bestselling novel *Fear of Flying* (1973), written when the author was in her early thirties, to novels and autobiographical writings published in her midlife and later years. In doing so, Stončikaitė's study tackles the prevailing myth that conflates artistic creativity with youth. As her contribution shows, looking at a fictional writer's work in conjunction with their autobiographical writings can yield fruitful insights into an author's creative processes in older age, in particular with regard to the narrative construction of a mature sense of self. This is especially pertinent with regard to Jong, who has acknowledged her 'fear of writing' and her reticence in asserting a female point of view in her early writings owing to culturally ingrained perceptions of women's writings and experiences as somehow lesser than men's. Jong has commented on her sense of liberation as an older writer who, confident in her own voice, no longer seeks approval and affirmation, in that sense becoming 'fearless'. This fearlessness is perhaps also reflected in her blurring of genre boundaries, notably life writing and fiction, thus defying cultural and readerly expectations. As Stončikaitė's article demonstrates, the writer's process of growth, facilitated precisely by Jong's continual reflections on her writing practice and her place in society as a woman writer past and present, effectively challenges the pervasive narrative of ageing as decline, thus turning her into a role model for younger writers in particular. As such, Jong is part of a number of iconic second-wave feminists such as Greer and Segal, who embarked on the process of exploring their older age, thereby helping to move the theme of ageing from the margins to the centre of feminist discourse.

Yet, as Lucinda Rasmussen's article reveals, biographical work on seventies icon Farrah Fawcett is situated within a reactionary discourse precisely undermining second-wave feminism. A postfeminist culture perpetuates conservative gender norms, including ageism, by naturalising and amplifying control of women. This culture is exemplified in the beauty industry, wherein practices of commodification centring on the body package and sell idealised, youthful femininity as a form of power. Exploring the effects of such conflations of youth and success, age and illness, Rasmussen refers to Sally Chivers, who writes that within celebrity culture, 'old age is akin to disability in the ways that they are socially constructed [...] as bodily, threatening, and signalling failure' (2011, 23). In this context, Rasmussen examines a trajectory which takes place across auto/biographical narratives by and about Fawcett, demonstrating how Fawcett's celebrity persona, constructed as perpetually young and beautiful, serves as an impediment in her later years, drawing indictments of the 'grotesque' as she seeks to maintain it. Turning to an illness narrative entitled *Farrah's Story* (2009), a documentary depicting Fawcett's experiences with terminal cancer, Rasmussen opposes critical tendencies to interpret Fawcett as a victim of contemporary celebrity culture. This narrative, Rasmussen argues, with reference to Gullette, 'is inevitably yoked to a set of naturalized ageist rhetorical and visual practices'. Countering this trend, Rasmussen instead locates the strategic self-representation that provides for Fawcett to question celebrity culture, an invasive media and their brutal treatment of older women. In Rasmussen's reading, *Farrah's Story* represents a deliberate and powerful life narrative.

Three of the articles in this collection adopt autoethnography wherein, using self-reflection and qualitative research, the researchers' personal narratives are expressed through the embodied experience of performance (Anne Webster-Wright), meaning-making through objects (Hannan et al.) and reflecting on films (Ferris-Taylor et al.) to explore the subjectivities of older women and in connection critique wider social and cultural representations. Integral to this approach is the idea of 'thinking with age', which as Rita Ferris-Taylor, Jane Grant, Hannah Grist, Ros Jennings, Rina Rosselson and Sylvia Wiseman set out in their article on old age and care encounters in film, provides for exploring and speaking back to cultural scripts by way of harnessing a repository of life course experiences. Thus, the articles collected here seek to overcome the distance between the researchers and the subjects of research, so that older women exploring personal experience, both resembling and diverging from cultural representations, produce new critical evaluations. The experimentation and agency represented in these articles opens out new and exciting possibilities for the stories and experiences of older women to contribute to our understanding of women and ageing, private meaning and social lives, by intervening in the silences and taboos which often surround issues of old age.

Anne Webster-Wright's article 'Grace and Grit: The Politics, Poetics and Performance of Ageing as a Woman' harnesses an autoethnographic approach to explore what the author calls 'the poetics and potential of ageing' and to find an answer to the basic question: 'How am I to live my life as an older woman?' Eschewing the bio-medical perspective that tends to foreground decline, Webster-Wright draws together insights from feminist and philosophical works, notably Simone de Beauvoir and Paul Ricoeur, recent research in cultural gerontology, as well as her own experiences of 'restorying' her life upon turning sixty. As Webster-Wright argues, in view of the demographic shift towards an ageing population in most Western societies, the dominant decline narrative needs to be replaced with alternative visions of ageing that allow for creative agency and growth. Her argument that the demographic group of 'Baby Boomer' women currently in their sixties are in the process of transforming 'the face of ageing' just as they once altered 'the makeup of the workplace', is illustrated by her own experiences of tapping unknown creative resources when joining a dance group for older women. As she writes, 'my newly found creative agency [...] has taken the philosophical idea of an embodied storied self to a new visible form. I've moved from theories and frameworks to action and protest, and in doing so, I've come alive again'. Webster-Wright's vivid description of performing with the WaW Dance group also gestures towards performative aspects of ageing in general, suggesting how the ways older women 'perform' their age are often influenced by negative cultural stereotypes, which in turn can be challenged by reinventing and 'restorying' their lives.

Similarly, in their article '"A View from Old Age": Women's Lives as Narrated Through Objects', Leonie Hannan, Gemma Carney, Paula Devine and Gemma Hodge point to the issue that though the ageing population are often in the news, reports tend to oscillate between care home horror stories and neoliberal dismissal of older people as a financial burden on the young. This group are furthermore polarised in the popular imaginary into categories of wise old age or fragility and decline. The result of such one-dimensional reasoning and occlusion is that those with experience of living a long life are not represented in public forums about them and their needs. In light of this misrepresentation, the authors developed a collaborative cross-disciplinary project inspired by Penelope Lively's memoir *Ammonites and Leaping Fish: A Life in Time*, in which Lively proposed that 'people's possessions speak of them' (2013, 199). Accordingly, in their project, the researchers asked a cohort of Northern Irish men and women over sixty to choose six objects in their possession that said 'something of who I am'. The resulting article included here uses interview data from three women over sixty to analyse their narration of their own biographies. The chosen objects shed light on the complex and contradictory experiences of women's ageing and provide insights into the ways in which an individual's personal history mirrors the historical and social changes they have lived through. One aspect which comes to the fore through objects as a means of communication is the significance of relationships. 'In tracing their life histories', the authors note, 'relationships with others formed a central focus—both as a means of creating narrative structure and as a way of making sense of the self'. Fostering a close collaboration between researchers, practitioners and participants, this project culminated in the sharing of objects, quotations and interpretations in a public exhibition entitled 'Something of Who I Am'.

One aspect recently highlighted by cultural gerontologists and critical age scholars is the importance of care work in later life. This concerns members of the so-called 'fourth age' in need of care as well as the younger generation, often women, who either work as professional carers or tend to their frail family members. In recent years a number of films have explored the emotional, physical and psychological implications attached to a situation dreaded by most: being old, frail and dependent on care. Films such as *Amour* (Haneke 2012), *Chronic* (Franco 2015) and *A Woman's Tale* (Cox 1991) narrate much-needed, partly controversial stories about end-of-life care from the perspectives of both the elderly and their carers. Aiming to read these three films through an autoethnographic lens, two researchers, Hannah Grist and Ros Jennings, from the Centre of Women, Ageing and Media at the University of Gloucestershire, UK, teamed up with four women from diverse social, cultural and national backgrounds who were, at the time of writing, members of the Brent University of the Third Age Older Women in Film Group. Their co-authored article included here, 'Reading Film with Age through Collaborative Autoethnography: Old Age and Care, Encounters with *Amour* (Haneke, 2012), *Chronic* (Franco, 2015) and *A Woman's Tale* (Cox, 1991)' is the outcome of this exciting intergenerational collaboration. Their project as outlined in this article foregrounds the idea of 'thinking with age' and by doing so privileges the individual voices and perspectives of older women as they provide nuanced readings of the films, and by extension the themes of care and old age, inflected by their own experiences and life stories. In bringing together experiential and academic analyses, this innovative project not only provides a model of how older women's voices can be inscribed into the discourse of old age and care but also highlights the importance of intergenerational dialogue and collaboration as a catalyst for personal growth and cultural change.

As the articles in this collection demonstrate, the figure of the older woman is often veiled by the expectations of dominant discourse. Thus, the project of foregrounding women, ageing and life writing calls for stylistic experimentation and the reconsideration of generic hierarchies. G. Thomas Couser writes about how the rise of the terms 'life writing' and 'life narrative' might appear to imply a decline in the notion of genre, yet this usage 'reflects the vitality of life writing generally and the recognition of hitherto overlooked kinds of life writing (and new forms, like weblogs)' (2005, 142). This broadening of genre is particularly pertinent to providing for forms in which to inscribe subjective experiences of identity formation in later life, thereby evading traditional constructions of older age fixed in dominant modes of expression. Thus, the contributions in this collection by Elisabeth Hanscombe and Cathy Fowley respectively harness the reflective nature of the essay genre to chronicle the authors' experiences of growing older and finding a voice in the context of the bonds of family and friendship, as Hanscombe explores her relationship with her mother, and Fowley reflects on connections formed with women in an online community in the early days of the world wide web. Hanscombe, in 'Now That I'm Old: Life Writing, Women and Ageing', explores how her mother's reluctance to give voice to certain memories and her idealisation of the past in her memoir impacted on Hanscombe's own life writing, compelling her to searching self-reflection and the resistance of self-censorship or nostalgia. Fowley, in 'Writing Life and Death Online', documents how as a member of a community of older women formed through life writing in a shared forum, Women2women, she found mentors in ageing and a space to express emotions in writing, beyond everyday life and the immediate worlds of friends and family. A connection may be read between these essays in the sense of release informed by life writing, as an undertaking which is private yet also socially engaged, and which contributes to personal meaning-making as one grows older. For Hanscombe, the voice of her mother, as her internal critic, encourages her to follow her thoughts and frees her to release her memories as she ages. For Fowley, writing her life in connection with other women involved deep engagement with others' narratives of illness, dying and grief, as the group collectively aged. What ultimately comes to the fore in both Hanscombe's and Fowley's narratives is compassion through the negotiation of loss, and patterns of meaning in older age across space and generations.

In putting together this special issue, we are indebted to the School of Languages, Literatures and Cultures, Gender Arc, and the Moore Institute for Research in the Humanities and Social Studies for funding support and a Moore Institute Visiting Fellowship to facilitate our ongoing collaboration and enable us to host a research symposium on 'Women, Ageing and Life Narrative' at the National University of Ireland, Galway in May 2018. We would also like to thank Maureen Perkins for her enthusiasm and support for this special issue, and the peer reviewers for their invaluable guidance, indispensable especially in the context of such an interdisciplinary endeavour. Finally, we express our heartfelt thanks to the contributors for their scholarship, dedication and goodwill. As the articles in this collection demonstrate, life writing by and about older women often necessitates opening out literary forms and modes of critique, searching for narrative and performative strategies, and creating spaces in which to inscribe subjective experiences. Relationships, intergenerational connections, and visual and material cues are often integral to these analyses, which assert the richness of older women's life narratives that all too often risks being obscured by persisting cultural stereotypes. It is our hope that in bringing studies of women, ageing and life writing together, this special issue will contribute to the ongoing work of inserting personal, lived experiences into broader social discourses as part of effecting positive change.

Notes

1. de Beauvoir (1972); Sontag (1972). NZ.org: Periodicals, Books and Authors. http://www.unz.org/Pub/SaturdayRev-1972sep23-00029; Greer (1992); Friedan (1993); Segal (2013); Applewhite (2016).
2. This conference was funded under the Irish Research Council New Foundations scheme and held at the University of Limerick, Ireland, with support of Gender Arc, the Centre for German-Irish Studies and the Faculty of Arts, Humanities and Social Sciences. It has

given rise to the Women and Ageing Research Network and ongoing collaborations including *Ageing Women in Literature and Visual Culture: Reflections, Refractions, Reimaginings*, edited by Cathy McGlynn, Margaret O'Neill and Michaela Schrage-Früh (Cham: Palgrave Macmillan, 2017), this special issue of *Life Writing*, and a forthcoming special issue of the journal *Nordic Irish Studies* on 'Women and Ageing in Irish Literature and Film', edited by Margaret O'Neill and Michaela Schrage-Früh.

References

Applewhite, Ashton. 2016. *This Chair Rocks: A Manifesto Against Ageism*. New York: Networked Books.

Chivers, Sally. 2011. *The Silvering Screen*. Toronto: University of Toronto Press.

Couser, G. Thomas. 2005. "Genre Matters: Form, Force, and Filiation." *Life Writing* 2 (2): 139–156.

de Beauvoir, Simone. 1972. *The Coming of Age*. New York: G.P. Putnam's Sons. (first published in Paris under the title *La Vieillesse* in 1970).

Friedan, Betty. 1993. *The Fountain of Age*. New York, NY: Simon & Schuster.

Greer, Germaine. 1992. *The Change: Women, Ageing and the Menopause*. New York: Penguin.

Greer, Germaine. 2017. "Afterword." In *Ageing Women in Literature and Visual Culture: Reflections, Refractions, Reimaginings*, edited by Cathy McGlynn, Margaret O'Neill and Michaela Schrage-Früh, 321–325. Cham: Palgrave Macmillan.

Gullette, Margaret Morganroth. 1997. *Declining to Decline: Cultural Combat and the Politics of the Midlife*. Charlottesville, VA: University of Virginia Press.

Gullette, Margaret Morganroth. 2017. *Ending Ageism or How Not to Shoot Old People*. Camden, NJ: Rutgers University Press.

Lively, Penelope. 2013. *Ammonites and Leaping Fish: A Life in Time*. London: Fig Tree.

Ray, Ruth E. 2000. *Beyond Nostalgia: Aging and Life-Story Writing*. Charlottesville and London: University Press of Virginia.

Segal, Lynne. 2013. *Out of Time: The Pleasures and Perils of Aging* London: Verso.

Sontag, Susan. 1972. "The Double Standard of Aging." *The Saturday Review*, September 23, 1972. 31. *NZ.org: Periodicals, Books and Authors*. http://www.unz.org/Pub/SaturdayRev-1972sep23-00029

Twigg, Julia. 2004. "The Body, Gender, and Age: Feminist Insights in Social Gerontology." *Journal of Aging Studies* 18: 59–73.

Woodward, Kathleen. 1999. "Introduction." In *Figuring Age: Women, Bodies, Generations*, edited by Kathleen Woodward, ix–xxix. Bloomington and Indianapolis: Indiana University Press.

Wyatt-Brown, Anne M. 2010. "Resilience and Creativity in Aging: *The Realms of Silver*." In *A Guide to Humanistic Studies in Aging: What Does It Mean to Grow Old?* edited by Thomas R. Cole, Ruth E. Ray, and Robert Kastenbaum, 57–83. Baltimore, MD: Johns Hopkins University Press.

Contemplation as Resistance to Ageism, and its Historical Context: Mexican Writers Carmen Boullosa, Guadalupe Nettel, and María Rivera

Emily Hind

ABSTRACT

Carmen Boullosa's (1954) daring "Mis cadáveres" (My Cadavers, 2003) shares achievements with Guadalupe Nettel's (1972) "El cuerpo en que nací" (The Body in Which I Was Born) (2011) and María Rivera's (1971) "Variaciones para una autobiografía" (Variations for an Autobiography) (2011). The three autobiographical essays by Mexican women writers describe such sexuality-related moments as losing one's virginity (Nettel), masturbating (Boullosa), and giving birth by caesarean section (Boullosa and Rivera). The pioneering nature of these texts becomes visible through contextual details regarding earlier Mexican women artists Nellie Campobello (1900), Frida Kahlo (1907), Griselda Álvarez (1913), Elena Garro (1916), Clementina Díaz y de Ovando (1916), and Guadalupe Amor (1918). The archives on the Centro Mexicano de Escritores (Mexican Center for Writers, 1951–2006) help to illuminate the nature of ageist pressures exerted on Díaz y de Ovando, as well as on Ángeles Mastretta (1949), Ana Cecilia Treviño (1932), and Amparo Dávila (1928). Writing by more recent generations of writers represented by Boullosa, Nettel, and Rivera suggests that ageism can be overcome in part by exiting the narrative arc of autopathology in favour of meditation, which points to a solution of emptying out the self, contemplating the present moment, and valuing community over individuality.

Marc Augé's maxim, "Age is to aging intellectuals what beauty is to women" applies best—and perhaps only—to men intellectuals (2016, 14). If women intellectuals can be assumed to exist at all under Augé's rule of thumb, his comment anticipates the fact that looks *do* matter. Women intellectuals find themselves caught in the conundrums of ageism that affect careers in the entertainment industry, namely that "women's youth is a prized commodity that loses value with age" (McGlynn, O'Neill, and Schrage-Früh 2017, 3). The devalued intellectual woman can be hard to notice because, in one way or another, she begins to disappear as she ages (2017, 3). By contrast and in the spirit of Augé's adage, "men are allowed to age in the media and the celebrity culture" (Fairclough-Isaacs 2015, 363). Ageism has intensified to such an extent that Kristy Fairclough-Isaacs proposes that no middle ground exists between two age categories; subjects are perceived as "either young or old" (2015, 365).

The invisibility that comes with women's ageing controls even posthumous appreciation of their work. If "greatness" for a woman artist requires performance of youth, then the effect of this association of talent and youth is to conjoin the terms *Shame and the Aging Woman*, as Brooks Bouson's recent monograph argues. Bouson cites research that finds older women articulate an alienated interpretation of their own ageing bodies, especially viewing their aged faces as "deviant or pathological" masks or disguises, and therefore a betrayal of their inner younger selves (2016, 10). The sea change involved in interpreting wrinkles as positive—as indicators of a good mood, for instance (2016, 17)—is measured in the unfamiliar vocabulary related to an anti-ageist stance, i.e. the unexpectedness of the term *ageful*, which gerontologist Molly Andrew celebrates (Bouson 2016, 31). The scholar responsible for the disciplinary label *Age Studies*, Margaret Morganroth Gullette, wrestles with the paradox that links the older person to other minorities: a plight of both "invisibility and hypervisibility" (2017, xxi). This tricky status as either too-visible or invisible reflects the association of ageing with narratives of decline and death, which frames ageing women as symbols of dreaded deterioration to the degree that they become "deaths' heads" (2017, 14).

What was it like to be a "death's head" in a time when nearly no one identified the problem as such? One habit among celebrities from the last century was to lie about their age, as explored in the first part of this article on Mexican women writers. As the internet made it impossible to pull off creative age mathematics, however, a new crop of writers began to praise a contemplative absence from the demands of narrative itself. That release in meditation concerns the second part of my article, which suggests mindfulness as one secret for living "agefully," in Ashton Applewhite's neologism (qtd. in Gullette 2017, 82).

An overview of Mexican women artists and writers who faced ageing by way of reticence and misdirection highlights tactics evinced by Nellie Campobello (b. 1900), Griselda Álvarez (b. 1913), Elena Garro (b. 1916), Guadalupe Amor (b. 1918), and Frida Kahlo (b. 1907). To start with the least celebrated artist, the poet and sometime governor of Colima, Griselda Álvarez, published a memoir, *Cuesta arriba* (*Uphill*) (1992), that leaves out more dates than one would think possible in a detailed review of a political career. Álvarez omits the years of her birth, her marriage, her child's birth, her tenure in lower-level administrative positions, and the exact years of her governorship, though she never hesitates to drop the names of contemporaries who end up dating her; these peers span Mexican presidents from López Mateos (1958–1964) to de la Madrid (1982–1988) (1992, 71, 164). The difficulty of playing down age in the context of professional achievement appears in the contradiction, articulated by age scholar Stephen Fineman, between the "age signposts" embedded in educational and work history and the fact that to eliminate age complctely on a CV "would effectively erase the person" (2011, 62). Álvarez cannot divorce the timeline from her narrative of public accomplishment, and thus the open secret of her age places her in a kind of glass closet.

The same futilely closeted attitude toward age appears in publicity regarding Mexican intellectual Clementina Díaz y de Ovando (b. 1916), who apparently tried to solve the problem in print by leaving almost no personal writings among her many academic books and by revising her birth year. The obituaries agree that Clementina Díaz y

Ovando was born in 1916, though her file in the Centro Mexicano de Escritores has her born in 1920, a mistake repeated elsewhere (Domínguez Cuevas 1999, 116). Thus, Díaz y de Ovando was about 37 years of age, four years older than she claimed to be, when she received a writing grant for the year 1953–1954 (Domínguez Cuevas 1999, 116; "Díaz y de Ovando").

In very old age, Díaz y de Ovando continued to dye her hair. Her final preference for a deep black shade causes the observer to stare. Take one of the photographs typical of those used in obituaries for the 95-year-old: Díaz y de Ovando, some four years prior to her death, sits in a wheelchair, dressed formally in a blouse and skirt suit, with resolutely artificial dark hair ("Fallece" 2012; see also Palapa Quijas 2012). The obituaries upon her death in 2012 fail to specify whether she married, had children, or left behind a partner. The dyed hair suggests Díaz y de Ovando's fear of irrelevance under ageism, which surely contradicted the celebration of her pioneering achievements, such as her status as the first woman to join the Mexican Academy of History (in 1974) and as the first woman to receive the National University Prize (in 1988) ("La Dra" 2011). Like Álvarez, Díaz y de Ovando suffers the paradox that to remain visible for her work as she ages is also to risk admitting her age and thus disappearing.

Maturity connotes sexual knowledge, and here again it seems that performance *does* matter in assessments of intellectual careers. Both Díaz y de Ovando and Álvarez largely elide personal details in writing and thus implicitly convey uneasiness with sexuality. Even when referring not to herself but to two long-deceased uncles and an STD that truncated their careers, Álvarez ventures only euphemism. Narrating from what must be more than fifty years of distance, Álvarez recalls that in Paris the uncles caught "la llamada peste blanca" (the so-called white plague) (1992, 18). Díaz y de Ovando never seems to broach the topic.

A third example of this exercise in aged willful innocence surfaces in Elena Garro's more literarily skilful memoire, published, like that of Álvarez, in 1992. The gossipy *Memorias de España 1937* (*Memories of Spain 1937*) emphasises at every turn Garro's ingenuousness during her visit to the Spanish Civil War and reveals almost nothing about her sex life, despite the fact that the trip doubled as a honeymoon with Octavio Paz (b. 1914). Garro's reliance on naïveté as a framing device irritates critic Christopher Domínguez Michael (b. 1962), who fails to recognise the motives for Garro's tactics, and he judges her impatiently: "Elena [...] se hace la tonta como recurso narrativo (recurso que hará escuela entre las escritoras mexicanas)" (Elena [...] plays the fool as a narrative technique [a technique that will create a following among the other Mexican women writers]) (2014, 86). Certainly, if age benefits (men) intellectuals, Garro opts to incarnate only beauty, along with ignorance.

Perhaps to bolster the impression of innocence, Garro had declared her birth year to be 1920, rather than 1916. Domínguez Michael quotes Paz's opinion regarding Garro's lie: she used the younger age to support her tale of the kidnapped bride (2014, 68). In his role as Paz's biographer, Domínguez Michael digs up the paperwork and debunks Garro's story of a wedding ambush (2014, 78–79). Only the birth certificates are missing from the marriage file, perhaps because Garro was seven months shy of the legal age of 21.

Women who circulated in the arts knew that maturity put them at risk of vanishing from even reflected light. Sara Potter neatly summarises twentieth-century customs of romantic ageism by way of the example of Surrealist men artists' sexual relationships, in which "female lovers or wives were generally much younger than their male partners"; the steadily widening age difference cast women as "part of an ever-rotating roster, as they were frequently traded in for newer, younger models" (Potter 2013, 75). The "trading down" of partners lasted well beyond the heyday of Surrealism. Take Max Aub's (b. 1903) diary entry on August 1, 1967, when he marvels at Octavio Paz's second act in life, facilitated by a second marriage: "Octavio Paz, rejuvenecido. ¿Tendrá uno siempre la edad de su mujer?" (Octavio Paz, rejuvenated. Is one always the same age as one's woman?) (Domínguez Michael 2014, 291). Though Domínguez Michael himself cites this passage, he seems largely oblivious to what these connotations might mean for Garro.

Of course, Garro subtracts far fewer years from her age than would-be contemporary Nellie Campobello. In her biography of the Mexican writer and dancer, Clara Guadalupe García implies the collusion necessary to pull off Campobello's false thirtieth birthday party: "[E]lla apagó treinta velitas sin que nadie sospechara que en realidad tenía cuarenta" ([S]he blew out thirty little candles without having anyone suspect that actually she was forty) (García 2000, 105). Complicity with Nellie's lie had party guests accept her autobiographically informed art on the Mexican Revolution, despite the fact that without the extra decade on her age, it would have been much more difficult for her to remember the details of that conflict. Like Garro's *Memorias de España 1937*, Campobello resorts to naiveté for the Revolutionary tales of *Cartucho* (Cartridge) (1931), and that innocence is emphasised in Elena Poniatowska's (b. 1932) late twentieth-century introduction to the fragmented narrative (Gano 2015).

Campobello's younger half-sister Gloria modified her age too. Dates given for Gloria's birth year range from 1913 to 1919; however, according to dance scholar Margarita Tortajada Quiroz, the real date is 1911 (2001, 70). Nellie's lie thus seems to have claimed Gloria's age for herself, which must have forced Gloria's revision of her age and dictated both women's self-imposed setbacks in artistic maturity—a regression that complements naïve narrative voices but frustrates feminist art. In its ultimate consequences, lying downward about age leads to feminism devoid of experienced feminists, though rich in eternal ingenues.

As predicted by the pattern of self-censorship regarding sexual experience, the artificially youthful Nellie and Gloria studiously denied personal sexual history. Like Garro's eventual habit of taking publicly known lovers, including Adolfo Bioy Casares (b. 1914), but never publishing straightforward autobiography on the practice, the Campobello sisters enjoyed heterosexual relationships outside of marriage without publicising these adventures. Tortajada Quiroz neatly summarises the contradiction in the sisters' exercised sexual freedom: "[P]or un lado ejercieron su sexualidad alejadas de las formas tradicionales y por otro se mantuvieron atadas a éstas y las reivindicaron públicamente (con su exigencia de ser llamadas señoritas, por ejemplo)" ([O]n the one hand they exercised their sexuality far from the traditional forms and on the other hand they remained attached to those and publicly claimed them [with their demand to be addressed as young ladies, for example]) (2001, 539). Scholarship has revealed that before Nellie became a famous dancer in Mexico City, she gave birth to a son in 1919, in Chihuahua, who until his death at age two was raised by Nellie's mother. Few people knew about this child, in part because "Nellie nunca reconoció haber sido madre" (Nellie never acknowledged having been a mother) (Tortajada Quiroz 2001, 270).

In an eerie parallel to Nellie Campobello's troubled maternity, Guadalupe (Pita) Amor had a child whom she did not raise and who accidentally drowned when he was about a year-and-a-half old. Amor's pregnancy at age 38 caused her lover to withdraw his financial support. Soon after the caesarean section, according to Poniatowska, Amor entrusted the child to a sister (2000, 48). Martha Zamora reviews that sad story in the context of a failed interview with Amor. Though Zamora fails to coax the poet to talk about Frida Kahlo, the true subject of Zamora's research, the latter expresses gratitude that Amor refrained from her worst tantrums (Zamora 2015, 98). Michael Schuessler's laudatory biography of Amor acknowledges that in her later years, Amor's abusive habits and eccentric look earned her the nickname, "la abuelita de Batman" (Batman's granny) (1995, 14). In anecdotes told by Poniatowska, Zamora, and Schuessler, the aged Amor needed no provocation on the sidewalks of Mexico City to shout racial insults at men and whack young women with her cane.

Before her shameless ending, Amor broke taboos in more artistically interesting ways. Though confessing sexual knowledge proved nearly impossible for some contemporaries, Amor publicly acknowledged her sexuality. Poniatowska's biographical essay on her aunt, who never married, claims that Amor's daring stunts included humiliating her mother with a shouted confession during mass: "I had an abortion!" (¡Tuve un aborto!) (2000, 41). Perhaps Amor's most groundbreaking gesture is a repetitive and brief story about a woman protagonist who spends time alone, masturbating. The text is titled "La solitaria" (The solitary woman) and appears in *Galería de títeres* (Puppet Gallery) (1959). This writing marks the first published mention of female masturbation by a Mexican woman writer that I can name. However, no sexual discovery appears in Amor's autobiographically inspired novel *Yo soy mi casa* (I Am My House 1957).

Even the daring Frida Kahlo, who painted her experiences with abortion and miscarriage for all to see, manipulated her age. Eva Zetterman's research manages to intertwine these two topics by citing a clinical history, written in 1946, that at once repeats Kahlo's invented birth year of 1910, rather than the actual date of 1907, and marks Kahlo's three interrupted pregnancies, in 1929, 1932, and 1934 (2006, 231). Zetterman attributes published repetition of a "miscarriage myth" on Kahlo as the basis for converting it into the "established truth" (2006, 233). Convention also has biographers tend to excuse Kahlo's false birth year as a patriotic urge, and few invest much thought in Diego Rivera's traded-down partners. For instance, a children's biography introduces these points without much critique: "Diego casi duplicaba la edad de Frida: él tenía 42 y ella solo 22" (Diego almost doubled Frida's age: he was 42 and she just 22) (Morán 2012, 19). That statistic uses the correct math for Kahlo, and the biographer explains, "Frida, que nació en 1907, siempre se quitaba tres años. No por vanidad, sino para que su nacimiento coincidiera con la Revolución Mexicana (1910), con la que siempre se identificó" (Frida, who was born in 1907, always erased three years from her age. Not out of vanity, but so that her birth would coincide with the Mexican Revolution) (Morán 2012, 31).

In order to assess the ageist pressures that influence these distortions, I turn to another group of women writers whose struggles appear in the archive on the Centro Mexicano de Escritores (Mexican Center for Writers), the CME, which operated from 1951 to 2006. Relevant authors who applied for a year-long writing grant from this Mexico City institution include Ángeles Mastretta (b. 1949), Ana Cecilia Treviño (b. 1932), and Amparo Dávila (b. 1928). To start with that first figure, I note that an image search on Google reveals Mastretta's surgically rejuvenated face; she joins the ranks of the would-be ageless, along with Chilean novelist Isabel Allende (b. 1942). I turn to the CME archive for more data on the pressures that might have led Mastretta to, on the one hand, chase an ageless self-performance, and, on the other hand, write daringly, such as including an early lesson from a gypsy on female masturbation in the bestselling novel *Arráncame la vida* (*Tear this Heart Out* 1985).

The file on Mastretta preserves evaluations from the CME application process. The most cutting of these three early opinions is issued by Salvador Elizondo (b. 1932), who sighs, "Los lugares comunes en estos libros de mujeres que se sienten adolescentes. Siempre la misma cosa" (Clichés in these books by women who feel like adolescents. Always the same thing) (Mastretta, "Archivo" 64-3). Elizondo's negative judgment on Mastretta as a perpetual adolescent proves one thing, at least: her age performance and age-appropriate behaviour mattered. All three evaluators' notes are prefaced with Mastretta's age of 24, which in Juan Rulfo's (b. 1917) evaluation appears written by hand (64-1). The fact that Rulfo would imitate the typed headings on the notecards for his entirely hand-written letter of evaluation suggests that the judges took seriously the matter of age.

Nearly ten years before Mastretta's winning application, the social columnist Ana Cecilia Treviño won a CME grant for 1964–1965. The evaluation notecard in her file begins with the typewritten "GIRONELLA, CECILIA TREVIÑO DE / Edad: 32 años" (Age: 32 years). Below that heading, three brief handwritten opinions appear by the director Margaret Shedd (b. 1900), and the writing tutors Juan Rulfo, and Juan José Arreola (b. 1918) (Treviño 17). Shedd's English-language comments read in full: "Seems to be a very interesting project, and an attractive girl" (Treviño 17). The idea that a well-known thirty-two-year-old social columnist for *Excélsior* could seem a "girl" and that her competitiveness as a candidate had to do with this girlishness indicates the problem of ageing into maturity as a woman writer. At the time, Treviño may have been older than 32. A Facebook post from 2015 by the Instituto de Investigaciones Bibliográficas (Institute of Bibliographic Research) at the National Library, lists Treviño's birth year as 1929, against the Center's record of 1932—the year also repeated in Domínguez Cuevas's history of the CME (1999, 402). The possible three-year fudging of Treviño's birthdate should strike my reader as plausible. After all, if "Bambi," as Treviño was known pseudonymously, competed successfully as "an attractive girl," what better career boost than youth?

If Treviño did lie for the Center's paperwork, she stands in good company. Even Juan Rulfo, a man writer, subtracted a year from his age on the grant application. Biographer Fernando Barrientos del Monte attributes Rulfo's creative mathematics to age rules issued by the CME requiring authors to be under age 35. Record of early rules has vanished, and thus no proof for this suspicion exists. Barrientos del Monte himself acknowledges that Rulfo also represented himself as one year younger on his marriage certificate and on the birth certificate for his second child (Barrientos del Monte 2007, 41). Setting aside Rulfo's hazy motives for deception, it remains clear that ageism intertwines with sexism to pressure women more than men. As Gullette observes, "Gender always has an age too, although theorists rarely notice this" (2004, 160).

The imbrication of sexism and ageism emerges in the evaluations for the grant cycle 1966–1967 with judges' handwritten opinions on a single notecard headed in typescript: "DAVILA, AMPARO. Edad: 38 años / Divorciada" (Age: 38 years / Divorced) (Dávila 28). I did not find another instance of civil status appearing on the notecards. The salience of Dávila's marital status hints at the reasons earlier women artists, like the Campobello sisters, Garro, and Amor, took pains to omit or rewrite their own sexual histories. In Poniatowska's memorialising journalism of Dávila's truncated marriage to Pedro Coronel, she explains vaguely, "Creo que tuvieron dos hijas, porque después perdí a Amparo de vista" (I think they had two daughters, because later I lost sight of Amparo) ("Poniatowksa 2016 El renacimiento"). Dávila disappeared from her own career, a plight that had Emmanuel Carballo (b. 1929) lament at a national homage for her in 1998 that only a few university teachers and literary critics appreciated Dávila's out-of-print stories (Hernández García 2002, 8).

Today's grant competitions in Mexico, such as the national *Jóvenes Creadores* (Young Creators) and *Tierra Adentro* (Land Within) programmes, tend to use applicants' ages to differentiate between one category of competition and another, often with the age of 34 or 35 as a dividing line, so some values have not changed. However, in another sense, the internet has eliminated a central conceit here: when writers today hit maturity, they cannot lie convincingly about it.

Although I have pitched one angle here as the importance of writers' sexual forthrightness, before arriving at the last grouping of writers I want to temper my own enthusiasm by citing Gullette's observation that "sexuality is the main narrative we are currently being trained to read for" (2004, 16). Narratives of sexuality are complicit with a prejudicial system. To the extent that ageism today discriminates against women after menopause —making them both hypervisible and invisible—it does seem that Carmen Boullosa (b. 1954), Guadalupe Nettel (b. 1972) and María Rivera (b. 1971) take the lesson inherent in figures such as Amor, Campobello, and Garro. Rather than risk dismissive labels like "crazy" so easily applied to the earlier artists, these more recent generations stake careful claim to *restored* mental health. That is, each of the more contemporary texts assures the reader that the author has *already* overcome a mental health problem. Alongside this framing appropriation of sanity, the three autobiographical essays by Boullosa, Nettel, and Rivera likely fail to engage fully what Thomas Couser calls *autopathography* (1997, 5). Emphasis in the Mexican essays falls not on pathology, with its comic tropes and obsession with autonomy, but on a process or pathway—a mode attuned not to narrative, but to the contemplative.

Boullosa's daring autobiographical essay "Mis cadáveres" (My Cadavers, 2003) was first published online in a feminist journal and is available there as a PDF, from which I borrow the page numbers used below. The piece was later republished in her book of essays, *Cuando me volví mortal* (When I Became Mortal) (2010). While Boullosa's essay has not garnered much attention, various and mixed reviews on the Mexican home front greeted Nettel's essay "El cuerpo en que nací" (The Body in Which I Was Born) and the later book version of the same title, published in 2011 (2011a). A well-received English-language translation of the book appeared in 2015. Nettel's essay is available online in the 2009 *Letras Libres* magazine edition, along with María Rivera's contribution, "Variaciones para una autobiografía" (Variations for an Autobiography). Both Nettel's and Rivera's essays were republished in *Trazos en el espejo* (Penstrokes in the Mirror) (Nettel 2011b, Rivera 2011), the anthology that reorganised the original magazine project to include only autobiographies of Mexican writers under the age of 40. I take the page numbers below from that anthology.

By contrast to the persistent attention given to Nettel's work, Rivera's "Variaciones para una autobiografía" attracted an enthusiastic reception that soon lapsed into silence. Rafael Lemus (b. 1977), as well as Ricardo Muñoz Munguía (1970), approved of Rivera's intimate essay, although the former rejected Nettel's piece as "una narrativa de lo más tradicional: relatos lineales con un yo sólido y estable al centro" (a narrative in the most traditional style: linear stories with a sold and stable "I" at the centre) (Lemus 2011). For Nettel's book-length version, which some critics view as more of a novel, *Letras Libres* published two reviews: Geney Beltrán Félix (b.1976) issued an ambivalent opinion along the lines of Lemus's quibble (2012), and Christopher Domínguez Michael (b. 1962) admired Nettel's prose and praised a scene of masturbation with the railing of a stairway (absent from the essay), but he failed to acknowledge the pioneering nature of that description for a Mexican woman writer (Domínguez Michael 2012, n.p.).

If Boullosa admits her age as nearly fifty years old, a detail inserted at the end of "Mis cadáveres," Rivera and Nettel reveal their ages mostly by reminiscing about the tumultuous events of the 1990s. Nettel's explicitly anti-(sexually) romantic acquaintanceship with Subcomandante (Deputy Commander) Marcos, the leader of the Zapatista Army of National Liberation (ELZN), occurred when she was a university student returned from France, and she never changes tone when jumping from the personal to the political, as in a previous unromantic comment that at age 16 she lost her virginity "de una manera poco memorable" (in a forgettable way) (2011b, 162). Just as Nettel matter-of-factly narrates her rejection of that boyfriend who subsequently attempts suicide, she reveals in unpretentious detail that Marcos eventually ejected Nettel from the rebellion, because she accepted a governmental subsidy in the form of a *Jóvenes Creadores* writing grant. Perhaps to anchor the lack of grandiosity, Nettel views this history as dreamlike: "Nunca volví a pisar el territorio zapatista. Me sigo preguntando si su existencia es realmente geográfica o si es algo que se lleva por dentro, como un sueño recurrente o una existencia paralela" (I never set foot in Zapatista territory again. I still ask myself if its existence is really geographic or if it's something that one carries inside, like a recurring dream or a parallel existence) (2011b, 173). The scorecard for ageism seems uncertain: Nettel dates herself only to suggest the unreality of history.

Rivera's essay pulls the same move. She looks back on her life as it intertwines with historic events and notes, "Los días, los años se superponen y mirados tan de cerca dan la impresión de no ser nada, de nunca haber pasado" (The days, the years overlap and examined closely they give the impression of not being anything, of never having happened) (2011, 12). The dissolving nature of linear time justifies disinterest in narrative arcs, articulated insistently in Rivera's fragmented poetic notion that her essay must "hacer menos una trama y más un cuadro impresionista" (make less of a plot and more of an impressionist painting) (2011, 12). To wit, "Variaciones para una autobiobrafía" starts over in eight of the nine sections. Eight times the essay launches a variation of the phrase, "Tendría que empezar así:" (I would have to begin like this:) and varies the second part of the sentence. The last, ninth, section changes the anaphora and states: "Tendría que acabar así: últimamente la noción de estilo me causa repugnancia, no dejo de pensar en él como una domesticación del alma" (I would have to end like this: lately the notion of style disgusts me, I can't stop thinking about it except as a taming of the soul) (2011, 28). This dismissal of *style* suggests humility as an individual that might benefit the goal of a collective endeavour.

The theme of shunning individual ego for meditation arrives explicitly in Nettel's brief admission of a depression years in the making that finally caught up with her in Paris. The problem is no sooner mentioned than solved; she recovers by way of a birthday gift, a Tibetan book about the art of dying, which leads her to explore Buddhism, to visit India and a French retreat centre, and finally to write a short story. Nettel achieves a newly emptied state as a fiction writer; that is, she compares the enterprise of crafting the short story with the mind-emptying task of automatic writing: "Me aferré a él [el cuento] como quien busca en la escritura automática las claves de su existencia. Lo titulé 'Bonsái'" (I clung to it [the short story] like someone who searches for the keys to her existence in automatic writing. I titled it "Bonsái") (2011, 176). Again, Nettel seems to write not so much an autopathography—*that* would be the suicidal ex-boyfriend's story—but an example of self-revelation that resists the plotting that makes self-revelation so difficult for women. To slip out of the ageist trap without leaving behind her experience—to include both *the* age and *her* age—Nettel meditates on her own ordinariness.

That meditation on common human qualities *includes* the sensation of being an outsider and may contradict to some degree the scholarly work on Nettel's writing that engages disability studies.[1] Finding oneself as part of the world by way of the not-plotted body concerns an interview conducted on the publication of *El cuerpo en que nací*. There, Nettel proposes her autobiographical goal of self-revelation as just another being:

> Quería sobre todo resaltar la idea del trilobite: de la cucaracha que va encontrando el camino hacia su reconciliación con ella misma. ¿Y quiénes son las cucarachas? Las que vienen de atrás, las sobrevivientes de miles de cosas. Me puse en la perspectiva de "no soy la única cucaracha, no soy la única *outsider*". Ha existido toda una corriente oculta del trilobite, desde los tiempos remotos hasta nuestros días y yo me reconozco como heredera de ella. (Espinosa de los Monteros 2011, 34)

> I especially wanted to highlight the idea of the trilobite: of the cockroach that is finding the path to reconciliation with itself. And who are the cockroaches? The ones that come from behind, the survivors of thousands of things. I put myself in the perspective of "I'm not the only cockroach, I'm not the only outsider". There has been a whole hidden current of the trilobite, from ancient times to our days and I recognize myself as its heir.

Even as Nettel places herself in a kind of impersonal and deep time, this eternal present and ordinariness give way in the book-length *El cuerpo en que nací* to a final paragraph that subscribes to a narrative of decline:

> Mi propio cuerpo [...] me aparece ahora como un vehículo en descomposición, un tren en el que he ido montada a lo largo de todo este tiempo, sometido a un viaje muy veloz pero también a una inevitable decadencia. (My own body [...] seems to me now a vehicle in decay, a train I have been riding this whole time, subject to a very fast trip, but also to an inevitable decline 2011, 195–196)

Nettel's switch from a contemplative essay to an ageist book finalised with the decline trope inspires me to wonder whether meditative reflection, like allegory and the fable, is best realised in a genre with a short word count.

For her part, Rivera never revises her essay into a book and thereby preserves the integrity of the meditative approach. To critic Lemus's delight, the fragmented "Varations" do place into doubt a narrative "I" that would justify an autobiographical plot arc. Rivera hints at momentarily emptied-out self-identity as a means of combating overly determined narrative designs, particularly when she describes a trio of delirious experiences. Under the category of "la misma placidez somnífera" (the same sleepy pleasure), Rivera remembers outdoors drunkenness in Paris on Ranelagh street, nighttime drunkenness on a lawn in Ohio, and sedation after a caesarean section; though narrated in the above order, the latter experience is chronologically situated between the two drunken episodes abroad (2011, 15). As a poet, Rivera seems to enjoy these non-narrative states of sedation or drunkenness ("que es lo mismo" [which are the same]) (2011, 15). For reasons of word count, I skip the lyricism of Rivera's unusual review of her Caesarean section and highlight only the meditative moment of Rivera's first gaze upon her daughter: "Decir todo esto es no decir nada. Las palabras se me angostan, el lenguaje no me alcanza para expresar el silencioso sueño de mi hija, la mirada de sus ojos azorados cuando me ve como a una extraña cosa" (To say all this is to not say anything. The words narrow on me, language falls short of expressing my daughter's quiet dream, the look in her alarmed eyes when she views me like a strange thing) (2011, 16).

Against the development of an arc of would-be autopathology that chooses between the miraculous normalcy or the sick strangeness of motherhood, Rivera alludes only vaguely to the mental health problems that afflicted her before the birth, during a lengthy troubled period, from around 2000 to 2005. That reckless problem period appears largely in the past tense, as in the following passage:

> Cuando tras años de vivir al límite, me encontré agotada y enferma. Cuando la herida que me acicateaba, una herida que se convirtió en una vía de conocimiento, se volvió un costurón invisible y mi lamento, una cantaleta. Cuando encontré que no tenía caso seguir caminando en esa dirección, que esos días como rayos encendidos habían dado ya toda la luz posible. (2011, 17)

> When after years of living on the edge, I found myself exhausted and sick. When the wound that spurred me on, a wound that turned into a path of knowledge, became an invisible scar and my wail, a whining refrain. When I found that there was no point in continuing to walk in that direction, that those days like burning bolts had given all the light possible.

Rivera's return to health does not arrive in linear history, just as Nettel's illuminations seem to turn away from politics. Rather than a Buddhist treatise, however, Rivera finds relief in the cyclical domestic bliss of having a child and a partner. The constantly restarting "Variations" on an autobiography thus hint that writing well reflects a present-moment meandering; note the similarity between trance-like moments of drunkenness and sedation, and Rivera's notion of poetic writing, "un camino hacia 'quién sabe dónde', que es como yo llamo a la poesía" (a path to "who knows where," which is what I call poetry) (2011, 10).

Finally, Boullosa reaches this same destination-irrelevant path by arranging her autobiographical essay around the theme of dead bodies. Of special interest here is a childhood pathway to relief from rational thought processes, accessed by staring at a desiccated bat. As a child, Boullosa practiced imaginative trances by staring at the bat, amusingly classified as the largest specimen among a childhood collection of preserved insects:

> Pasé muchos ratos observando atentamente al murciélago. Lo encontraba muy atractivo, y lo usaba como una base. Lo veía, pero me viajaba mirándolo. Era mi base para imaginar. Abría

> la caja, acercaba mi carita a la de él, fijaba en él los ojos, y ¡adiós mundo!: me iba. A mi manera yo estaba enamorada de él. (2003, 35)
>
> I spent many hours intently observing the bat. I found it very attractive and used it as a base. I saw it, but I traveled watching it. It was my base for imagining. I would open the box, bring my face near his little face, fix my eyes on him, and Goodbye world! I would check out. In my way I was in love with him.

The imaginative base of the preserved bat, like Nettel's glossed interest in Buddhism and Rivera's escape into sedation, eludes the problems of narrative and therefore does not include much of the contemplative experience itself. Just as Nettel never recounts the details of "Bonsái," (which the curious reader can find in the oeuvre anyway), and just as Rivera does not present her poetry in her description of the delights of taking a path to the unknown, Boullosa chooses not to recount any particular fantasies inspired by the bat. The process and not the plot matters.

In "Mis cadáveres" Boullosa takes the unusual step for Mexican women writers of confessing sexual discovery. For instance, a first memory of genital pleasure took place under a faucet when a grandmother washed "Carmelita's" "colita" (little tail). The grandmother, nicknamed *Mami*, does not comprehend Boullosa's enthralled request for more (2003, 30). The described *trance* in the passage links the notion of meditative escape with sexual pleasures of the body, shared with the grandmother who both participates in and fails to register the event. Another memory in this vein places a four-year-old Boullosa seated alone at a table, pressing her crotch against her foot in a darkened room and experiencing genital pleasure tinged with a sense of isolation. Boullosa claims an epiphany: "De golpe, he comprendido que yo acabo en mi piel, que irremediablemente yo termino en ese límite" (Suddenly, I have understood that I end at my skin, that inevitably I terminate at that edge) (2003, 28). Just as Rivera experiences her C-section alone in a room of people and Nettel feels herself isolated in childhood due to an eyepatch that attentive doctors instruct her to wear, Boullosa tests the limits of her separation as an individual within the context of care. "Mis cadáveres" thus shares the theme of commonness and community that Rivera's and Nettel's meditations suggest; Boullosa's expression of belonging is also meditative and attained through bodily experience.

I hope to take the lesson from these three essays. Rather than attempt to pull these meditations by Boullosa, Nettel, and Rivera into my diagnostic narrative arc, I want to close by locating these groundbreaking autobiographies on a collective family tree. A previous generation left sex and infants out of the story: Guadalupe Amor, Nellie Campobello, and Elena Garro, among others, never emphasise the birth of their one child. These women and their peers also tended to erase their true ages, to bury lovers, and otherwise to silence their affairs. Boullosa, Nettel, and Rivera allow the audience to see flashes of another way. I applaud this switch in answering questions about one's age from "Um" to "Om," particularly in view of the ineffectiveness of lying. Abandoning the narrative structures that encourage ageist discrimination marks the first step in a more mindful approach to assessing our own and other women's ageful lives. This task of assessment requires balance between recovering the historical context and letting go of that same past, in an embrace of beginner's mind that is not so much a tool of ingenuousness as a process of seeing anew.

Note

1. Maricruz Castro Ricalde (2017) summarises nicely some of that disability-themed criticism in her article on the short story "Pitosis".

Acknowledgements

Thanks to Narciso Rojas Moreno at the Archive for the Center for Mexican Writers.

Disclosure statement

No potential conflict of interest was reported by the author.

ORCID

Emily Hind http://orcid.org/0000-0003-3244-3669

References

Álvarez, Griselda. 1992. *Cuesta arriba: Memorias de la primera gobernadora*. Mexico: Universidad de Colima, Fondo de Cultura Económica.

Amor, Guadalupe. 1959. *"La solitaria." Galería de títeres*. Mexico: Fondo de Cultura Económica.

Augé, Marc. 2016. *Everyone Dies Young: Time Without Age*. Translated by Judy Gladding. New York: Columbia P.

Barrientos del Monte, Fernando. 2007. *Juan Rulfo: El regreso al paraíso*. Guadalajara, Jalisco: Universidad de Guadalajara, Editorial Universitaria.

Beltrán Félix, Geney. 2012. La certidumbre del monstruo." *Letras Libres* 160 http://www.letraslibres.com/mexico/libros/la-certidumbre-del-monstruo.

Boullosa, Carmen. 2003. "Mis cadáveres." *Debate Feminista* 28: 23–50.

Boullosa, Carmen. 2010. *Cuando me volví mortal*. Mexico: Cal y Arena.

Bouson, J. Brooks. 2016. *Shame and the Aging Woman: Confronting and Resisting Ageism in Contemporary Women's Writings*. New York: Palgrave Macmillan.

Castro Ricalde, Maricruz. 2017. "'Pitosis' de Guadalupe Nettel y otras historias." *Revista Chilena de Literatura* 95: 61–84.

Couser, G. Thomas. 1997. *Recovering Bodies: Illness, Disability, and Life Writing*. Foreword by Nancy Mairs. Madison: University of Wisconsin Press.

Dávila, Amparo. Archivo Centro Mexicano de Escritores, Box 11, File 56, Fondo Reservado of the Biblioteca Nacional, Universidad Nacional Autónoma de México, Mexico City.

Díaz y de Ovando, Clementina. Archivo Centro Mexicano de Escritores, Box 11, File 59, Fondo Reservado of the Biblioteca Nacional, Universidad Nacional Autónoma de México, Mexico City.

Domínguez Cuevas, Martha. 1999. *Los becarios del Centro Mexicano de Escritores, 1952-1997.* Mexico: Aldus and Cabos Sueltos.

Domínguez Michael, Christopher. 2012. "Una novela de madurez." Review of Guadalupe Nettel's *El cuerpo en que nací. Letras Libres* 7 June. http://www.letraslibres.com/mexico-espana/una-novela-madurez.

Domínguez Michael, Christopher. 2014. *Octavio Paz en su siglo.* Mexico: Penguin Random House.

Espinosa de los Monteros, Silvina. 2011. "Libro autobiográfico de Guadalupe Nettel: El doloroso enigma de la identidad." *El Financiero* 8466: 34.

Fairclough-Isaacs, Kristy. 2015. "Celebrity Culture and Ageing." In *Routledge Handbook of Cultural Gerontology,* edited by Julia Twigg, and Wendy Martin, 361–368. London: Routledge.

Fallece la historiadora Clementina Díaz y de Ovando, miembro de Academia Mexicana de la Lengua. 2012. *Sin Embargo.* 19 Feb. http://www.sinembargo.mx/19-02-2012/155374.

Fineman, Stephen. 2011. *Organizing Age.* New York: Oxford UP.

Gano, Geneva M. 2015. "Campobello's *Cartuchos* and Cisnero's Molotovs: Transborder Revolutionary Feminist Narratives." *Journal of Transnational American Studies* 6 (1): 1–28. https://escholarship.org/uc/item/8dm6d1fz.

García, Clara Guadalupe. 2000. *Nellie: El caso Campobello.* Mexico: Cal y Arena.

Garro, Elena. 1992. *Memorias de España 1937.* Mexico: Siglo XXI.

Gullette, Margaret Morganroth. 2004. *Aged by Culture.* Chicago: U of Chicago P.

Gullette, Margaret Morganroth. 2017. *Ending Ageism or How Not to Shoot Old People.* Camden, NJ: Rutgers UP.

Hernández García, Alma Gloria. 2002. "La literatura fantástica en dos cuentos de Amparo Dávila, como recurso para plantear un conflicto existencial." (*B.A. Thesis*). Universidad Nacional Autónoma de México.

Instituto de Investigaciones Bibliográficas. 2015. Facebook post. 15 Oct. https://www.facebook.com/BiblioNacMex.HemeroNacMex.IIBUNAM/posts/974375029268459.

La Dra. Clementina Díaz y de Ovando recibe el primer Premio de Equidad de Género Miguel Alemán Valdés. 2011. Boletín de la Federación Mexicana de Universitaras AC. 113 (Oct): 1.

Lemus, Rafael. 2011. Review of "*Trazos en el espejo: 15 autorretratos fugaces*" *Letras Libres* 149 (1 May). http://www.letraslibres.com/mexico/trazos-en-el-espejo-15-autorretratos-fugaces-varios-autores.

Mastretta, Ángeles. Archivo Centro Mexicano de Escritores, Box 24, File 130, Fondo Reservado of the Biblioteca Nacional, Universidad Nacional Autónoma de México, Mexico City.

McGlynn, Cathy, Margaret O'Neill, and Michaela Schrage-Früh. 2017. "Introduction." In *Ageing Women in Literature and Visual Culture: Reflections, Refractions, Reimaginings,* edited by Cathy McGlynn, Margaret O'Neill, and Michaela Schrage-Früh, 1–20. New York: Palgrave Macmillan.

Morán, José. 2012. *Frida Kahlo: El dolor convertido en arte.* Ilustrated by Acacio Puig. Madrid: Susaeta Ediciones.

Muñoz Munguía, Ricardo. 2011. Review of *Trazos en el espejo. Siempre* 24 Dec. http://www.siempre.mx/2011/12/trazos-en-el-espejo/.

Nettel, Guadalupe. 2011a. *El cuerpo en que nací.* Barcelona: Anagrama.

Nettel, Guadalupe. 2011b. "El cuerpo en que nací." In *Trazos en el espejo: 15 autorretratos fugaces,* 155–176. Mexico: Universidad Autónoma de Nuevo León.

Palapa Quijas, Fabiola. 2012. "Murió la escritora y académica Clementina Díaz y de Ovando." *La Jornada* 20 Feb. http://www.jornada.unam.mx/2012/02/20/cultura/a10n1cul.

Poniatowska, Elena. 2000. *Pita Amor." Las siete cabritas.* Mexico: Era.

Poniatowska, Elena. 2016. "El renacimiento de la gran cuentista Amparo Dávila." *La Jornada* 20 Mar. http://www.jornada.unam.mx/2016/03/20/opinion/a04a1cul.

Potter, Sara A. 2013. "Disturbing Muses: Gender, Technology, and Resistance in Mexican Avant-Garde Cultures." (*Dissertation*). Washington University in Saint Louis.

Rivera, María. 2011. "Variaciones para una autobiografía." In *Trazos en el espejo:15 autorretratos fugaces,* 9–28. Mexico: Universidad Autónoma de Nuevo León.

Schuessler, Michael Karl. 1995. *La undécima musa: Guadalupe Amor.* Mexico: Diana.

Tortajada Quiroz, Margarita. 2001. *Frutos de mujer*. Mexico: CONACULTA, INBA.
Treviño, Ana Cecilia. Archive Centro Mexicano de Escritores, Box 42, File 243, Fondo Reservado of the Biblioteca Nacional, Universidad Nacional Autónoma de México, Mexico City.
Zamora, Martha. 2015. *En busca de Frida*. Huixquilucan, Estado de Mexico: Self-published, 2015.
Zetterman, Eva. 2006. "Frida Kahlo's Abortions: With Reflections From a Gender Perspective on Sexual Education in Mexico." *Konsthistorisk Tidskrift Journal of Art History* 75 (4): 230–243.

Ageing, Creativity, and Memory: The Evolution of Erica Jong's Literary Career

Ieva Stončikaitė

ABSTRACT
Taking a life-course perspective, this article considers the intersections of creativity, memory, and ageing in Erica Jong's middle and later works, and explores underlying changes in the author's self-perception as a writer. It demonstrates the substitution of Jong's initial "fear of writing" by increased self-knowledge, courage to speak her mind, and gradual capacity to ignore negative criticism in later years. Although her later life works and her most recent personal accounts reveal that ageing does not render the creative process easier, in Jong's case the act of life writing becomes fearless with age. An examination of the relationship between memory processes and the narrative construction of a sense of self through the act of writing demonstrates how the writer becomes more self-assured, grounded, and mature over time, which challenges the pervasive narrative of decline and helps to better understand the complex realities of ageing and the artistic achievements of older adults.

No trouble, no tale. (Randall and McKim 2008, 118)

From "fear of writing" to growth of confidence

The meanings that older people attach to their life cycle and, especially, to the experience of their later years, can reveal important insights into the development of their creativity and self-perception and, at the same time, provide a nuanced picture of older adults' inner worlds and experiences of ageing (Cohen-Shalev 1989, 21). Anne M. Wyatt-Brown argues that one of the best ways to determine the effects of ageing on an artist's life is to examine the transformation of creative processes, with a special focus on memoirs and other works produced in late adulthood (1989, 175). According to Wyatt-Brown, "[o]nly by combining research with novels and memoirs can we begin to comprehend the varieties of ageing experience in our time" (2010, 57). These statements are relevant to Erica Jong's works, especially her middle and later writings, which reveal how the writer becomes more self-assured, grounded, and mature over time. Jong's thoughts on creativity, confidence, and ageing echo other works produced by ageing writers, such as Ruth Raymond

Thone (1992) and May Sarton (1997), who show that the ageing process prompts people to be more inclined to speak their mind and become more self-assured and less concerned with external opinions and criticism. Drawing from her personal experiences, in her article "Toward Another Dimension" Sarton confesses that age has given her more courage to express herself openly: "I have found that the greatest joy is that one can be absolutely open, say outrageous things if they are true" (1997, 230). She states that, with age, we "have greater freedom than ever before to be our true selves. Everything is opening out inside and around us", and we "are permitted to be eccentric" because "there is less tension, less drive, [and] the margin for giving is wider" (1997, 230–231). Further research findings contribute to these assertions, as they demonstrate that older people become more "experienced, accomplished, and seasoned", which leads them "into an increasingly harmonious whole" (Ross and Mirowsky 2008, 2393). These ideas are distilled in Jong's middle and later works, as well as in her most recent personal accounts, which aid in better understanding the complex realities of ageing and contribute to challenging the negative connotations associated with the artistic achievements of older adults.

Jong, one of the key figures of the second-wave women's liberation movement, has been an important spokesperson for women of her generation ever since she gained worldwide popularity with the publication of her bestselling book, *Fear of Flying* (1973). Although Jong's tendency to incorporate intimate personal experiences and to use sexual references mixed with humour in her fiction generated much controversy and even misogynist comments, she has continued to explore women's emotional, professional, and sexual needs in her works. This article provides an analysis of the evolution of Jong's literary career from a life-course perspective and argues that the development of her voice and confidence is wedded to a complex process of remembering and ageing. This process challenges negative notions of old age and the assumption that creativity is related to youthful energy.[1]

In her early career as a writer, Jong was fearful of addressing the problems, anxieties, and aspirations of women of her generation. She was convinced that for a woman to obtain literary recognition, to be accepted and to be heard, it was necessary to adopt a "male" voice. Thinking that the majority of "serious novels were about men", Jong "tried to sound either male or neutral" (1974, 264, 1980, 118–119). As Jong confessed, since her childhood, she had been used to reading books written by men and, unconsciously, she "identified with male heroes" (1994, 145). At the age of thirty-one, the author wrote:

> [...] there is still a feeling that women's writing is a lesser class of writing, that to write about what goes on in the nursery or the bedroom is not as important as what goes on in the battlefield, that to write about relationships between men and women is not as important as writing about a moon shot. Somehow there is a feeling that what women know about is a lesser category of knowledge. [...] There is a kind of patriarchal prejudice which infuses our whole culture. I think it is not always malicious on the part of men – it's often purely unconscious. (as quoted in Templin 2002, 8)[2]

Following the same line of thought, in one of her midlife memoirs, Jong said that "[a] poem under a man's name smells *virile*. Under a woman's name, the same poem smells thin" (1999, 41, emphasis in original). The author was also aware of the fact that it was harder for a woman writer to obtain literary recognition than for a man. As a young woman, Jong observed that if women "were good, they were good *in spite of* being women. If they were bad, it was *because* they were women" ([1972] 1980, 118, emphasis in original). Hence, it comes as no surprise that in her first attempts to write, Jong tried to imitate a man's style and sought to create male protagonists.[3] However, writing from a man's perspective could not reveal her inner voice, and, as the writer herself stated, it "was false" and "lacked life and authenticity" (1974, 264–265).

Jong's decision to write *Fear of Flying* from a woman's perspective in her early thirties can be viewed as a first successful step towards her growth in confidence as a writer. Yet, the writing of this novel was accompanied by fear of being rejected and misunderstoodthe author was afraid that nobody would publish her book. Aged thirty-five, she confessed: "It was terrible. I wrote *Fear of Flying* in a constant state of tremor. I was so scared my hands and feet kept getting cold. I kept thinking, 'What are you doing, what are you putting on the page, you nut, you can't publish this'" (as quoted in Templin 2002, 79). Her poem "The Hole" from the collection *Loveroot* (1975), which was written around the time she was writing *Fear of Flying*, vividly depicts her insatiable need to write, as well as her fear of failing, and insecurity after having completed the book:

> She is frightened when the book is done.
> The novel whose scrawled yellow pages
> have filled her heart from seven years
> is snatched away.
> The book-in-progress
> was the mattress of a bed
> where her past made love
> to her future,
> She has no choice - she will begin again. (106)

Although writing from a woman's perspective was challenging, it helped Jong to find her inner voice and to learn about the art of writing, as exemplified in these lines:

> At times, the writing was hell and at times it was bliss. At times I would grow bored with Isadora and long to be in another consciousness, and at times I would love her and learn from her things I had never known about myself. I sensed I was doing something new with this book in certain ways and anticipated great resistance. (1974, 266)

At sixty-four, the author again admitted that she was very "young and green" when the novel came out, but she felt proud to have written *Fear of Flying* because "it has guts and juice two things [she] prize[s]" (2006, 2–3). In her midlife memoir *Fear of Fifty* (1994), Jong acknowledged that when she hit midlife, she could write from a man's perspective if she wanted, because she "had lived with enough men to know their feelings as if from the inside" (146). Yet, the author refused to do so, because many women needed "their own stories to be told" from a woman's point of view (1994, 146). *Fear of Flying* was a sincere manifestation of her thoughts and encouraged other women writers to voice their concerns and to lose their fear of writing. Writing this novel helped Jong to realise that the act of creation could grant the strength, confidence, and self-assurance to continue exploring issues that concerned the women of her generation.

Ageing, writing and self-development

As Jong grew older, she came to consider that the process of writing was far more rewarding than the feedback she received, because the act of creation was about listening to her inner voice, rather than about looking for external approval. According to the author, only by openly expressing ourselves can we find joy and fulfilment in the experience of writing, which is sometimes painstaking and fatiguing, but also rewarding and gratifying. Jong's poem "Flying at Forty", from the collection *Ordinary Miracles* (1983), written when she was forty-one, illustrates that, with age, the author became more self-assured and less afraid to speak out about her concerns; fear of rejection and criticism no longer inhibited her:

> [f]ear was my element,
> fear my contagion.
> I swam in it
> till I became
> immune.
> The plane takes off
> & I laugh aloud.
> Call me courageous.
> I am still alive. (82)

In *Fear of Fifty* (1994), Jong again stated that the greatest "compensation for being fifty in a culture that is not kind to older women is that you care less about criticism and you are less afraid of confrontation" (xxvi). Similar thoughts are also conveyed in this statement by fifty-one-year-old Jong: "I have reached the point, hitting my fiftieth birthday, where everything terrible has been said about me, right? I can't lose. I'm no longer afraid" (as quoted in Templin 2002, 189). In various late-life interviews and memoirs, the author emphasised that writing must come out of love and not interest in profit, because

> no money will ever be enough and eventually you will start imitating your first successes, straining hot water through the same used tea bag. It doesn't work with tea, and it doesn't work with writing. You must give all you have and never count the cost. (1999, 181)

In one of her recent interviews, Jong also remarked that ageing is not loss, but, on the contrary, an opportunity for new discoveries and alternative points of view:

> […] age is the last taboo, and it's so wrong because, in a weird way, life is just beginning. You're confident. You're good at your work. I've more imagination now than ever. I've come into my own. I'm not afraid of anyone. (Cooke, 25 Oct. 2015)

These quotations clearly show that, as the author ages, her value system and goals in life change. The things that she considered important in her younger days, such as fame, her social position, or literary recognition, become less significant in later years. Over her life course, the writer gained more power, self-confidence, and imagination in her later creative output. For Jong, old age is a stage in life marked by new discoveries and a greater capacity for artistic expression, which challenges the narrative of decline (Gullette 2004), according to which ageing individuals are seen as dependent and frail.

The evolution of Jong's understanding of the experience of ageing is also mirrored in the transformations of her characters, who become more introspective and mature as they grow older. Through Leila, a protagonist of the novel *Any Woman's Blues* (1990), written when the author was approaching her fifties, Jong shows that ageing grants women a possibility to go back in time to find lost selves that have vanished because of family and social obligations:

> Nature gives us thirty years of blindness to male bullshit so we can make the maximum number of babies. And when the estrogen begins to wane, and we come back to ourselves again. We return to the bliss we knew as nine-year-olds, coloring in our coloring books. We get our lives back, our autonomy back, our power back. (161)

Her other late-life works and interviews continue to highlight that life is a continuous process of becoming, characterised by a greater sense of wholeness, maturation, and of harmony. The author also states that as people age, they tend to have fewer regrets, as exemplified in this interview, conducted when Jong was seventy-three: "we become ourselves more when we get older, we know who we are and we like who we are. [...] The important thing about getting older is that we are more unapologetic about who we are" (Finch, 13 Nov. 2015). According to the writer, everything in life teaches us something that is valuable, which gives a sense of power and confidence.

Jong and her fictional characters' acceptance of mistakes and their positive view towards the process of growing older echo Catherine E. Ross and John Mirowsky's (2008) research findings on the relationship between age and the balance of emotions. The scholars show that as people approach the second half of their lives, the quality of their emotions tends to shift from negative to positive, and from active (excitement) to passive (serenity). The results from the emotions module of the 1996 U.S. General Social Survey reveal that, as people grow older, they experience less anxiety and negative emotions, due to greater maturity and fewer time pressures and regrets, which helps them to function more "efficiently and successfully" (Ross and Mirowsky 2008, 2392–2393). Similar thoughts are also expressed in Germaine Greer's (1991) view of older age as liberating and empowering. In *The Change* (1991) Greer sees menopause as a major turning point, and argues that, as women grow older, they come into their true selves and seize their own power out of their newfound invisibility and resistance to the male gaze.[4] It is worth mentioning that even though both Greer and Jong agree that age grants women more power, maturity, and confidence, contrary to Greer, Jong continues to advocate sexual practices in later years.[5] Jong's later fiction is also similar to the *Reifungsroman*, a novel of "ripening" (Waxman 1990). This literary genre, identified by Barbara Frey Waxman (1990), provides significant insights into ageing, presenting it as an ongoing process of growth rather than a narrative of decline in an older woman's life. Jong's late works, in particular, share the patterns of the *Reifungsroman* as, through her heroines' increased sense of maturity and wholeness, they create space for positive associations with the experience of growing older. In fact, Jong adopts this genre to recall her memories and to tell her life story through the vantage point of her later years, which shows that ageing is not bound to a loss of creativity.

Writing or telling one's life-story is inevitably linked to the evocation of memory, turning points in life, and creative processes. As the story of one's life grows longer and thicker with time, so does the necessity to share it with others (Randall and Elizabeth McKim 2008, 118). As William L. Randall and A. Elizabeth McKim argue, "the longer our life, the greater the potential and capacity for meaning, and the greater our need for it as well" (2008, 178). Memory processes are an inherent part of ageing in that they are never static and linear but encompass complex meanings and require a continual re-making and interpretation of life. The act of remembrance, like ageing, can be regarded as a continuous interplay between loss and gain, which shapes our sense of self and provides us with different understandings of old age and the process of ageing itself. In connection, research in literary gerontology shows that midlife is a creative turning point in a writer's career, and that the works produced around this stage in life can provide new meanings about an artist's self-development and creative and memory processes (Wyatt-Brown 1989; Casado, Domínguez, and Worsfold 2016). The capacity to regard the process of growing old as a constructive change, rather than construing it as loss and the lack of creativity, also helps to reconcile our past and present selves, and to acquire new meanings in what can come to be an advantaged and transformative stage in life. As Linda J. Vogei observes, growing older and a desire to tell one's life story is both a transforming and transformative process that is characterised by an increased self-assurance and rethinking of one's life (1995, 75).

Jong's midlife memoirs and her later works attest to these statements, as they show that ageing does not limit her creative processes, but, on the contrary, grants new visions of old age that emerge from her accumulated life experience and increased self-knowledge. Compared to her earlier writings, the writer's memoirs, such as *Fear of Fifty* (1994), *What Do Women Want* (1999), and *Seducing the Demon* (2006), produced around her midlife, reveal a more consolidated authorial voice and a deeper examination of her life experiences. In them, Jong revives her unresolved inner conflicts and "fear of writing" and attempts to rework her frustrations through the combined act of remembering and writing. Her growing self-confidence as a writer and her lesser concern about public opinion are, for instance, exemplified in her "Twenty-One Rules for Writers", which appear in *Seducing the Demon*, published when she was sixty-four. The author sets up some rules for young writers, in which she states that, in order to succeed in the literary domain, one must have faith, not be afraid of change, and not expect approval (2006, 4). Jong's midlife memoirs and her explorations of her intimate life from the perspective of mother, writer, and wife, suggest that ageing has granted her more confidence and has reduced her concerns about external opinions and criticism. According to the writer, with time, her writing improves because she is no longer constrained by the fear of writing. As she states: "I'm 73, and my writing is better than it's ever been" (Burns, 8 Sept. 2015).

The challenges of late-life creative processes

Although Jong has become more self-assured as a writer, her works also reveal that it takes time and effort to learn to trust one's inner voice and be confident in writing. This observation reminds us that confidence is gained through a life-long reflective process. Jong, aged seventy-two, reinforces the idea that age brings greater serenity, knowledge and maturity, and she reminds her readers that even though "[y]outh still beguiles us" and we wish to revive it, it is a delusion, because ageing grants other abilities and capacities that are absent in youth (2014, 85). At the age of seventy-two, the author looks back at her life from the vantage point of her more mature self and applies a developed sense of irony and a "double vision which innocence cannot have" (2014, 86). This observation bespeaks her increased confidence and reveals her capacity for introspection, the search for meaning in her creative processes, and the development of her critical thought.

Yet, Jong also acknowledges that sometimes this double vision has its downsides, because it lacks the naivety and innocence of small children, attributes that she used to have as a young writer (2014, 86). In fact, Jong states that the act of creation becomes more challenging with age because it is harder to find a "middle voice" that speaks for both young and aged people:

> The search for a voice in our books becomes more difficult as we age. When young we only had to learn to write as we spoke – both aloud and in our own heads. As we grow older we strain to find a voice that both age and youth will thrill to – a much harder task. (2014, 86)

To illustrate her claim, the author looks back at the writing trajectory of well-known writers, such as Ernest Hemingway, Kurt Vonnegut or J. D. Salinger, and highlights that public interest in their books decreased as they grew older because they could no longer interest the same readers who had looked for innovation and youthful inspiration in their earlier works:

> Youth has a kick, the excitement of the new. Age may sound too world-weary. Think of the writers who thrilled you with their viridity, if not virility – Ernest Hemingway, Kurt Vonnegut, J. D. Salinger – and see how they aged. Hemingway's voice palled unless he was writing out of his youth, as in *A Moveable Feast*. Vonnegut became grumpy unless he has a real historical event to describe, like the fire-bombing of Dresden in *Slaughterhouse-Five*. And Salinger refused to age at all. Where are his hidden unpublished books? (2014, 86–87)

In Jong's eyes, writing is even more challenging for older women writers because the image of the ageing woman is often correlated with that of the crone or witch:

> And for women writers, as we deepen from the voice of the ingénue to that of the wise woman, it's even worse. Few have mastered this metamorphosis except in memoir. Maybe this is because of our prejudice against old crones – wise or not. And why do we hold on to this prejudice? Out of fear' Intimidation? […] Perhaps it is the Crone's breadth and depth of experience we find so threatening. (2014, 87)

Jong's comments about the increasing difficulty of expressing her thoughts and appealing to a broader audience as an ageing female artist reveal the persistence of sexism, ageism and the narrative of decline in Western society.

According to Jong, these days people are interested in youth, love, sex, and the new. As the writer ages and incorporates older women in her books, she realises that her readership becomes more limited and her works less popular in mainstream culture, in comparison to her earlier works:

> I never expected to get this old […]. I get excited about writing a poem as I ever did. The question is whether other people get as excited about poems about aging as they do about poems of first love. […] And our society is in love with the new. As we age, our writing ages with us and sometimes we wonder if anybody cares but other women of a certain age. Yes, they are the most avid readers, but often they are readers whose taste goes unconsidered and unmarked. The young are the important tastemakers, and if we write about the ironies of aging, perhaps they can't identify. (2014, 84–85)

In an interview following the publication of *Fear of Dying*, Jong expresses the idea that with age it becomes more difficult to write and to express one's thoughts in a frank way. In fact, she "found it very, very hard to write [the novel *Fear of Dying*] because of the shadow of fame still cast by Isadora Wing":

> The fact was, everybody kept wanting me to write a book about Isadora Wing, […] And I honestly tried, but I felt that it as a character she had so much baggage that it was hard to

> write. And I thought, 'I'm not there any more. I'm in a different place in my life, and the voice should be a different voice'. (Larsen, 4 Oct. 2015)

Similarly, in another interview conducted the same year, Jong said that in order not to disappoint the audience, she made Isadora, the protagonist of her ground-breaking book, *Fear of Flying*, a minor character in the novel:

> The other reason was I couldn't find a voice for the book. Everybody wanted me to write the last Isadora book, and Isadora just had too much baggage. And it was only when I was almost finished with the book that I introduced her as a minor character who was best friends with my major character. (Lacher, 18 Sept. 2015)

These assertions suggest that the process of growing older helps Jong to reconsider her values and preferences—she can no longer identify with the youthful and frenetic Isadora. Instead of reviving her famous heroine, the writer creates a more grounded and mature fictional character, Vanessa. Committed to her readers, mainly to women of her generation, Jong seeks to communicate that women should express themselves freely, and age the way they want to.

Although Jong inspires women to voice their fears and anxieties, and challenges the notion that creativity decreases with age, in her works the author also expresses her concerns about the "double standard" of ageing and the representation of older women as deformed, desexualised, frail, sagging, and unattractive, which leaves them vulnerable and invisible (Sontag 1972). Jong's *oeuvre*, in particular her middle and later-life writings, show that women's individual satisfaction is closely related to the desire to reshape and rejuvenate their ageing bodies. Jong's fictional characters seem to have a sense of discordance between their youthful inner selves and their exterior images, which may negatively influence the development of their creative capacity and generate ambiguous and conflicting feelings. For instance, the heroine Vanessa in *Fear of Dying* is so displeased with her ageing body and the loss of her charms, that she would sell her soul to the devil if he could promise her the recovery of her beauty and the power of seduction:

> Now I believed I was old, and I didn't like it. I didn't like the hairs on my chin. I didn't like dyeing my eyebrows. I wanted my youth back – even with all its miseries. I envy the young and they don't know they are enviable. *I* certainly didn't know it when I was young. I hate, hate, *hate* getting older. I would sell my soul to the devil to stay young. (2015, 151, emphasis in original)

These internal discrepancies generate ambiguous and conflicting feelings and reveal a profound fragmentation of one's identity. Jong's writings also suggest that even if older women should accept the natural process of growing older and regard the signs of ageing as footprints of their life experiences, they are constrained by a powerful anti-ageing discourse, which limits their choices and self-expression. In her works, the female characters are grounded in prejudiced sociocultural realities and subjected to the patriarchal tyranny to always remain youthful and sexually attractive. In her midlife memoir *Fear of Fifty*, Jong writes that as she grows older, she feels younger and more liberated; however, her body and society become more unforgiving: "when we are dewy-faced and tender-looking we tend to be horribly tough on ourselves. At fifty, we are more ready to forgive. And this is when the flesh becomes most unforgiving" (1994, 61). The obsession with rejuvenation and the cult of youth is not only visible in the desire to stop the ravages of age, but it is also reflected in the writer's wish to adjust to readers' preferences. As Jong ages, she becomes empowered by her more mature and self-confident voice; yet, she is disempowered by a society that, as she states, "is in love with the new" (2014, 84–85). However, even if Jong feels constrained by social expectations and readers' preferences, the author does not seek to renounce her confidence in writing and the courage to speak her mind. Jong claims to find pleasure in writing about "who we are now, as we age in utterly unexpected ways" (2014, 86).

Conclusion

In Jong's later works, self-reflexive narratives and her most recent personal accounts, the process of growing older is characterised by new understandings of life, enhanced confidence, maturity, and an increased sense of inner strength. Over time, Jong has learnt to lend more importance to the process of creation, the discovery of her inner voice, and her individual style, rather than to the perceived outcome or reception of her works. Instead of fading into invisibility and despair after the negative criticism that her earlier works received, the author emerges as a consolidated writer, whose later life writings shatter the prejudices associated with older women's creative inactivity, invisibility, and lack of intellectual capacity. Although Jong's mid- and later life works reveal that ageing does not render the creative process easier, and that the "double standard" of ageing makes women more vulnerable and invisible, in her case the act of life writing becomes apparently fearless with age. A constant interaction between memory processes and a willingness to resolve past struggles suggests that the author learns to come to terms with her ageing process, creative mechanisms, and the evolution of her literary persona. Memory processes also help her to deal with the "fear of writing" and the ghosts of the past that no longer inhibit her writing but, on the contrary, deliver the strength and courage to continue her life story well into old age. Moreover, her later works demonstrate a balanced vision of the process of growing older, which challenges the narrative of decline and negative connotations associated with the creative drive in later years. As Mike Hepworth states, since fiction is "a creative mental activity requiring author and reader to extend her or himself imaginatively into the minds of other characters", it "evidently adds a further dimension to our understanding of the quality of the ageing experience" (2000, 5). A creative drive that is expressed through life narratives allows for a more successful adaptation of both the writer and reader to old age and an understanding of how memory shapes the perception of our changing selves.

Jong's life narratives and her ability to look inward can encourage new ways of thinking about the future of ageing and can help to reconsider the notions associated with old age and late-life artistic expressions. At the same time, her later works challenge prejudiced sociocultural realities that inform the process of growing older, and inspire women of her generation to face ageing without fear. This approach may be viewed as a new beginning accompanied by inner strength and courage to speak one's mind, as exemplified in these lines, taken from one of the recent interviews with Jong:

> I'd say I'm ageing very gracefully. I'm happy and happier with every passing year and I feel more empowered in my writing and even more empowered when I have to do a book tour because it reminds me that I don't suffer fools gladly. I have absolutely no problem saying to people, 'That's a stupid question, move on!' (Finch, 13 Nov. 2015)

In sum, Jong learns to transform her inhibiting initial fears into personal "victories" and courageous "flights" as she moves towards maturity and a sense of transcendence during her life journey into older age. Over time, the older writer realises that the "fear of flying" is not justified because, paraphrasing the author, only by doing the things that we most fear in life can we progress, grow, and age in harmony with ourselves and the external world (1999, 125).

Notes

1. Creative achievement has predominantly been identified with the period of youth, as exemplified in the works of well-known Romantic poets who died young: Keats died of tuberculosis, Lord Byron of cholera in Greece, and Shelley drowned (Cohen-Shalev 1989, 25). Similar ideas are also observed by Emma Domínguez-Rué, who argues that artists of the first decades of the twentieth century associated ageing with the loss of their creative potential, which led to personal conflicts and anxieties (2004, 63). These notions are reflected in the works of some well-known writers, such as T.S. Eliot in his "Love Song of J. Alfred Prufrock" (1915), F. Scott Fitzgerald in his *Tender Is the Night* (1934), or Evelyn Waugh in his *Brideshead Revisited* (1944). Yet, Cohen-Shalev claims that the assumed power of youthful creativity is a cultural construct and depends on dominant ideologies about age in different historical periods (1989, 25).
2. The writer did not blame men for ascribing an inferior status to women writers. According to her, men take in this notion through mainstream culture and patriarchal discourses, which make women's writing seem less valuable, weaker, and more sentimental. Although Jong has achieved celebrity status as a writer, past her midlife, she continues to think that women are less represented in male-dominated literary circles. For the author, "[a] woman writer must not only invent the wheel, she must grow the tree and chop it down, whittle it round, and learn to make it roll. Then she must clear a path for herself" (1994, 145). Even though men, like women, also struggle to be recognised in the literary domain, they are not obliged to "convince the world that [they have] the *right* to find [their] voices" (Jong 1994, 145, emphasis in original).
3. In her early forties, Jong confessed that since graduate school she considered Nabokov as the "cleverest writer in the world" (as quoted in Templin 2002, 146). She attempted a Nabokovian style novel under the title *God on West End Avenue* about a young mad poet who considered himself God (1974, 264).
4. Germaine Greer's view on old age might be considered too simplistic as it seems to offer the other extreme of the narrative of decline.
5. On Erica Jong's attitudes towards sexual practices and the perception of sexuality in later years, please see: Ieva Stončikaitė. 2017. "'No, My Husband Isn't Dead, [But] One Has to Re-Invent Sexuality': Reading Erica Jong for the Future of Aging."

Disclosure statement

No potential conflict of interest was reported by the author.

References

Burns, Carole. 2015. "Erica Jong is Back – as Fearless as Ever." *The Washington Post*. Accessed September 8. www.washingtonpost.com/entertainment/books/erica-jong-is-back--as-fearless-as-ever/2015/09/08/2dd30a18-55d7-11e5-b8c9-944725fcd3b9_story.html.

Casado, Núria, Emma Domínguez, and Brian Worsfold, eds. 2016. *Literary Creativity and the Older Woman Writer: A Collection of Critical Essays*. Bern: Peter Lang.

Cohen-Shalev, Amir. 1989. "Old Age Style: Developmental Changes in Creative Production from a Life-span Perspective." *Journal of Aging Studies* 3 (1): 21–37.

Cooke, Rachel. 2015. "Erica Jong: 'There are a Million Ways of Making Love … .'" *The Guardian*. Accessed October 25. www.theguardian.com/books/2015/oct/25/erica-jong-million-ways-of-making-love-interview.

Domínguez-Rué, Emma. 2004. "I May Not be a Lady, But 'I'm All a Woman': Triumphant Middle Age in Ellen Glasgow's *Barren Ground*." In *The Polemics of Ageing as Reflected in Literatures in English*, edited by Brian J. Worsfold, Maria Vidal-Grau, and Núria Casado-Gual, 63–73. Lleida: Servei d'Edicions i Publicacions de la Universitat de Lleida.

Finch, Hannah. 2015. "Erica Jong Explores the No-strings Sex Lives of the Over Sixties." *WMN Western Morning News*. Accessed November 13. www.westernmorningnews.co.uk/Erica-Jong-explores-strings-sex-life-sixties/story-28169086-detail/story.html.

Greer, Germaine. 1991. *The Change: Women, Ageing and the Menopause*. London: Hamish Hamilton.

Gullette, Margaret Morganroth. 2004. *Aged by Culture*. Chicago: The University of Chicago Press.

Hepworth, Mike. 2000. *Stories of Aging*. Buckingham: Open University.

Jong, Erica. (1972) 1980. "The Artist as Housewife." In *In Her Own Image: Women Working in the Arts*, edited by Elaine Hedges and Ingrid Wendt, 115–120. New York: Feminist Press.

Jong, Erica. 1974. "Writing a First Novel." *Twentieth Century Literature* 20 (4): 262–269.

Jong, Erica. 1975. *Loveroot: Poems*. New York: Holt, Rinehart and Winston.

Jong, Erica. 1980. "The Artist as Housewife" (*Mr. 1972*). In *In Her Own Image: Women Working in the Arts*, edited by Elaine Hedges, and Ingrid Wendt, 115–120. New York: Feminist Press.

Jong, Erica. 1983. *Ordinary Miracles: New Poems*. New York: New American Library.

Jong, Erica. 1990. *Any Woman's Blues*. London: Arrow Books.

Jong, Erica. 1994. *Fear of Fifty, A Mid-life Memoir*. New York: Harper Collins Publishers.

Jong, Erica. 1999. *What Do Women Want? Bread, Roses, Sex, Power*. London: Bloomsbury.

Jong, Erica. (1973) 2003. *Fear of Flying*. New York: A Signet Book.

Jong, Erica. 2006. *Seducing the Demon: Writing for My Life*. New York: Penguin.

Jong, Erica. 2014. "Breaking the Final Taboo." In *A Story Larger than My Own. Women Writers Look Back on their Lives and Careers*, edited by Janet Burroway, 84–93. Chicago: Chicago Press.

Jong, Erica. 2015. *Fear of Dying*. New York: St. Martin's Press.

Lacher, Irene. 2015. "Why Erica Jong Decided to Take on Mortality in *Fear of Dying*." *LATimes*. Accessed September 18. www.latimes.com/books/jacketcopy/la-ca-jc-conversation-fear-of-dying-20150920-story.html.

Larsen, Peter. 2015. "Erica Jong and Her Characters Grow Up." *The Orange Country Register*. Accessed October. www.ocregister.com/articles/jong-685876-book-says.html.

Randall, William L., and A. Elizabeth McKim. 2008. *Reading Our Lives. The Poetics of Growing Old*. Oxford: Oxford University Press.

Ross, Catherine E., and John Mirowsky. 2008. "Age and the Balance of Emotions." *Social Science and Medicine* 66 (12): 2391–2400.

Sarton, May. 1997. "Toward Another Dimension." In *The Other Within Us: Feminist Explorations of Women and Aging*, edited by Marilyn Pearsall, 229–233. Boulder: Westview Press.

Sontag, Susan. 1972. "The Double Standard of Aging." *The Saturday Review* 23: 29–38.

Stončikaitė, Ieva. 2017. "'No, My Husband isn't Dead, [But] One Has to Re-invent Sexuality': Reading Erica Jong for the Future of Aging." *Societies* 7 (2): 11.

Templin, A. Charlotte, ed. 2002. *Conversations with Erica Jong*. Jackson: University Press of Mississippi.

Thone, Ruth Raymond. 1992. *Women and Aging: Celebrating Ourselves*. New York: Haworth Press.
Vogei, J. Linda. 1995. "Spiritual Development in Later Life." In *Aging, Spirituality, and Religion: A Handbook I*, edited by A. Melvin Kimble, and Susan H. McFadden, 74–87. Minneapolis: Augsburg Fortress Press.
Waxman, Barbara Frey. 1990. *From the Hearth to the Open Road: A Feminist Study of Aging in Contemporary Literature*. New York: Greenwood Press.
Wyatt-Brown, Anne M. 1989. "Creativity in Midlife: The Novels of Anita Brookner." *Journal of Aging Studies* 3 (2): 175–181.
Wyatt-Brown, Anne M. 2010. "Resilience and Creativity in Aging: *The Realms of Silver*." In *A Guide to Humanistic Studies in Aging: What Does It Mean to Grow Old?*, edited by Thomas R. Cole, Ruth E. Ray, and Robert Kastenbaum, 57–83. Baltimore, MD: Johns Hopkins University Press.

From Girl to Grotesque: Exploring the Intersection of Ageing, Illness, and Agency in Auto/biographical Narratives About Seventies Icon Farrah Fawcett

Lucinda Rasmussen

ABSTRACT

This article examines life narratives by and about seventies television celebrity Farrah Fawcett (1947–2009). It begins by examining how Fawcett's success at the height of her popularity is connected to life narratives which present her as perpetually young, or girlish, an image which bolsters the heteropatriarchy while undermining feminist work being done to counter gender inequality. By tracing Fawcett's celebrity construction throughout a selection of auto/biographical narratives over her career, including some coinciding with the rise of postfeminism, I situate my analysis of her girlish persona within discussions about celebrity culture and ageism. In this way, I argue that Fawcett's girlish persona, once a source of her power, deeply complicates her ageing process, particularly when she sets about to create an illness narrative titled *Farrah's Story* (2009), a television documentary depicting her experiences with terminal cancer. While there has been some tendency to interpret *Farrah's Story* as evidence that Fawcett was a victim of celebrity culture, I locate Fawcett's agency in my interpretation of this work, to argue that *Farrah's Story* is strategically created to depict Fawcett's personal growth as she begins to question what constitutes social accountability within an invasive media culture known for its negative treatment of women.

Farrah Fawcett, best known for her role as Jill Munroe on the seventies television detective drama *Charlie's Angels*, died on 25 June 2009 at age 62 of anal cancer. As a pre-teen viewer, I was an enthusiastic fan of *Charlie's Angels*, and my favourite of the three female protagonists was Fawcett's character. My admiration was shared by many North-American girls of my age at the time. Elana Levine, for instance, recalls how a group of fourth-grade girls identified "Farrah Fawcett-Majors" as the celebrity whom they would most like to emulate (2007, 123).[1] Levine explains that many of these girls chose Fawcett as a role model on the basis of her appearance (123). Likewise, Whitney Womack recalls how, at six-years-old, "[her] most treasured possession was a plastic bust of Farrah Fawcett, complete with her trademark feathered hairdo and blindingly white smile" (2003, 151). While perhaps not immediately apparent, these girls were responding to a constructed image of Fawcett as emblematically young. Indeed, several biographies about Fawcett emerged in the seventies, each of which presented an account of her rise to stardom organised, significantly, around descriptions of Fawcett's youthful brand of heteronormative femininity.[2] One of these, *Farrah: An Unauthorized Biography* (1977), was the book that provided me with what I, as a pre-teen girl, took as an accurate account of Fawcett's life, while also ushering me into the world of fashion and beauty consumption. Written by Patricia Burstein and published by Penguin in 1977 (the year I turned 12 and during the first season of *Charlie's Angels*), *Farrah* is part a celebrity biography and part instruction manual, rife with details on how to copy Fawcett's hairstyle and exercise routine, as well as her approach to career and romantic relationships. The point I want to emphasise is how Burstein throughout her biography helps to inscribe Fawcett as an exemplar of young womanhood, by describing her as variably as "fresh, outdoorsy, and quiety sexy" (1997, 71), or as a beauty who "keeps her golden look by running on the beach and playing a competitive game of tennis" (101).

While *Farrah* (1977) chronicles Fawcett's rise to celebrity status in the late-seventies, some 30 years later Fawcett's autobiographical cancer documentary is a very different type of work. *Farrah's Story* (2009), which originally aired on television shortly before Fawcett's death, and which runs about ninety minutes, follows Fawcett through her experiences with the conventional health system in the United States, as well as through an alternative treatment plan that she underwent in Germany. Throughout the documentary, Fawcett touches on several social issues, including her concern that "more research [needs to be] done on certain types of cancer" as well as her worry that the conventional healthcare system fails to "embrace alternative treatments that have proven to be successful in other countries." In addition, *Farrah's Story* holds both the American health system and especially the gossip industry accountable for breaching her privacy, an event that happened when a UCLA healthcare worker leaked news of her cancer diagnosis to the tabloids. While *Farrah's Story* touches on these important topics, it also includes considerable footage to show how Fawcett looked in the seventies. These images starkly contrast those of Fawcett when she is sick, and consequently, while *Farrah's Story* prompts viewers to contemplate social concerns, it does so by inviting them to mourn Fawcett's lost youth. In this way, *Farrah's Story* contributes to what Margaret Morganroth Gullette (2017) refers to as "decline ideology." What this means is that as a woman who, in addition to being ill, has clearly begun to age, Fawcett's cancer narrative is inevitably yoked to a set of naturalised ageist rhetorical and visual practices, practices Gullette locates in the "Visual, discursive, medical, economic, political, bureaucratic [and] legal" spheres of contemporary culture (xviii). Thus, I argue that to fully grasp the significance of *Farrah's Story*, one must take into account Fawcett's status as a female celebrity who is ageing in a postfeminist media culture that is undeniably hostile toward older women.

Situating Fawcett's *Farrah's Story* (2009) in a conversation about ageing provides an opportunity to reflect on critical responses to this documentary, including my own. Initially, I found Fawcett's illness narrative difficult to watch—not merely because it is unpleasant to witness another person suffer but because my pre-teen experiences as her fan meant that I had come to associate Fawcett with my youth, and thus to see her in the end stages of her life reminded me of my own mortality. While Fawcett's cancer narrative on its surface is not about ageing, in it she is visibly older, an observation which, alongside the realisation that Fawcett has stage four cancer, is anxiety producing, not least because it conflates the social scripts of ageing and terminal disease. Sally Chivers, in her discussion of celebrity, ageing, and disability, explains why fans experience anxiety when witnessing celebrities' "previously ideal bodies deviat[ing] from their own previous youthful standard" (2011, 43). In her view, fans fear the personal impacts of ageing when it becomes apparent that "if even Hollywood stars age, then so too must we" (43). Chivers goes on to explain how celebrities once admired can become subjects of scorn as their bodies and appearances change: "This horror [which fans experience]," writes Chivers, "ironically allows the audience members to distance themselves from the [ageing] process" (43). This distancing process can materialise as the audience's disavowal of the ill person's efforts to share their pain, a response that one can locate in some reactions to *Farrah's Story*. For instance, on 16 May 2009, Alessandra Stanley with *The New York Times* described *Farrah's Story* in an online review as "awful" with its "maudlin music, gauzy slow-motion film, and pseudo-revealing interviews with friends, coworkers, doctors and hairdressers reminiscing about a former star." Stanley's criticism is partly a response to a scene at the documentary's end where Fawcett's son, shackled while on a compassionate leave from his prison sentence for narcotics possession, is filmed at his mother's sickbed. Fawcett is gravely ill, and it is uncertain to what extent she is aware of her son's presence or the cameras during this intimate moment. For such reasons, Stanley condemns *Farrah's Story* for its tabloid excesses, and is concerned that Fawcett may have been exploited in the process of the documentary's creation.[3] Elsewhere, Coline Covington, in an essay titled "Farrah Fawcett in Denial as She Films Cancer Battle," is kinder, but implies that Fawcett's decisions surrounding her medical care plan may have been poorly made, and speculates that Fawcett's fear left her "particularly susceptible to exploitation and false promises" (2014, 72). Taking a different approach, Christopher Kelly praised *Farrah's Story,* as a "genuine public service" (2009, 62). For this commentator, the documentary constitutes Fawcett's finest work, but here the writer also reads Fawcett's work leading up to *Farrah's Story* as evidence she was "a kind of victim" within celebrity culture (62), as well as "intransigent and reckless" in her refusal to heed physicians' advice (64). In my view, each of these commentaries is problematic for its failure to ascribe Fawcett agency when it came to determining her own healthcare plan and preparation for her death. One way to locate Fawcett's agency within these difficult circumstances is to consider them alongside her ongoing work to construct a self-representation that allowed her to navigate attitudes toward ageing women both in *Farrah's Story* and in other narratives about her life.

When those who witness an auto/biographical performance question its creator's capacity to act, it says as much about the culture in which the work has been produced as it does about the life narrator. Sidonie Smith and Julia Watson remind readers that "people tell stories of their lives through the cultural scripts available to them, and they are governed by cultural strictures about self-presentation in public" (2001, 42). Fawcett clearly understands this reality and how it pertains to her as an actress who is both ageing and ill. For example, towards the end of *Farrah's Story* (2009), Fawcett expressed frustration over how tabloid reporters "[were] always trying to get" a photograph of her in a wheelchair. Coincidentally, when writing about Joan Crawford's age in the film *Whatever Happened to Baby Jane*, Chivers argues that filmmakers put Crawford's character in a wheelchair because it made it easier for viewers to "accept the aging of Crawford if she is seen as also disabled" (2011, 40). Fawcett's acute awareness of the tabloid photographers' objectives suggests her awareness of mainstream culture's reliance on particular tropes to dismiss ageing female celebrities, as well as women more generally, who "become utterly devalued—and thus marginalized and excluded—if they become disabled or suffer from debilitating health conditions as they age" (Bouson 2016, 136). Given Fawcett's clear awareness of cultural tropes, watching *Farrah's Story* should lead viewers to consider the ways in which ageism has been naturalised in contemporary mainstream culture, to the extent that the actress and those who create and consume *Farrah's Story* must be understood as grappling with a deeply connotative understanding of Fawcett as a seventies icon of youthful femininity. It is precisely because Fawcett, in the words of her romantic partner Ryan O'Neal, is so emblematic of "young American womanhood" (2012, 12),[4] that any life narratives constructed about her are always irrevocably linked to discursive practices that give rise to ageism. To understand this problem and its implications, it is essential not only to read *Farrah's Story* as a life narrative about illness, but as a narrative about ageing, celebrity, and postfeminism. As Chivers writes with regard to the first two of these terms, an intersectional approach to the study of ageing and celebrity is vital since within celebrity culture, "old age is akin to disability in the *ways* that they are socially constructed [...] as bodily, threatening, and signalling failure" (2011, 23). Fawcett clearly understood what was at stake when creating *Farrah's Story*, and thus she and those who help her to make the documentary seek to counter certain hostilities to which ageing women in Hollywood are often subjected. These hostilities belong to what Kirsty Fairclough describes as a broader set of "post-feminist trends" (2012, 95), and they are perpetuated by a "gossip industry [where] famous women and their ageing narratives are configured in terms of disintegration and invisibility" (93). As an ageing actress in the first decade of the twenty-first century, Fawcett faced a number of social strictures that complicated the narrativisation of her cancer experience, particularly given the extent to which, at the high point of her popularity, the success of her self-presentation hinged on her girlish appeal. At the same time, it would be fair to assume that Fawcett's performance of girlishness throughout her career was a reason that some viewers found it difficult to trust her decision-making at the end of her life.

To examine *Farrah's Story* (2009) for what it can reveal about ageing, celebrity, and postfeminism, this article draws on auto/biographical traces found within texts from several genres and mediums where auto/biographical anecdotes about Fawcett are recounted: these include memoirs by famous men who wrote about her (O'Neal and Bernstein), a celebrity biography (Burstein), Fawcett's illness documentary (*Farrah's Story*), Fawcett's short-lived reality television programme (*Chasing Farrah*), and magazines (*Playboy* and *People*). In particular, Burstein's *Farrah* will be discussed because traces of its type of rhetoric surface frequently in later life narratives about her—an observation which supports my claim that an understanding of Fawcett's seventies persona and the mythology it engenders is central to understanding the narrative of her illness nearly three decades later. The trajectory taking place across these seemingly disparate platforms for auto/biographical utterances, while necessary to gain an appreciation of *Farrah's Story* as it is discussed in the latter part of this article, does require some qualification. To understand how Fawcett's celebrity persona can be read across multiple forms, it is useful to draw on Marshall and Barbour's definition of persona as "the construction, constitution, and production of the self through identity play and performance by the individual in social settings" (2015, 2). A celebrity's persona is constructed and marketed through many auto/biographical moments, all created to satisfy one or more of the public's desires across different social contexts, which also "intersect with biographical and autobiographical studies, and the related areas of life writing in their exploration of the presentation of the public figure in all sorts of environments" (Marshall and Barbour 2015, 9). Marshall and Barbour's observations are usefully considered alongside Smith and Watson's view that life narrators who "explore the body and embodiment as sites of knowledge and knowledge production [...] [must] negotiate cultural norms determining the proper uses of bodies" (2001, 41). While Smith and Watson refer to auto/biographical narratives in a general sense, it goes without saying that the public's perception of what constitutes a woman's "proper use" of her body shifts and changes over time. By examining a trajectory which takes place across auto/biographical narratives by and about Fawcett, it becomes possible to understand how Fawcett's celebrity persona is, through a series of related auto/biographical moments, constructed as girlish in the seventies, but how, as she ages as a subject of postfeminism, this same identity surfaces as an impediment.

Fawcett's status as an exemplar of youthful heteronormative femininity in seventies America is indisputable. While a popular television celebrity of the time in her own right, she was also the wife of Lee Majors, famous for the television programme *The Six Million Dollar Man.* In addition to her high-profile marriage and work on *Charlie's Angels*, Fawcett's "red swimsuit" poster brought her fame, with the poster reportedly achieving sales of some "eight million copies in 1976 alone" (Gough-Yates 2001, 93). The poster's success is of particular interest for the way it is predicated on an image of Fawcett as an exemplar of successful ageing. Burstein's way of writing about Fawcett in *Farrah* also emphasises her youthfulness, an approach which situates the biography within a reactionary discourse undermining second-wave feminism. In other words, Fawcett's image as it is presented in works such as *Farrah* fulfils a social need, which is to alleviate some of mainstream patriarchal society's anxiety over the emergence of a strong women's movement.

Insight into the discursive system designed to promote Fawcett in the seventies can be located in Jay Bernstein's memoir *Starmaker* (2011), in which he remembers his work as Fawcett's publicity agent and reveals how the construction of her celebrity persona is grounded in a narrative of successful ageing. Unsurprisingly, Bernstein takes credit for Fawcett's success, stating that Fawcett's status as "America's new role model" (130) happened in part because she allowed him to "reveal her age in a publicity campaign" (132). In Bernstein's view, this move facilitated what would become the hugely successful dissemination of the red swimsuit poster. As Bernstein explains, "Farrah was [at the time of posing for this photograph] almost thirty [whereas] [t]raditionally, the perfect celluloid woman was under twenty-five" (132). According to Bernstein, Fawcett, who looked younger than 30, heeded his advice to share her age with the public, whose response to this disclosure was enthusiastic: in his words, "[Fawcett] received a half-million letters from young women, saying in effect, 'I'm twenty-six, and I thought I was over the hill. Thanks to you, I realize I've got a few more years to get my life together'" (133). Bernstein's memoir shows that part of the poster's success as a marketplace commodity can be connected directly to an image of Fawcett as a woman who does not visibly age. Consequently, Fawcett's life story in the seventies operates as a type of "time panic"—a phrase Diane Negra identifies as one of the "signature attributes of postfeminist culture" (2009, 47)—

by suggesting to women that to have value after the age of 30, they must still look and behave like girls.

This point prompts a return to the earlier claim that *Farrah's Story* (2009) and indeed all of Fawcett's auto/biographical representations are, by virtue of being about ageing, also linked to discourses and tropes associated with postfeminism. Postfeminism, an ideology that becomes particularly pervasive as a manifestation in popular culture in the late 1990s and into the twenty-first century, actively seeks to undermine or interfere with feminism as a social movement that is invested in bringing about gender equality (McRobbie 2009, 2015). Angela McRobbie tracks "a line of connection between the forces of the new right which from the start of the 1970s, mobilised against the women's movement through various actions and strategies" (2009, 8). This timing is significant when considering the evolution of Fawcett's persona over the course of her life, particularly as Fawcett was growing older in the nineties and early-twenty-first century, a time when, as Fairclough (2012) notes, aggressive ageism practiced within the postfeminist gossip industry was particularly heightened. By extension, the ways in which *Farrah* helps to establish Fawcett's life story as part of a discourse that rebukes feminism predicts a pattern that McRobbie associates with a postfeminist ideology. As she has shown, each time feminism "re-enter[s] political culture and civil society, there is, as though to hold this threat of new feminism at bay, an amplification of control of women, mostly by corporeal means, so as to ensure the maintenance of existing power relations" (2015, Abstract). Cultural critics have studied the ways that women who encounter this ideology and who buy into its premises will participate in discursive practices whereby they present themselves as having *chosen* to conform to what is ultimately a rather conservative set of gender norms (McRobbie 2009; Negra 2009; Gill and Scharff 2011; Gill 2016). Burstein's *Farrah* works in precisely this way. Fawcett's success in the seventies—constructed on the basis that she was a 30-year-old woman who looked beautiful, and who deferred demurely to her husband —suggests that her celebrity persona was manufactured in ways that align it with work countering the women's movement.

Bernstein's disclosure helps to contextualise earlier work by Burstein, who in *Farrah* helps to create "The Farrah Phenomenon" (1977, 1). This earlier work, which coincides with Fawcett's rise in popularity, informs readers that Fawcett is 30 years old (Burstein 1977, 102), while drawing attention to Fawcett's youthful appearance and conventional femininity. Specifically, Burstein repeatedly makes the point that Fawcett is both girlish and by extension wholesome: for instance, she refers to Fawcett as "the 100 percent girl [who] wears the 100 percent look" (78–79), as well as an "old-fashioned girl baking cookies" (103). Burstein also frequently cites powerful men in the entertainment industry who explain why Fawcett is irresistible; for example, producer Barney Rosenzweig describes Fawcett as having a "sensuality that appeals to every guy and the little girl about her that brings out the paternal instinct" (as quoted in Burstein 1977, 93). Elsewhere, television director Allen Baron refers to Fawcett's "childlike nature" (as quoted in Burstein 1977, 97) while Ray Browne, "a professor of Popular Culture," describes Fawcett as:

> [...] virginal. She is the very attractive girl next-door rather than the sex goddess down the street at the movie house. She does not represent sex except in the safest sense of the word. She is too young to be sexy [...]. Farrah is the young girl whom you look at and don't touch and *strikingly* don't *want* to touch. (As quoted in Burstein 1977, 130–131)

The biographer's characterisation of Fawcett as childlike is juxtaposed with comments about her infamous brand of innocent sex appeal, which is presented as non-disruptive to conventional gender hierarchies.

Indeed, one contributor to Burstein's *Farrah* locates in Fawcett the answer to the question of "what constitutes sexuality in an age of sexual freedom?" (Rosenblatt quoted in Burstein 1977, 133). The answer provided implies that Fawcett's girlishness is a quality to emulate—after all, "*nobody* takes offense at this gorgeous sex symbol" (Burstein 1977, 2). Burstein makes clear that Fawcett understands how to behave appropriately in public life, noting that "[even] [t]hough Farrah is on the advisory board of the Women's Bank of Los Angeles, she does not embrace feminism" (124–125). Consequently, the biography, in inviting women to emulate Fawcett, suggests that feminism has no bearing on whether or not a woman will be successful: indeed, a properly feminine woman (like Fawcett) will distance herself from feminism so as to participate in public life without threatening heteropatriarchy. *Farrah* even goes so far as to explicitly identify Fawcett as a representation of "the Total Woman" (Burstein 1977, 1). The phrase refers to Marabel Morgan's 1973 advice manual of the same title, a work that disavows feminism's goal of gender equality while teaching its female reader that within the heterosexual marriage, "[c]ommitment involves a woman's full surrender to her man" (113).[5] Ultimately Morgan's goal is to teach her presumably female reader how a husband "wants the girl of his dreams to be feminine, soft, and touchable when he gets home" (92). Burstein aligns Fawcett with this model of correct womanhood by repeatedly emphasising how Fawcett's role as Lee Majors' wife "takes precedence over every other facet of her life" (117).

While I am arguing that Fawcett's popularity in the seventies emerges from cultural scripts that undermine feminism, some criticism of Fawcett has taken a different route by suggesting she and her co-stars on *Charlie's Angels* can be read as feminist role models. Anna Gough-Yates acknowledges that many academic commentators have identified the programme as misogynistic, while also "interpret[ing] the show as part of a wider 'backlash' against feminism in the American media during the late 1970s" (2001, 83). However, she also notes that the programme "engaged with shifting discourses around feminism and the lifestyles of single women in a meaningful [...] way" as a liberal feminist text (96). Such views only confirm that an optimistic reading of *Charlie's Angels* is possible. However, Burstein's *Farrah* makes it clear that the character Fawcett impersonates on *Charlie's Angels* and Fawcett are different in one key way. While Burstein admits that Fawcett is similar to Jill Munroe in that each is "sexy, athletic and outdoorsy" (1977, 83), she clarifies that Jill Munroe's attitude toward relationships differs from Fawcett's. As Burstein remarks, Munroe's "relations with the opposite sex are active," whereas Fawcett is in a monogamous relationship as the wife of "the Six-Million-Dollar Man" (83). As this biography demonstrates, Fawcett's image reified a heteropatriarchal worldview which presented Fawcett as a double standard; specifically, it showed her as sexually self-aware by virtue of the character she played on television, but also as appropriately submissive when making choices about how to conduct herself in her personal life. Understood in this fashion, Fawcett's celebrity persona at the height of its success is modelled to equate female empowerment with gender conformity.

However, Fawcett's decision to leave *Charlie's Angels* as well as to eventually divorce Majors after separating from him in 1979 were at odds with the public persona that had been constructed of her at that point in time. After *Charlie's Angels,* Fawcett would go on to have roles in a number of television films and motion pictures, such as *Extremities* (1986) and *The Burning Bed* (1984)—works that respectively condemn men for sexual violence and domestic abuse, and which did earn her some acclaim.[6] However, while Fawcett's popularity in the seventies meant that she could play a sexually autonomous character on television without fear of reprisal, when she separated from Majors and began a new romantic relationship with actor Ryan O'Neal, her private life no longer neatly mapped onto the celebrity persona that she and those Hollywood patriarchs who promoted her had worked to create. Obviously, Fawcett's decisions demonstrated her unwillingness to fully conform to patriarchal authority: these acts also coincided with her growing older and rendered her susceptible to criticism. In her analysis of what makes female pop stars in the music industry successful, Kristin Lieb writes that female entertainers with life stories about the "men who have saved them [...] at different points in their careers" (2013, 126) can leverage a "*protected status,* most commonly through [...] marriage to an industry insider" (91). Lieb's argument applies here as well, particularly since within Fawcett's celebrity narrative, Majors was generally represented as teaching Fawcett how to survive "the brash, tough world of Hollywood" (Burstein 1977, 54). The image of Fawcett as in need of a male protector recalls the sort of naiveté that would be associated with someone who is young and inexperienced and thus maps well onto the celebrity construction of Fawcett as a girl wed to and under the protection of an American hero. It is incongruent with the person who Fawcett later becomes after she divorces Majors, makes films about domestic and sexual violence, and remains unmarried to the man with whom she eventually has a child.

It has been demonstrated that Fawcett's popularity in the seventies was due to her girlish persona, part of which involved a particular type of self-presentation predicated on the public's willingness to accept her as a girl, and by extension as someone who was reliant on male authority. However, whereas prior representations of Fawcett as both sexy and innocent seemed to garner her praise while she was in her 30s, Fawcett's efforts to remain visible as an older unmarried actress were fraught. Tabloids would describe Fawcett as "the angel who fell from grace" while also remarking on Fawcett's status as an unwed mother (Darrach 1984, 55). For instance, a writer for the December 1984 issue of *People* reports that despite being pregnant Fawcett "at 37" had no plans to "marry the baby's father, though Ryan has proposed repeatedly" (Darrach 1984, 55). In this article, O'Neal, whose age is not given, is represented sympathetically, while Fawcett is subtly criticised for refusing his proposal. Later, in March 1997, *People* would report that the couple had ended their relationship while continuing to emphasise how "Fawcett declined O'Neal's [proposals]" (Schneider 1997, 94).

While a full exploration of Fawcett's career and relationship with the media is beyond the scope of this paper, it does seem important to consider how, as she grew older, she had far more difficulty in presenting a successful face to the public. As a female celebrity once known for looking younger than her biological age, Fawcett's challenge was growing older in an industry that affords mature women few opportunities to continue to work, and which often derides them as they attempt to remain in the public eye. One way for the mature female performer to maintain visibility "in the spotlight" is, of course, to present herself as a woman who does not "look her age" (Fairclough 2012, 94). As Fawcett approached her 50th birthday, she did in fact attempt to present herself once again as an exemplar of ageing through work as a pin-up model, this time by posing on two occasions in *Playboy*. In the first of these features, published in December 1995, the photographer states that Fawcett has "the body of an 18-year-old" (Factor as quoted in "Farrah!" 1995, 147). Here Fawcett works to rebirth that image of herself as girlish: "I'm shy, even with Ryan," she states within the article. "After 14 years I still can't let him see me change clothes!" (Fawcett quoted in "Farrah!" 1995, 147). Similar rhetorical play is used 2 years later when, at the age of 50, Fawcett once again appeared in *Playboy*, as well as on a pay per view feature *All of Me*. Glenn O'Brien, author of the feature article in *Playboy* magazine, reports that Fawcett still looks like she is 30—specifically he states that she looks "like she was born in 1968"—while also explaining how Fawcett self-identifies as "basically a shy person" (1997). Both *Playboy* articles aim to present Fawcett as an exemplar of successful ageing while also working to show that Fawcett has maintained her girlish brand of sanctioned sex appeal. However, these efforts did not meet with success. In particular, Fawcett's performance in an infamous talk show interview with David Letterman, during which she chose to play the infantilising role of a dumb blonde as she promoted her work in *Playboy*, was derided.[7] One online think piece by Anne Taylor Fleming refers to Fawcett as "a spaced-out, aging sex symbol" (2009). This same commentator discusses Fawcett's appearance in *Playboy* at age 50 as "one of those stops on the way down for beautiful women of iffy talent who still feel it necessary to strut their stuff." Fawcett's tendency to perform using an exaggeratedly infantile method of speaking was also the approach she often took during her short-lived, failed reality television show, *Chasing Farrah*.[8] This programme was likewise dismissed through references to Fawcett's age, with Alessandra Stanley reporting that "many older actresses are trapped in comeback comedies where the joke is mostly on them" (2005). As Stanley goes on to report in her assessment of *Chasing Farrah*, "Farrah Fawcett [...] [is] more Blanche Dubois than 'Charlie's Angels'."

These self-representations and certain responses to them suggest that as Fawcett grew older, the same behaviours she employed as a young actress were read as "'grotesque'" with regard to a mature woman playing an "eccentric or 'sick,' 'under the influence,' or even 'possessed'" role (M. C. Kolbenschlag as quoted in Morey 2011, 103). Why did Fawcett choose to risk this type of criticism by behaving in ways deemed inappropriate for a woman of her age? The difficulties she experienced with managing her persona have much to do with postfeminist media culture and its heightened ideological reach through the late nineties and into the first decade of the twenty-first century. Significantly, McRobbie explains that a young postfeminist woman at the time was permitted to, for instance, attend a lap-dancing club or expose her breasts in public as evidence of her liberation (2009, 18). However, McRobbie acknowledges that the ideal postfeminist subject will not receive positive attention for such behaviours once she grows old (2009, 84). Elsewhere, Chivers posits that some ageing female celebrities "risk scandal to remain on screen" (2011, 42). As she draws from Russo, Chivers explores the possibility that celebrities might "act *against* [their] age, that is, of not conforming to normative ideas of age-appropriate behaviour" (41). Of course, celebrities who behave against their age might well encounter "ridicule, contempt, pity, and scorn" (Russo as quoted in Chivers 2011, 41), which is precisely what happened to Fawcett. "Nonetheless," writes Chivers, "Russo encourages hazarding such a scandal since the dangers of not taking that risk are equally, if not more, intimidating [...] [because] [a]cting one's age means buying into damaging cultural prescriptions for later life" (41). What is also required of the older female celebrity in order to remain visible is her demonstrated willingness to behave as if being subjected to scrutiny on the basis of age is no big deal. After all, "celebrities who appear in complete control of their lives in terms of career, ageing and personal lives are routinely celebrated" (Fairclough 2012, 95). Fawcett would eventually work to demonstrate her maturation when it comes to ageing on an episode of *Chasing Farrah* titled "Tonight's Guest" (2005), where she explains that people frequently ask her if ageing bothers her. According to Fawcett, "not as much as it seems to bother everybody else." She continues by casually remarking that ageing is "the law of nature." Fawcett's move here is strategic, explaining to her audience that her performance on Letterman was done in fun, and that she is ageing well, this time by conforming to a version of a sanctioned social script in which she articulates that she is comfortable with growing older.

Fawcett's calculated work to remain visible in a postfeminist media culture that has naturalised ageist rhetoric in efforts to manage female conduct is the backdrop against which her final life's work in *Farrah's Story* must be read. By doing so, Fawcett's agency is clear, allowing for the recognition that she has been complicit in the perpetuation of ageist stereotypes, but also with the recognition that her performances had strategic components, insofar as she wanted to establish herself as a performer who had valuable insight to offer. The opening credits of *Farrah's Story* include rolling footage of what is presumably the interior of Fawcett's home. There is a montage of photos in ornate frames taken of the actress at various stages of her life, several of which were also included in Burstein's biography *Farrah*, and one of which is the famous image of Fawcett in the red swimsuit. Within the first 15 minutes of the documentary, Fawcett's internalisation of her youthful persona becomes further apparent, when she refers to herself as "the girl who always believed in change." At the beginning of this documentary, especially, viewers are reminded of Fawcett's fame and with it, her youth. The effects are worth noting since, as Smith and Watson observe, "when we read or listen to an autobiographical narrative, we listen for and attend to the role of remembering—and conscious forgetting—in the act of making meaning out of the past and present" (2010, 30). They show how consumers of autobiography "may notice an emphasis on particular acts of remembering or particular moods and voices identified with certain memories [and that audiences] may glimpse the triggering devices that stimulate certain memories" (2010, 30). Smith and Watson's ideas help elucidate how *Farrah's Story* works to remind audiences of how Fawcett's persona constructed an image of her as girlish, young, and healthy.

The documentary's aim to have viewers recall Fawcett's youth is, however, complicated by a later scene when Fawcett, who is beginning to lose her hair from chemotherapy, makes the decision to shave her head. As the scene proceeds, Fawcett and her hairstylist sing a round of the song, "When I grow up, I want to be an old woman." Fawcett—who is clearly hesitant to participate in the song—ends the segment by asking "am I ready now?" On one level, the scene is problematic for the way it conflates Fawcett's illness experience with ageing, as well as for the stylist's clichéd voiceover reminding viewers how "all that really matters is growing old." On another level, Fawcett's bravery in having the scene filmed constitutes a moment whereby she casts off her seventies celebrity persona. The magnitude of the gesture is emphasised when O'Neal mourns that Fawcett's "head of hair was for real [and] it's gone now." Although O'Neal problematically suggests that Fawcett's identity is contingent on her trademark hair, his comment also conveys the import of

Fawcett's decision to shave her head, and demonstrates how rhetoric naturalising Fawcett's youthful beauty has become the established way of understanding her life—a factor which suggests that this scene was included so that Fawcett might show her depth of character in what she is prepared to do on camera as she moved away from narratives celebrating her for her youthful appearance.[9]

In summary, while *Farrah's Story* draws on Fawcett's past self-representation as a young girl, thereby conveying that the loss of her youthful beauty is the tragedy of her cancer, I believe that there is much more going on. Commentators have noted that Fawcett lacks agency, and with that have suggested her story lacks credibility; for example, Covington notes with scepticism Fawcett's refusal to undergo a colostomy as per her American physicians' advice (2014, 71). However, these commentators are perhaps not seeing the story that Fawcett sought to tell. The idea that Fawcett embodies aspects of the grotesque has already been raised, and is a point to which this essay will now return. Morey has shown that part of

> the trajectory of the typical female performer of the grotesque during the studio era moves her from a youthful persona that emphasizes her physical attractions, to the role of the mother in one or more maternal melodramas, to a maturity in which her embrace of the grotesque acknowledges her prowess as an actress. (2011, 105)

As a celebrity life narrative, *Farrah's Story* is a curious articulation of this portion of Morey's pathway. First, it includes reminders of Fawcett's iconic brand of youthful beauty in the seventies, as well as the previously mentioned intimate, if melodramatic moment she shares with her troubled son. Moreover, the scene in which Fawcett shaves her head while contemplating whether or not she is old is clearly constructed to show Fawcett's maturation. This observation is important because, as Morey shows, "grotesquerie may be a source of professional and even personal power, given the frequent overlap between the dramas played out on the screen and those associated with certain stars' personal lives" (104). In the context of an auto/biographical documentary, Fawcett's performance of the grotesque and her real-life situation are conflated in what becomes her powerful attempt to challenge audiences to confront social problems to which celebrity contributes, such as the gossip industry's brutal treatment of women. The difficulties associated with this mission are considerable since, as medical humanities scholar Arthur Frank notes, "Society prefers medical diagnoses that admit treatment, not social diagnoses that require massive change in the premises of what that social body includes as parts of itself" (2013, 113). While Fawcett may have made questionable health decisions—a physician on the documentary states, for instance, that Fawcett's chemotherapy regimen was initially created so as not to cause hair loss—it bears noting that many "ageing women" who suffer from medical concerns like chronic pain also "tend to delay consulting medical specialists because they assume their aches and pains are signs of old age" (Bouson 2016, 97).[10] If Fawcett's agency is acknowledged in the decision making process, viewers must confront the reality that the way they participate and consume celebrity gossip has costs, one of which is that it is a contributing factor in many women's feelings of shame over growing older, to the extent that those women's health could be impacted because they have internalised negative beliefs about ageing. Fawcett's own performance of a girlish persona throughout much of her career contributes to this problem for other women, but when it comes to *Farrah's Story,* Fawcett begins to ask all participants in tabloid culture to acknowledge their roles in this system, particularly as she actively works to refuse the gossip industry's efforts to inscribe her as a failed model of ageing femininity.

Farrah's Story includes a concluding image of Fawcett sitting alone on a park bench looking old and ill. I have struggled with how to interpret the documentary's final few moments, asking whether such imagery consigns Fawcett to decline ideology, or shows her transcending the limits of a celebrity culture obsessed with youth. Gullette has suggested that photographs taken of old people "often [show them as] isolated—on a park bench, along an empty stretch of beach" (2017, 39). For Gullette, such images are problematic because they convey the old person as "having been abandoned" (39). Fawcett's isolation in this moment could be read in the way Gullette suggests. However, this image could also be symbolic of her refusal of the gossip media's work to objectify her, an interpretation that makes sense when *Farrah's Story* is set against the backdrop of other narratives about her life. While the image of Fawcett alone on a bench shows her isolation, Fawcett is showing her sick and ageing body on her terms. Tellingly, in the final moments of the documentary, she reverses the camera toward the audience and asks them two questions: "How are you? What are you fighting for?" These questions are in proximity to footage of Fawcett angrily shredding a tabloid magazine. The documentary's ongoing return to a critique of the gossip industry throughout should prompt viewers to interpret these questions as an invitation to re-examine media culture's reification of beauty standards. The work of life writing criticism, which assumes "human beings [...] [are not] passive pawns in social games or unconscious transmitters of cultural scripts" has hopefully been instructive in allowing for this possibility (Smith and Watson 2001, 42). I am not suggesting *Farrah's Story* is unproblematic, for it does reinforce stereotypes of ageing and decline: I am suggesting that when traces of Fawcett's conscious efforts to remain viable in an ageist media culture are located in her work, she can teach us about the costs of belonging to an unchecked social order that celebrates youthful femininity at the expense of feminist ethics. Commentators can dismiss the narrative stating that Fawcett was exploited, but the fact that *Farrah's Story* is often interpreted in ways that ignore social accountability has a lot to do with the ways ageism is used to discipline women in contemporary western culture.

Notes

1. In 1977, Fawcett was known as Farrah Fawcett-Majors, marking her high-profile marriage to actor Lee Majors. When the couple divorced, she became Farrah Fawcett.
2. In addition to *Farrah: An Unauthorized Biography*, at least two other biographies about Fawcett were published at about the same time. *Farrah & Lee* by Connie Berman discusses Fawcett's marriage to Lee Majors describing them as "this golden duo" (1977, 145), while *Welcome to Farrah's World* by Claire Susans presents the story of "the hottest actress in the country" (1977, 11).
3. Alleged disputes between Fawcett's romantic partner Ryan O'Neal and the producer of *Farrah's Story* Craig Nevius contribute to concerns that Fawcett may not have had full creative control of her documentary. See Shain (2009).
4. In *Both of Us: My Life with Farrah*, O'Neal tends to regard Fawcett in ageist terms, particularly when referring to Fawcett's menopause as "nature unleashed [with] Farrah headed toward the eye of that storm" (2012, 118). O'Neal's comments are made after Fawcett's death, and with respect to the dissolution of his and Fawcett's relationship, which he ties

to Fawcett's ageing body as it "[began] to rebel with recurring maladies" (118). The fact that O'Neal thinks of Fawcett this way further suggests the extent to which ageist rhetoric is naturalised as a part of the story told about her.

5. In *Farrah & Lee*, Berman likewise refers to Fawcett as a "Total Woman," noting that Farrah's attitudes toward marriage are not "fashioned according to the dictates of women's lib" (1977, 36).
6. See *American Legends: Farrah Fawcett* (2014).
7. Fawcett's appearance on *David Letterman* took place on 6 June 1997. It was derided by critics and has been referred to as a "lights-out appearance" (Justin 2015). For footage of that interview, see also, "Farrah Fawcett Drugged on Letterman" (2009), https://www.youtube.com/watch?v=RYo7u6GUTEY.
8. *Chasing Farrah* was a short-lived reality television show featuring Fawcett: its premise was that cameras would follow Fawcett during her daily activities. It premiered in 2005.
9. Fawcett's hairstyle from her *Charlie's Angels* days is iconic. Burstein summarizes it best stating that Fawcett's hair is "that fresh sporty feeling that really spells 1977" (1977, 73).
10. Dr Lawrence Piro explains that initially treatments were chosen "that were likely to work on the tumour, but that were [also] likely to spare her hair." After the cancer progressed, he goes on to state that eventually Fawcett "knew we needed to bring our best A game to the fight that we had at this moment" (*Farrah's Story* 2009).

Disclosure statement

No potential conflict of interest was reported by the author.

References

American Legends: Farrah Fawcett. 2014. Charles Rivers Editors.

Berman, Connie. 1977. *Farrah & Lee*. New York: Grosset & Dunlap.

Bernstein, Jay. 2011. *Starmaker: Life as a Hollywood Publicist with Farrah, the Rat Pack, and 600 More Stars Who Fired Me, as Told to Larry Cortez Hamm with David Rubini*. Toronto: ECW Press.

Bouson, J. Brooks. 2016. *Shame and the Aging Woman: Confronting and Resisting Ageism in Contemporary Women's Writings*. Cham: Palgrave Macmillan.

Burstein, Patricia. 1977. *Farrah: An Unauthorized Biography*. New York: Signet.

Chivers, Sally. 2011. *The Silvering Screen*. Toronto: University of Toronto Press.

Covington, Coline. 2014. "Farrah Fawcett in Denial as She Films Cancer Battle." In *Shrinking the News: Headline Stories on the Couch*, 71–74. London: Karnac.

Darrach, Brad. 1984. "Farrah Fawcett." *People Weekly*, December 24.

Fairclough, Kirsty. 2012. "Nothing Less Than Perfect: Female Celebrity, Ageing and Hyper-Scrutiny in the Gossip Industry." *Celebrity Studies* 3 (1): 90–103. doi:10.1080/19392397.2012.644723.

"Farrah Fawcett Drugged on Letterman." Youtube, June 29, 2009, lucienpsinger. https://www.youtube.com/watch?v=RYo7u6GUTEY.

"Farrah!" 1995. Playboy: Entertainment for Men, December.
Farrah's Story. 2009. "Executive producers Farrah Fawcett, Alexandra Gleysteen, and Craig Nevius, Featuring Farrah Fawcett et al." *NBC News*, May 15.
Fleming, Anne Taylor. 2009. "Fallen Angel: From 'It' Girl to Stricken Reality Star, Farrah Fawcett Reflects Our Obsession with Fame." *Las Angeles Magazine*, June 1. http://www.lamag.com/citythinkblog/fallen-angel/.
Frank, Arthur. 2013. *The Wounded Storyteller: Body, Illness and Ethics*. 2nd ed. Chicago, IL: University of Chicago Press.
Gill, Rosalind. 2016. "Post-Postfeminism?: New Feminist Visibilities in Postfeminist Times." *Feminist Media Studies* 16 (4): 610–630. doi:10.1080/14680777.2016.1193293.
Gill, Rosalind, and Christina Scharff. 2011. "Introduction." In *New Femininities: Postfeminism, Neoliberalism, and Subjectivity*. London: Palgrave. 1–17.
Gough-Yates, Anna. 2001. "Angels in Chains: Feminism, Femininity and Consumer Culture in *Charlie's Angels*." In *Action TV: Tough Guys, Smooth Operators and Foxy Chicks*, edited by Bill Osgerby and Anna Gough-Yates, 83–99. London: Routledge.
Gullette, Margaret Morganroth. 2017. *Ending Ageism or How Not to Shoot Old People*. New Brunswick: Rutgers University Press.
Justin, Neal. 2015. "Top 10 Reasons We Love David Letterman." *Star Tribune*, May 5. http://www.startribune.com/top-10-reasons-we-love-david-letterman/302175441/.
Kelly, Christopher. 2009. "Angel Heart." *Texas Monthly* 37 (8): 62–64.
Levine, Elana. 2007. *Wallowing in Sex: The New Sexual Culture of 1970s American Television*. Durham, NC: Duke University Press.
Lieb, Kristin. 2013. *Gender, Branding, and the Modern Music Industry: The Social Construction of Female Popular Music Stars*. New York: Routledge.
Marshall, David P., and Kim Barbour. 2015. "Making Intellectual Room for Persona Studies: A New Consciousness and a Shifted Perspective." *Persona Studies* 1 (1): 1–12.
McRobbie, Angela. 2009. *The Aftermath of Feminism*. London: Sage.
McRobbie, Angela. 2015. "Notes on the Perfect: Competitive Femininity in Neoliberal Times." *Australian Feminist Studies* 30 (83): 3–20. doi:10.1080/08164649.2015.1011485.
Morey, Anne. 2011. "Grotesquerie as Marker of Success in Aging Female Stars." In *In the Limelight and Under the Microscope: Forms and Functions of Female Celebrity*, edited by Su Holmes and Diane Negra, 103–124. New York: Continuum.
Morgan, Marabel. 1973. *The Total Woman*. New Jersey: Fleming H. Revell.
Negra, Diane. 2009. *What a Girl Wants: Fantasizing the Reclamation of Self in Postfeminism*. New York: Routledge.
Nevius, Craig, and Farrah Fawcett. 2005. "Tonight's Guest: Farrah Fawcett." Chasing Farrah. TV Land.
O'Brien, Glenn. 1997. "Farrah: All of Me." *Playboy* 44 (7), July. Factiva Inc. ISSN: 0032-1478.
O'Neal, Ryan, Jodee Blanco, and Kent Carroll. 2012. *Both of Us: My Life with Farrah*. New York: Crown Archetype.
Schneider, Karen S. 1997. "End of the Affair." *People Weekly*, March 10.
Shain, Michael. 2009. "Not Farrah's 'Story': She's Never Exposed Son to Scrutiny or Push 'Angels': Ex-Producer." *New York Post*, May 18. https://nypost.com/2009/05/18/not-farrahs-story/.
Smith, Sidonie, and Julia Watson. 2001. *Reading Autobiography: A Guide for Interpreting Life Narratives*. 1st ed. Minneapolis: University of Minnesota Press.
Smith, Sidonie, and Julia Watson. 2010. *Reading Autobiography: A Guide for Interpreting Life Narratives*. 2nd ed. Minneapolis: University of Minnesota Press.
Stanley, Alessandra. 2005. "Older Woman Role: Tough or Ladylike." *New York Times*, March 15.
Stanley, Alessandra. 2009. "TV Watch: 'Farrah's Story.'" *The New York Times*, May 16. https://artsbeat.blogs.nytimes.com/2009/05/16/tv-watch-farrahs-story/.
Susans, Claire. 1977. *Welcome to … Farrah's World*. New York: Dell.
Womack, Whitney. 2003. "'Re-Evaluating Jiggle TV': *Charlie's Angels* at Twenty-Five." In *Disco Divas: Women and Popular Culture in the 1970s*, edited by Sherrie A. Inness, 151–171. Philadelphia: University of Pennsylvania Press.

"A View from Old Age": Women's Lives as Narrated Through Objects

Leonie Hannan, Gemma Carney, Paula Devine and Gemma Hodge

ABSTRACT
This article uses interview data gathered during a collaborative cross-disciplinary project undertaken in 2016 to explore experiences of longevity in qualitative detail with a small cohort of Northern Irish participants. The project was inspired by Penelope Lively's autobiography *Ammonites and Leaping Fish: A Life in Time* (2013, 4, 199), which documents the author's feelings about her life through focused reflections on her own possessions. Lively chose objects which she felt "oddly identified" her life and proposed that "people's possessions speak of them". We devised a series of activities to be undertaken with participants over the age of 60, with the intention of using material things as a lens on longevity. In this article we use interview data with three female participants to analyse women's narration of their own biographies. The aim of this article is to explore the role of the possessions in narrating women's lives and to consider how themes of ageing, memory, relationships, and the self are articulated through objects. The theoretical context for this exploratory work refers to cultural gerontology, material culture studies, gender studies and scholarship on life history. We conclude that objects offer a useful, tangible means of articulating and communicating the complexity of women's longevity.

This article uses interview data gathered during a collaborative cross-disciplinary project undertaken in 2016 to explore experiences of longevity in qualitative detail with a small cohort of Northern Irish participants. While the ageing population is seldom out of the news, reports tend towards the one-dimensional. News stories swing between horror at the mistreatment of residents in care homes to neo-liberal ideologues" dismissal of older people as greedy for having bankrupted their children's future (Howker and Malik 2011; Willits 2011). Reporters rarely speak directly to those with the experience of living a long life. One outcome of simplistic reasoning in public debate is the absence of an informed discussion about *what it actually means to live a long life*. It is hoped that the methods trialled during this project, and its initial findings, can contribute to enriching and enlivening debates about the meanings of old age.

The narration of a life through objects provided the inspiration for this project. Specifically, Penelope Lively's autobiography *Ammonites and Leaping Fish: A Life in Time* (2013,

4, 199), which documents the author's feelings about her life through focused reflections on her own possessions. Lively chose objects which she felt "oddly identified" her life and proposed that "People's possessions speak of them". A group of researchers and practitioners took up Lively's proposal and devised a series of activities to be undertaken with participants over the age of sixty, with the intention of using material things as a lens on longevity. Over a period of 12 months, 3 women and 3 men were involved in a multi-disciplinary project which began by asking them to choose six things in their possession that said "something of who I am". The participants were recruited through the authors" networks established through the ARK Ageing Programme (see ark.ac.uk/ageing) and through project collaborator, Lorraine Calderwood, in her role with the Arts and Older People Programme at Arts Council Northern Ireland.[1] An individual interview was conducted with each person. Four weeks later, they met as a group and worked with visual artist, Gemma Hodge, to explore the materiality of their chosen objects at an arts workshop.[2] The project culminated in a public exhibition entitled "Something of Who I Am', which displayed their objects, quotations from the interviews, and Hodge's interpretation of their objects.[3] Whilst the exhibition provided a finale to the project's activities, the path taken and the end result were left open and what resulted was the product of close collaboration between researchers, practitioners and participants. The third author ran a reflective focus group with participants one month following the exhibition.

Here, the analysis focuses on the three individual interviews with female participants, each taking between an hour and an hour and a half to conduct. The aim of this article is to explore the role of the possessions in narrating these women's lives and to consider how themes of ageing, memory, relationships and the self are articulated through objects. The theoretical context for this exploratory work refers to cultural gerontology, material culture studies, gender studies and scholarship on life history.

The view from old age in gerontology

Feminist gerontologists have written about the experience of ageing from a woman's point of view for decades (Arber and Ginn 1991; Calasanti 2006, 2007, 2010, 2016; Cruikshank 2003; Estes, Biggs, and Phillipson 2003; Gullette 1997, 2013, Laws 1995; Ray 2004; Woodward 2003). Some of the "baby boomer" generation of the 1960s had experience of second wave feminist activism earlier in the life course and have subsequently chosen to write about their own ageing (Hanson 2013; King 2013; Segal 2013). As a result, there is now a growing and exciting literature in the humanities and social science branches of gerontology in which women use feminist methods (including narration) to write about their own and their societies" ageing (Applewhite 2016; Garner 1999; Gullette 2013, 2017; Karpen 2017; Woodspring 2015). Their work speaks directly to the theme of this special issue: the social context and meaning of women's private lives.

Feminist writing about old age has a pedigree which extends at least as far back as Simone de Beauvoir's *The Coming of Age* (1972) and Friedan's (1993) *Fountain of Age*. These *grandes dames* of feminism found that personal experience of growing older prompted them to write about ageism (Sontag 1972). Though now focused on ageism, their motivation came from the same place as Friedan's *Feminine Mystique*; to name and claim their experience of discrimination. More recent work by boomers such as

Applewhite (2016) comes from a similar place. In each case, the story of women's later lives is placed in a political context, particularly in terms of women's rights. These women's narrations are imbued with a sense of gender relations having shaped their life experience, including the experience of growing older. For Friedan (1993) and de Beauvoir (1972), their experience of ageism mirrors earlier experiences of sexism. This study is informed by this literature and sees the personal as political in the sense outlined by de Beauvoir and Friedan.

Growing recognition of lived experience in gerontology

Amongst gerontologists, the personal has become an increasingly important factor in research that seeks to understand the experience of growing older (Carney and Gray 2015; Carney 2017; Gilleard 2018). In 2017, for the first time since it was first published in 1961, flagship journal *The Gerontologist* published a special issue "Aging—it's personal', in which older gerontologists were asked to write about the relationship between their personal ageing and their research and teaching in gerontology (Pruchno 2017). Meanwhile, in British gerontology, a Leverhulme Trust funded project *The Ageing of British Gerontology* "explores the evolution of the study of ageing in Britain from 1971 to the present day'.[4] Bernard and her team have interviewed and photographed 50 leading researchers in the UK about their personal and professional experiences of ageing. Their respondents display an ambivalence towards accepting their own ageing, and an acknowledgement that academic knowledge of ageing is sometimes useless in the context of personal experience of growing older. This acknowledgement, of the role of the personal as relevant to understanding ageing, is long overdue, particularly given that living a long life is now an expected feature of life in the countries in question (UK and US). It may indicate that the lived experience of ageing by researchers themselves is beginning to make even gerontologists see that the vulnerability of ageing stems from physiological changes as much from personal experience, such as the dying off of one's "co-biographers" (Hagestad and Settersten 2017). The more nuanced understanding of what it actually means to live a long life is raising new questions for a discipline that has been dominated by resource-focused issues such as "how will we fund the care of "the elderly"?' The fact that "the elderly"—that amorphous and undifferentiated mass of the old—is a fictional whole that exists only in the minds of the commentator is becoming apparent. Lively's memoir voices frustration with the homogenising of "older people': "All that we have in common, we in this new demographic, are our aches and pains and disabilities ... For the rest of it, we are the people we have always been—splendidly various, and let us respect that" (Lively 2013, 21). It would seem that there is a growing chasm between the experience of ageing, and how it is perceived in the wider population. The self-reported distance between the lived experience of old age, and the wholesale appropriation of "old age" as a *bad thing* by mass media motivated Friedan (1993) and latterly Lively (2013, 3) to write about their experiences: 'One of the few advantages of age is that you can report on it with a certain authority; you are a native now, and know what goes on here'.

The distance between the experience of ageing, and its study was clear to the gerontologists who contributed to the special issue "Aging—it's personal". In some cases, the impact of personal experience on understanding of ageing was profound. For example, behavioural psychologist Scheidt (2017, 110) was humbled by the experience of ageing:

"Now I am experiencing my own aging ... I share a few observations and thoughts about my daily struggle to preserve a healthy sense of self amidst this thievery of my personhood by *ageism'*.

The uniquely illuminating perspective of ageing feminists

Elsewhere, Carney has claimed that the ageing feminists within the cohorts of baby boomers have a uniquely useful set of experiences (Carney and Gray 2015; Carney 2017). Having lived through the changes brought about by the activism of the women's movement, these women have a particularly politicised perspective on life. They also have the powers of description, the tools and the language to articulate how life looks from the viewpoint of the oppressed. A leader in the gerontology of the humanities, Ruth Ray has published widely as a feminist gerontologist (Ray and Fine 1999; Ray 2004). She was also one of those who wrote an essay for the "Aging—it's personal" special issue for *The Gerontologist.* In her essay, Ray (now Ray Karpen) focuses on women's experiences of retirement, specifically noting the inequalities between women and acknowledging her privilege as belonging to what she refers to as "The Top 20%' of women—those who are the first women to retire after a long career and with a decent pension. She asks: "What will they be doing all those years? Given their strong attachments to paid work and its rewards, what will take its place? How might they use this time to redefine the meaning and purpose of retirement?' (Karpen 2017, 103). Ray Karpen's responses to these questions offer a number of insights on the experience of ageing, which are shared by the women whose lives are narrated in this article.

Ageing is full of contradictions. It is simultaneously a status and a stage of life. It is intensely personal, conflicted, challenging and rewarding, which goes some way to explaining the relationship between feminist thinking and the study of ageing, as both necessarily embrace ambiguity in relation to personal experience. The Janus-faced nature of the experience of living a long life is often ignored in both science and culture. Popular media present polarised images of serenity, wisdom and financial security, or of loss, impairment and decline. Neither of these extremes captures the whole, which is, more likely, composed of elements of both, mixed with other random, as yet unidentified factors. Drawing on the work of Holstein (2015), Karpen (2017, 104) acknowledges this ambiguity in terms of women's retirement: "it is a complex emotional, psychological, and spiritual process that changes over time, and it involves various types of work, both paid and unpaid". The life courses narrated by the Lively Project women are full of similarly challenging experiences. The objects that they use to communicate these transitions shed an important light on the intensely complex and personal struggle that it is to be a woman, trying to make one's way in the world, particularly after many decades of life where one's personal history mirrors the historical and social changes one has lived through.

Narrating age through things

In asking participants to tell something of themselves through objects that they own, this research necessarily engages with biography, narration and the methodological issues of analysing life stories (Bertaux 1981; Tedlock 1983; Denzin 1989; Bateson 1990; Josselson and Liebech 1995). As Tierney (2000, 539) reminds us, "Life history is a culturally produced artifact in one light and an interpretive document in another". The juxtaposition of artefact and document in this statement is significant. For many scholars in the humanities and social sciences, firmly wedded to language as evidence of human thought and action, material things still present certain analytical challenges (see Auslander 2005). However, work in the fields of anthropology, science studies and philosophy has sought to overcome the division between mind and matter (subject and object) and demonstrate the agency of things in our social worlds (Harman 2002; Latour 2005; Henare, Holbraad, and Wastell 2007; Bogost 2012). Or, as Appadurai (1988, 5) put it:

> we have to follow the things themselves, for their meanings are inscribed in their forms, their uses, their trajectories. It is only through the analysis of these trajectories that we can interpret the human transactions and calculations that enliven things. Thus, even though from a *theoretical* point of view human actors encode things with significance, from a *methodological* point of view it is the things-in-motion that illuminate their human and social context.

Further, interdisciplinary research is beginning to show the ways in which interactions that involve object handling, conversation and reflection can have specific effects on cognitive functioning. Research has variously attributed better educational (Paris 2002; Chatterjee and Hannan 2015) as well as health and wellbeing (Thomson and Chatterjee 2014; Solway et al. 2016) outcomes to multi-sensory engagements with objects.

As more researchers are drawn to the use of objects in their research practice, approaches that are self-conscious about their interpretive frameworks are particularly helpful. The study of objects as evidence necessitates a negotiation between the experiential and the intellectual, which is particularly intense in circumstances where items have been in a person's possession for many years. As archaeologist Carl Knappett has emphasised (2011, 12): "Things establish themselves in ways that are not entirely comprehensible, and they exert a powerful hold on human social and cognitive dynamics". By asking participants to discuss their lives through the things that they own, this project initiated a complex set of interactions: between researcher and researched; sensory and symbolic; object and memory; memory and narrative, and so on (Chatterjee 2008). These interactions are all contingent on time and place, but, as Svašek (2007) has argued, where people and objects move across time and space, objects offer the opportunity to overcome distances and to re-create the familiar, whilst undergoing shifts in meaning and emotional resonance. The potential of objects to jump register, to connect to distant times and places and to do so with particular sensory, emotional and cognitive implications is helpful for the study of gender and ageing.

The interviews analysed here were undertaken in the homes of the participants, and the objects chosen referred directly to domestic space—whether that was present or past homes. In two of the three cases, the participant was in a process of transition—having moved from or moving to a new home—and was therefore already engaged in a process of sorting and selecting possessions. As Miller (2008, 2) tells us, people

> put up ornaments; they laid down carpets. They selected furnishing and got dressed that morning. Some things may be gifts or objects retained from the past, but they have decided to live with them, to place them in lines or higgledy-piggledy [...] These things are not a random collection.

Of course, many people's homes represent a struggle with objects and space—where compromises have been made over decades, with the material whole departing significantly from the inhabitants" intentions. Some objects that are meaningful to an individual are, at the same time, disruptive.

Discussion of the objects we choose to display in our homes (and the meanings these selections have for our identities) often focuses on their aesthetic or utilitarian dimensions. As Sherry Turkle rightly highlights (2007, 5), "We are on less familiar ground when we consider objects as companions to our emotional lives or as provocations to thought". This is a productive way of thinking about the role of objects when they are used in the narration of life histories. Moreover, as literary scholar James Krasner has argued in his study of spatialised memory in the homes of the elderly (2005, 227), "understanding metaphorical self-representation" in domestic material accumulation can help carers and gerontologists to weigh up the psychological benefits or detriments of staying in the home. As Krasner acknowledges (2005, 210), qualitative gerontology has found "that long time home residence represents a crucial imaginative structure through which elders define themselves and their life stories', especially for those who live alone. In the object-based interviews analysed here, chosen possessions act in a number of ways—sometimes as lightning rods for a particular time or place, as a memory, and at other times as signifiers of the self or of an achievement. Sometimes the participants talked past their possessions, but often they spoke through them.

Given the importance of the home in the way possessions are stored, used and prioritised, it is worth noting the status of each participant in relation to their domestic space at the time of the interview. One participant (Mary, aged 62) had relocated recently and had moved into a temporary, rented home while she looked for a property to buy in her new city. Of the seven objects she selected, six had come with her to the rented house, which she regarded as significant of their meaning to her. Another participant (Penny, aged 80) was in the process of selling the house she had lived in for 54 years and was assessing the possessions she had in preparation for this transition. She said that she had welcomed the invitation to participate in this project because she was already involved in a process of sorting her possessions. The third participant (Ruth, aged 61), by contrast, remained in a home she had lived in for decades and had not engaged in any recent sorting or "de-cluttering". Ruth described her home as "an installation', equating home furnishing with artistic expression, and hers was the most materially crowded domestic space of the three.

The object-based narratives of three women

The interviews with three women discussed here offer a glimpse of the diverse and revealing ways lives can be told when objects anchor a conversation. The transcripts illuminate three distinct responses to the object-based approach, and the narratives that prevail negotiate the presence of objects in different ways. For participant Mary, the choice of objects was based on instinct, leading to a very solid sense that these were *the* objects that traced her life:

> [I chose my objects] immediately, absolutely immediately and I didn't waiver then, I thought those ones are among the chosen few. [...] there's all sorts of things that I could've chosen I suppose, that would have set off all sorts of trains of thought in different directions and brought up all sorts of different issues.

Mary was keen to stress that she was neither sentimental nor "an accumulative person', offering her tendency to let go of things rather than hold onto them as evidence of the intense meaning of her chosen things. By contrast, participants Penny and Ruth thought first about the aspects of their life they wished to characterise and then considered which possessions could speak to those times, places or relationships. Penny was chronologically focused: "Well, I try to think of each era of my life, I'm 80 now. I was thinking of my childhood and then my teenage years and early married life and then my career". In contrast, Ruth's selections emphasised activities in her adult life of which she felt proud, whether that was early motherhood, her professional achievements or pastimes that had been rewarding. She articulated the process of choosing as follows: "Right, number four is probably travel. The other two, one is travel and one is my band and the other is my yarn bombing. [...] Right, so those are my chosen areas". Hence from the start of the interview, very different patterns were in progress, patterns that related strongly to narrative structure—a conscious process of sifting that could produce a desired result.

It is worth acknowledging here that this decision-making was to a lesser or greater extent guided by the request that had been made of the participants. By asking them to think about their lives in relation to different possessions, an object per life stage was strongly implied as a method of selection. Likewise, however, the guidance notes asked participants whether objects reflected particular passions or interests, proffering the suggestion of an alternative organisational approach. As the telling of life histories relates closely to the sense of self, the request itself asked a lot of the participants in terms of their commitment to discuss deeply held feelings. Furthermore, by structuring the interview around objects, the process harnessed the material, symbolic, tactile, temporal and interpersonal meanings that are so often located in domestic possessions. The interview also placed an emphasis on relating the material presentation of a given thing to a range of memories or feelings.

To take the first of these issues, the participants sometimes referred directly to materiality. Mary commented that "Things that we keep close to us are things that we really want to hold onto, over and above the stuff that goes through our life"—emphasising tactile proximity and personal will with the phrase "holding onto". Likewise, some objects were redolent of a very particular time in life, a childhood toy was described as synonymous with that life stage for one participant: "That really pins me down". Penny's testimony celebrated the materiality of certain objects. She described in captivating detail the discovery made by her relation of an old box of letters:

> He and his young son were down there one day, and they noticed on the wall, the outline of a cupboard that had been papered over and they opened [it] up and he was quite excited to find this old tin box. Thought he'd maybe discovered the family fortune in there. [...] And was very disappointed to find a bundle of old letters that had been stitched together.

Penny became very involved with these letters and "spent a year or two years transcribing them all'; a not inconsiderable task of converting old paper and ink into a published text:

> They had been stitched together that they were higgledy piggledy, they weren't in order and you had to try and match the paper with the writing and the year. I finally got permission from his wife, [...] she allowed me to take the stitching out at the side and open the letters out that I could put them into better order.

By taking an object-based approach, certain episodes in life (such as the transcription of letters) were foregrounded over others. The object was not always decisive in the inclusion of recollections about a very significant life event—like having a child but in some cases, it was. In her interview, Penny remained alert to the losses that occur when the material is replaced by the digital, commenting of passports "they've lost all their kind of meaning [...] haven't they? They've become so electronic and everything" and regretting that the large school bell she had rung in the playground as a teacher had most likely been replaced by "somebody pressing a button". These reflections, somewhat removed from the main thrust of the narrative, speak to the sensory engagement generated by the process of choosing, handling and talking about personal possessions throughout the interview.

The materiality of some objects came through more strongly than others and the most acute example of this was in relation to an item that had been partially destroyed. Mary's first object was a teddy bear: "I was really, really attached and he came everywhere with me and he did do, he still remained with me all the time until a dog came and ate him". In describing her teddy's life before his encounter with the dog, Mary said:

> Yes, I suppose that originally he was covered in this nice, yellow fur. I actually never remember him like that. I remember him being pretty baldy and battered as you can see. [...] Unless it's just affection, years and years of being stroked and fondled and all the rest of it, this is what it does to a teddy bear, I don't know. [...] he's just much loved you see. Love comes at a cost too.

The dramatic loss of material form of an object that had been "held onto', "stroked and fondled" for years and which was regarded as the only surviving memento of early childhood had been devastating and its ongoing status as damaged was clearly troubling to Mary: "some things if you fix them, they're actually not the same. They have more integrity as the damaged original as the repaired thing, do you know?' In the end, Mary enacted her own repair to the bear's face in time to display him in the project exhibition. Her mending was done lightly and reversibly and, hopefully, in such a way as retained its original character. The care that Mary took in retaining the teddy's characterful ageing may offer some explanation of what she meant by "the cost of love'; she wanted the wear and tear of decades of giving and receiving love to show on the teddy.

All three participants presented at least one photograph as part of their chosen things. In the case of Ruth and Penny these photos were physical artefacts—either the product of film or printed digital images. The first object that Ruth presented was a clown doll, named Spike, which she had made for her infant son, but to underline the meaning of this object she produced a photograph of herself, her son and the doll. This image was taken on film and had been a chance discovery some years after it had been taken:

> my father died, and for some reason you have this flurry of clearing things out, [...] and I came upon two little undeveloped canisters of film. [...] in the black and white set, [...] and at the very end of the reel there was this one and another one, which I also have developed upstairs, and they're. I don't know what the word is, whether they're over exposed or whatever is wrong with them, but they are like that. They're almost like a a silhouette and I just loved it, ... I thought it was like art, really. It em, it lives beside my bed and so does another one, [...] the two at the end of the film. [...] Yes, he's holding Spike and we're having a conversation.

In this episode the materiality of the photograph is very present, the technology behind its creation contributing an element of chance to its creation and discovery. However, it is in the three silhouetted figures that Ruth found most material meaning, as it was the photograph rather than doll itself that sat by her bedside. Again, the emphasis on choosing objects in this interview scenario had prompted different repertoires of reflection, ones which considered the accumulation of personal possessions and their meanings over time.

Mary presented one digital photograph as her final object, apologising for not having had it printed. In this case, the different kinds of proximity brought by a digital image were discussed: "this photo was taken by my son and he Whatsapp'd it to me and I was abroad at the time when it arrived and I thought, "Oh that's lovely", so it is part of that inter-connectedness too you know?' This speaks to the way older women have engaged with dramatic changes in communications technology, proactively adopting in some instances and in others registering caution.[5] Nonetheless, Mary argued that "objects can sort of carry an awful lot more meaning" than photographs. By contrast, both Penny and Ruth used photographs flexibly alongside three-dimensional objects to bring to the fore the associations they found most compelling. For example, Penny had "looked out photographs" in order to make a small, silver spoon belonging to her sister who had died in childhood "more meaningful". Ruth took this approach further—she drew on her existing practice of arranging photographs and images in collages and displaying them in her home to help her construct the narrative of her adult life, much of the transcript relying on photographic illustration of particular episodes over and above the material presence of a particular artefact. For Ruth, the visual and the material were highly inter-related.

Without so many images to rely upon, objects occupied a more central role in prompting time and location-specific memories for Mary and Penny. As Mary reports, her teddy bear acted as a gateway to early childhood and her repetition of the phrases "it's the only thing" and "I've nothing else [...] nothing" seems significant.

> If I did want to think about my childhood, it would be through different things with the bear ... ... that would bring me back there, you know, it's like a kind of a touch stone? And it takes me right back and it's the only thing I have ... ... .yeah, it is absolutely the only thing I have [...] I've nothing else from that period in my life, nothing.

Sometimes these connections were drawn through a close relationship. Penny reports the purchase of a Toby jug for her father and the way she saw him in its expression: "But I just spied it and I thought, it just reminded me of my Father. He had a very quirky sense of humour [...] he really was very fond of it". She likewise locates this object in a domestic space and remembering the way it looked in that place offers further insight into her father's character:

> it sat up on top of a china cabinet and we didn't have electricity, until I was about 16 ... So he didn't put the lights on very early in the evening, that would be two years later. So it sat there and by the light of the fire, he imagined that the face was sort of winking at him or, he said, "He winked at me', when you talked to him.

Had Penny been asked about her father rather than about objects that were important to her, it is doubtful that the interview would have recorded this memory of the Toby jug and how it appeared in the firelight at home. But it is in Penny's description of its winking expression and the way that linked her to memories of her father that we gain particular insight into the quality of both her childhood experience and this parent-child relationship. The Toby jug is a good example of how objects can offer a tangible link backwards in time to a lost loved one, a former relationship or a formative experience.

The participants" selections of objects had slightly different biases. All three chose objects that primarily represented a relationship, although Mary did this more consistently than Penny or Ruth; Ruth was the least likely to tie her objects to specific relationships. All the participants chose at least one object that signified a personal or professional achievement, and Ruth was particularly focused on this as a way of organising her life narrative. Objects were also chosen across the piece that represented independent action, creativity or adventure (a passport, a bike, travel souvenirs). These objects sat alongside others that were symbolic of domesticity (a nappy pin, a dresser, a child's doll). None of the objects were especially valuable in either monetary or aesthetic terms, and many were quite the opposite; small and potentially insignificant things that had come to accumulate personal meaning. Likewise, Lively had imagined seeing her own chosen objects at a car boot sale—removed from the context of her memories and connections, they would instantly become mundane.

Mary's choice of an artificial flower fixed into a small glass vase prompted a reflection on the relationship it represented but also on the counter-intuitive aesthetic connotations of the object. The flower was purchased when Mary was on her way to visit her father in hospital with the idea in mind that it would "humanise his little environment". Mary was very close to her father and describes him as "an absolutely wonderful man". She explains the moment of purchase as follows:

> And you know the way in shopping centres, they have these kind of stalls in the middle of the mall, [...] and some of them are little things like this and some are large, big things, absolutely horrendous, I don't know who's buying them, but I just wanted to pick up something to put [by his bed]. And I just saw this and I just thought, ok that's a little red flower, it's going to be cheerful and slightly gaudy and very tacky, but so what, there it is!

In reflecting on the objectionable nature of the artificial flower, Mary asserts "Actually I cannot bear artificial flowers. I cannot bear them, I hate them, I abhor them!' Yet she bought the flower and has kept it with her ever since. She concludes: "So that will tell you the intensity of the emotion that's behind this, that I'm prepared to put up with an artificial flower, you know?' The disjuncture between Mary's dislike of artificial flowers and the very powerful feelings this red flower provokes reflects aspects of this time and the particularities of the relationship. Whilst her father was "wonderful" "he was [also] a very old fashioned man and he just did not talk about his emotions at all". The purchase of the artificial flower was prompted by the thought that fresh flowers would be purposeless because "he was going to be impervious one way or another". Perhaps the prospect of fresh flowers seemed less appealing because of their short life, or maybe the bright colour of this artificial flower felt bold enough to break through the sterile atmosphere of the hospital; to "humanise" it in some way. Mary remembered thinking:

> ok, it's a little flower and it's going to sit on his locker and it's going to be ... I don't know, an individual thing. Anyway I brought it in, I don't know if he took any notice of it at all, but it was there until he came home.

The very presence of the flower—perhaps unnoticed—was important in this instance and that became the case later when Mary brought it back to her own home. This part of the interview brings into focus women's subtle negotiations with the material world, and the way meaning attaches to objects through their roles in significant relationships and moments in life. It is this process of meaning-making that makes objects such powerful interpretive tools in a life history interview, both for the researcher and the interviewee.

In different ways, both Ruth and Penny engaged creatively with material representations of their lives. Ruth created collages out of photographs and other flat, visual materials:

> I used to do one every year, latterly I do it every 2 or 3 years. This one was done quite recently and it has some old pictures in it, from way back and it also has more recent pictures … it has a selection of different bits of my life.

Whilst these collages and other collected photographs documented Ruth's life, she explained these periods of time through the people she knew and worked with. In contrast, Penny's memory quilt made at the time of her mother's death was focused very much on what her mother had worked on during her lifetime. Penny explains: "After she'd died. I'm left with this heap of clothes to throw out, you know. I think the back was her dressing gown or something". The end result is a patchwork of fabrics and references to her mother's passions:

> She was a great one for alpine flowers and she, even in her 80's, was visiting Boulder, Colorado and going up mountains and looking at the plants and flowers … .this is the Red Cross. She was a great woman for chocolate cake. She baked chocolate cakes for all the birthdays, very good at shortbread. She was in Guiding, she was in W.I., as I was. She was a great walker, she was a historian, she was a great woman for stories and told all about various relations and stories about people in the area. … she was a botanist, … . you know, she left school at 14, but she was a self-educated botanist. She went over all the Latin names for flowers.

This attention to professional and intellectual interest down the female line is a strong feature of Penny's interview. Whilst her father's jovial manner can be glimpsed in her testimony, it is her mother's hard work, dynamism and enquiring mind that shines through most clearly. In describing the construction of the quilt, it's functionality in respect of memory becomes clear:

> And that was a button of her night-dress. So this was all made with her clothing, this was the jacket she was wearing, this was a dress, this was another […] it was quite difficult to put together, because this was silky material and this is cotton, so you know you were using different kinds of materials to … [it] could've twisted out of place very easily.

The different ways memory worked through things is an interesting dimension in these interviews. For some, the material manifestation of an object was the powerful factor, taking a person back to a specific time, place or person. For others, the objects could be constructed after the events they represent, memorialising particular people or experiences. Other objects functioned more as representations of a particular achievement or relationship, like the objects Ruth had collected while travelling abroad; things that reminded her of her adventures, but which were not individually potent in the same way as other items. The only object Mary had not been sure about including was a copy of her doctoral thesis, and this item operated differently in her interview; less materially resonant and designated as merely "representational". This was also the only object that she had needed to retrieve from storage and, as such, something that she had not chosen to bring to her temporary home as a matter of course.

Whilst based around personal possessions, the interviews are not a catalogue of things but a telling of the self. As such, the ways in which the participants presented themselves within their narrative is important. The participants gauged the expectations of the interviewer, sometimes checking that the result was on track. Ruth asked: "is it relevant for you to […] do you want to know the sort of the career history bit or is that not relevant?' Penny concluded: "That's everything, I'm sure you're bored silly"—modestly dismissing the value of her testimony. But despite any passing doubts, the three women all offered robust, purposeful accounts of parts of their lives. Ruth's interview provided the most narrative detail and, as it starts in adulthood, her discourse focuses very strongly on self-determination. Ruth is firmly in control of her own narrative, asserting: "Yep, drumming is very positive you see. Drumming is very good for the soul and it's very empowering for women', "You know, you've got to be a self-starter" and "Circus is quite life changing. I'm a real zealot, I'm an evangelist". Of the three women interviewed, Ruth's transcript is the one least influenced by the introduction of objects, retaining a flow of subjects and thoughts that had been given previous consideration by the participant. Penny's discourse is less explicitly about empowerment, but there is a firm authority in her statements about her achievements:

> I went off to Finland for a month, got married in December and went off in July to Finland for a month and it was through Guiding. […] that was a young leaders gathering in Finland, and through that I had a trip right up into the Arctic Circle, which was very exciting.

As a researcher herself, Mary was the participant most familiar with the interview scenario, although with roles reversed. Of the three participants, she drew out the connections between the objects, their meanings and her life most fully. Her damaged teddy bear prompting the reflection:

> I think to me there's a slight metaphor here, "cause this is the way life is … metaphorically the dog of life comes and eats your face off [laugh], it happens, you know and you just move on, you know.

She distinguished between the sensory and the symbolic, untangling layers of personal meaning from larger cultural associations:

> I think the dresser is very symbolic, and I don't know about maybe, in your part of the world, whether it would be the same. […] I lived in the West of Ireland for quite a while, and down there, like the dresser, […] the dresser is THE THING. […] [It refers to] the woman's realm, or that rite of passage or that sort of notion of domesticity continuing across the generation.

Conclusions and reflections

In conclusion, this exploratory research found objects to be a useful medium for connecting with older women's lives over many decades, helping to explore women's ageing in several ways. First, it is worth reflecting on the role of the objects in helping the women to narrate their life experiences. The benefits of using objects, as opposed to a straightforward narrative interview, were surprising to us as experienced qualitative researchers. The objects offered a tangible link to the past, or to a person who had passed. Objects allowed the interviewee to show, not just tell, how important a person, a relationship or an experience was to her. For younger researchers such as ourselves, it was enlightening and engaging to be drawn into the world of the past through the objects. The objects (such as Mary's mountain bike) also allowed us to see the everyday from the perspective of someone older than ourselves. It is difficult to imagine how similar insights could be drawn from conducting the same interviews without the guiding frame of the participant's personal possessions. Subsequently, our reflections substantiate what was found in the project evaluation—that the women's narration of their own life course was aided by speaking about their objects.[6] The objects foregrounded a different range of life events and relationships and did so in ways that offered deeper insight into the meanings of those times, places and people.

As researchers, we found that the objects ignited deeper discussion at interview, and even more strikingly at the public exhibition. As this article is based on the interview data only, we have offered evidence from those interviews of women clearly articulating their experience of navigating a long life course. Through their engagement with the accumulated meaning of their chosen objects, these women expressed a range of identities, sometimes adapting and changing according to what life threw at them. Objects such as nappy pins and children's toys were used by the women to demonstrate the intense experience of motherhood, a painful but enriching aspect of life. Sometimes, creative interventions with material things and images formed part of a personal curatorial practice, a habit that pre-figured participating in this project. Objects such as passports and travel memorabilia were used to demonstrate self-determination, adventure and escape from the sometimes stifling experience of living within prescribed gender roles in twentieth-century Ireland.

The most interesting finding was that objects can provide a window on the sometimes contradictory experience of women's ageing. None of the women sanitised their life histories. They were as keen to include objects that had sad associations, as they were keen to include happy emblems of success, such as Mary's bike, which reminded her of her flourishing relationships with children and grandchildren. Their object-based discourse moved deftly between the symbolic and the affective, and made connections between their experiences and larger social and cultural currents. The objects prompted them to describe their lives in different ways—ways that were rooted, inter-connected and emotionally illuminating. The women's ageing is both a fact of life, and a changing status. They have acquired years of perspective which allows them to "move on" when the metaphorical dog of life has ravaged them. They find comfort in relationships, they understand loss, and they choose to focus on experiences that have formed them, rather than those that have been particularly pleasant or comfortable.

All three of the women used their objects as symbols of the complex and subtle negotiations that make up relationships they have enjoyed or lost at various points in their life course. In this way, objects could be an important means of helping older women to communicate the significant impact of relationships in helping them to understand their place in the world once they reach old age. Objects also provide a tangible link to relationships that have formed them as individuals, but which may now be lost due to death, or the passage of time. In tracing their life histories, relationships with others formed a central focus—both as a means of creating narrative structure and as a way of making sense of the self. Objects were able to tunnel into very specific moments that shed light on the character of those relationships.

While none of the participants explicitly referred to the need to be an example to younger women, both Mary and Penny honoured their inheritance from previous generations of women. Mary referred to receiving her mother's dresser as a "rite of passage" and Penny's determined progress through life seemed to mirror the sense of purpose that defined her mother's life; a characteristic which Penny later captured in the quilt she made after her mother's death. Penny, at eighty years of age, offers plenty of evidence in response to Karpen's questions about what career women do with their retirement; write a book, join a club, work for the community, and take part in research.

The analysis presented here suggests that material culture has a potential role in communicating the complexity of living a long life to younger generations. Engaging seriously and methodically with our older generations on material pasts and presents could make a major contribution in terms of increasing public understanding of what it means to live a long life. Such a serious debate, informed by the lived experience of ageing, is a vital stage that we must not miss as we make the transition to a long-lived society and culture.

Notes

1. As a pilot project, the selection process prioritised participants who were able to commit to the project's activities, the only criteria being that they were over 60 years old, 50% men and 50% women and that they lived within easy reaching distance of where the arts workshop and exhibition were to be held.
2. See https://gemmahodge.com/ [accessed 18 January 2018].
3. https://thelivelyproject.wordpress.com/ [accessed 8 August 2017].
4. Bernard et al. 2017, "The Ageing of British Gerontology" exhibition material, https://ageingofbritishgerontology.wordpress.com/ [accessed 17 September 2018].
5. By contrast, Ruth had experimented with Facebook but found that this medium could reveal her life to a very large audience. She preferred instead the more intimate practice of making photo collages that represented the people that really mattered in her life.
6. The evaluation included a reflective focus group with all six participants, who expressed surprise at the extent to which the objects helped them to talk about their past.

Acknowledgements

We would like to thank our collaborators on that project: Gemma Hodge, Lorraine Calderwood, the Arts Council Northern Ireland and the Crescent Arts Centre, Belfast. Our greatest thanks go to the participants in the Lively project, who generously shared their lives and objects.

Disclosure statement

No potential conflict of interest was reported by the authors.

Funding

The authors thank the Wellcome Trust for a Small Grant that supported the research and public engagement activities upon which this article is based.

ORCID

Leonie Hannan http://orcid.org/0000-0003-0779-0773

References

Appadurai, A., ed. 1988. *The Social Life of Things: Commodities in Cultural Perspective.* Cambridge: Cambridge University Press.

Applewhite, A. 2016. *This Chair Rocks: A Manifesto Against Ageism.* New York: Networked Books Inc.

Arber, S., and J. Ginn. 1991. *Gender and Later Life: A Sociological Analysis of Resources and Constraints.* London: SAGE.

Auslander, L. 2005. "Beyond Words." *American Historical Review* 110: 1015–45.

Bateson, M. C. 1990. *Composing a Life: Life as a Work in Progress.* New York: Penguin.

Bertaux, D., ed. 1981. *Biography and Society: The Life History Approach in the Social Sciences.* Beverly Hills, CA: Sage Publications.

Bogost, I. 2012. *Alien Phenomenology or What It's Like to Be a Thing.* Minneapolis: University of Minnesota Press.

Calasanti, T. 2006. "Ageism and Feminism: From 'Et Cetera' to Center." *NWSA Journal* 18 (1): 13–30.

Calasanti, T. 2007. "Bodacious Berry, Potency Wood and the Aging Monster: Gender and Age Relations in Anti-Aging Ads." *Social Forces* 86 (1): 335–355.

Calasanti, T. 2010. "Gender and Applied Research on Aging." *The Gerontologist, (50th Anniversary Issue)* 50 (6): 1–15. doi:10.1093/geront/gnq085.

Calasanti, T. 2016. "Combating Ageism: How Successful is Successful Aging?" *The Gerontologist* 56 (6): 1093–1101.

Carney, G. M. 2017. "Toward a gender politics of aging." *Journal of Women & Aging*: https://doi.org/10.1080/08952841.2017.1301163.

Carney, G., and M. Gray. 2015. "Unmasking the Elderly Mystique: Why it is Time to Make the Personal Political in Aging Research." *Journal of Aging Studies* 35: 123–134.

Chatterjee, H. J., ed. 2008. *Touch in Museums: Policy and Practice in Object Handling.* Oxford: Berg.

Chatterjee, H. J., and L. Hannan, eds. 2015. *Engaging the Senses: Object-Based Learning in Higher Education*. Farnham: Ashgate.

Cruikshank, M. 2003. *Learning to Be Old: Gender, Culture and Aging*. Lanham: Rowman and Littlefield.

de Beauvoir, S. 1972. *The Coming of Age*. New York: G. P. Putnam's Sons.

Denzin, N. K. 1989. *Interpretive Biography*. London: Sage.

Estes, C., S. Biggs, and C. Phillipson, eds. 2003. *Social Theory, Social Policy and Aging: A Critical Introduction*. Maidenhead, UK: Open University Press.

Friedan, B. 1993. *The Fountain of Age*. New York: Simon & Schuster.

Garner, D. J. 1999. "Feminism and Feminist Gerontology." *Journal of Women and Aging* 11: 2–3. 3-12.

Gilleard, Chris. 2018. "Suffering: The Darker Side of Ageing." *Journal of Aging Studies* 44: 28–33.

Gullette, M. 1997. *Declining to Decline: Cultural Combat and the Politics of the Midlife*. Charlottesville: University of Virginia.

Gullette, M. 2013. *Agewise: Fighting the New Ageism in America*. Chicago, IL: University of Chicago Press.

Gullette, Margaret Morganroth. 2017. "Against 'Aging'—How to Talk about Growing Older." *Theory, Culture, & Society*, December 21. https://www.theoryculturesociety.org/margaretmorganroth-gullette-aging-talk-growing-older/.

Hagestad, G., and R. Settersten. 2017. "Aging: It's Interpersonal—Reflections from Two Lifecourse Migrants." *The Gerontologist* 57 (1): 136–144.

Hanson, A. 2013. "What's Wrong with Older Women Talking About The 70s?" *The Guardian*, August 19.

Harman, G. 2002. *Tool-Being: Heidegger and the Metaphysics of Objects*. Chicago: Open Court.

Henare, A., M. Holbraad, and S. Wastell, eds. 2007. *Thinking Through Things: Theorising Artefacts Ethnographically*. Abingdon: Routledge.

Holstein, M. 2015. *Women in Late Life: Critical Perspectives on Gender and Age*. Lanham: Rowman & Littlefield.

Howker, E., and S. Malik. 2011. *Jilted Generation: How Britain Has Bankrupted Its Youth*. London: Faber & Faber.

Josselson, R., and A. Liebech, eds. 1995. *Interpreting Experience: The Narrative Study of Lives*, 1–26. Thousand Oaks, CA: Sage.

Karpen, Ruth Ray. 2017. "Anti-Ageism: The Next Big Social Movement." Tikkun, December 7. http://www.tikkun.org/nextgen/anti-ageism-the-next-big-social-movement.

King, J. 2013. *Discourses of Aging in Fiction and Feminism: The Invisible Woman*. Basingstoke: Palgrave Macmillan.

Knappett, C. 2011. *An Archaeology of Interaction: Network Perspectives on Material Culture and Society*. Oxford: Oxford University Press.

Krasner, J. 2005. "Accumulated Lives: Metaphor, Materiality, and the Homes of the Elderly." *Literature and Medicine* 24 (2): 209–30.

Latour, B. 2005. *Reassembling the Social: An Introduction to Actor-Network-Theory*. Oxford: Oxford University Press.

Laws, G. 1995. "Understanding Ageism: Lessons from Feminism and Postmodernism." *The Gerontologist* 35 (1): 112–118.

Lively, P. 2013. *Ammonites and Leaping Fish: A Life in Time*. London: Fig Tree.

Miller, D. 2008. *The Comfort of Things*. Cambridge: Polity Press.

Paris, S. G. 2002. *Perspectives on Object-Centered Learning in Museums*. Mahwah, NJ: Lawrence Erlbaum Associates.

Pruchno, R. 2017. "Aging: It's Personal." *The Gerontologist* 57 (1): 1–5.

Ray, R. 2004. "Towards the Croning of Feminist Gerontology." *Journal of Aging Studies* 18: 109–121.

Ray, R., and M. Fine. 1999. "Researching to Transgress: The Need for Critical Feminism in Gerontology." *Journal of Women and Aging* 11 (2-3): 171–184.

Scheidt, R. J. 2017. "The Defence of My Aging Self: A Report from the Field." *The Gerontologist* 57 (1): 110–115.
Segal, L. 2013. *Out of Time: The Pleasures and Perils of Aging*. London: Verso.
Solway, R., P. M. Camic, L. J. Thomson, and H. J. Chatterjee. 2016. "Material Objects and Psychological Theory: A Conceptual Literature Review." *Arts & Health* 8 (1): 82–101.
Sontag, S. 1972. "The Double Standard of Aging." *Saturday Review of the Society*, 29–32. September 23.
Svašek, M. 2007. *Anthropology, Art and Cultural Production*. London: Pluto Press.
Tedlock, D. 1983. *The Spoken Word and the Work of Interpretation*. Philadelphia: University of Pennsylvania Press.
Thomson, L. J., and H. J. Chatterjee. 2014. "Assessing Well-Being Outcomes for Arts and Heritage Activities: Development of a Museum Well-being Measures Toolkit." *Journal of Applied Arts and Health* 5 (1): 29–50.
Tierney, W. G. 2000. "Undaunted Courage: Life History and the Postmodern Challenge." In *Handbook of Qualitative Research*. 2nd ed., edited by N. K. Denzin and Y. S. Lincoln, 537–553. London: Sage.
Turkle, S. 2007. *Evocative Objects: Things We Think With*. London: MIT.
Willits, D. 2011. *The Pinch: How the Baby Boomers Took Their Children's Future and Why They Should Give It Back*. London: Atlantic.
Woodspring, N. 2015. *Baby Boomers: Time and Aging Bodies*. Bristol: Policy Press.
Woodward, K. 2003. "Against Wisdom: The Social Politics of Anger and Aging." *Journal of Aging Studies* 17: 55–67.

Reading Film with Age Through Collaborative Autoethnography: Old Age and Care, Encounters with *Amour* (Haneke, 2012), *Chronic* (Franco, 2015) and *A Woman's Tale* (Cox, 1991)

Rita Ferris-Taylor, Jane Grant, Hannah Grist, Ros Jennings, Rina Rosselson and Sylvia Wiseman

[a]Older Women in Film Group, University of the Third Age, Brent, UK; [b]Centre for Women, Ageing and Media, University of Gloucestershire, Cheltenham, UK

ABSTRACT

This paper is primarily a study in research methods, reflecting on the application of an autoethnographic method as means to engage with a co-created intergenerational research project that focussed on reading films about older age and end of life care. Methodologically rich and complex, this paper outlines the research process through which six women at different stages of the lifecourse (Katz, Stephen. 2005. *Aging: Life Course, Lifestyle, and Senior Worlds*. Peterborough: Broadview Press) came together to critically analyse *Amour* (Haneke 2012), *Chronic* (Franco 2015) and *A Woman's Tale* (Cox 1991). The autoethnographic approach privileges the voices of older women who use their own life stories and experiences to produce nuanced readings of care and old age as they are represented on screen. From this innovative approach to film through autoethnographic reflection, new concepts of "reading with care," and "reading with age" emerge as important to our understandings of what it means to care and be cared for.

Introduction

This is a research methods paper that explores the use of autoethnography as a means to facilitate and capture the complexity and richness of a co-created process of intergenerational research. The paper presents a collaborative study of three films that focus on older people and experiences of caring (both caring for and caring about). The paper is, however, about much more than just the chosen films and the readings that are produced, although these elements are still of importance. Above all, it uses the self-reflexivity of autoethnography, to think with age (Jennings and Gardner 2012) about film and, by extension, about being/becoming an old woman. The idea of "thinking with age" is methodologically pivotal to the study as a whole because it is integral to its autoethnographic method. It forms the interpretative framework for the self-reflexive research process by saturating the autoethnographic process with life-course experiences. Age in this study is therefore more than a set of chronological markers from birth to death; age is a repository to think with and with which to read texts.

The aim of the paper is therefore to critically explore the Older Women in Film Group's (OWFG) desire to work with each other to comment on the films *Amour* (Haneke 2012), *Chronic* (Franco 2015) and *A Woman's Tale* (Cox 1991) from their perspectives as older women. This paper reflects on the process and outcome that emerged when two ageing studies scholars based in the Centre for Women, Ageing and Media (WAM) were invited into the mix, bringing with them autoethnography as a new approach to the project.

The project that is outlined in this paper is political and polemic in nature and presents a collective engagement between the members of the OWFG that changed in both content and process over time but never in its intent to offer readings about age, care, and film that are rarely heard; readings by older women. What follows is a co-constructed and intergenerational account of a research process. It draws together autographically inflected readings of three films set in three different locations: France (*Amour*), United States (*Chronic*), and Australia (*A Woman's Tale*), but analysed by an intergenerational, nationally diverse group of older women (US, European and Middle Eastern origin) in London, who were nonetheless mindful of their white Western privileges and gendered reading positions from the outset.

The provenance of the project is lengthy and grounded in grassroots experiential and feminist research on older women and film. Jane Grant, Rita Ferris-Taylor, Rina Rosselson, and Sylvia Wiseman were, at the time of writing, members of the Brent University of the Third Age (U3A) OWFG and Hannah Grist and Ros Jennings are members of WAM at the University of Gloucestershire, where Hannah is an Early Career Researcher and Lecturer in Media, and Ros is Professor of Ageing, Culture, and Media.

OWFG has an influential history in terms of the study of the representation of older women in film; including contributing data and materials that brought about a British Film Institute (BFI) Study Day (2006), a guide to *Older Women in Feature Films* (2006), and a paper presented by a former member of the OWFG at the *Ageing Femininities: Representation, Identities, Feminism* conference at the University of the West of England (2007). In addition, Rina established her *Ageing, Ageism and Feature Films* film blog (Rosselson 2017) and has also written for the feminist blog *The F Word*. The significance of this contribution lies not just in her reading of the films but in her drive to counter a statement once directed at her when she asked to be supervised for a PhD —"Who is interested in old women?"

Structure of the article

To try and do justice to the complexity of this process, this paper is unconventionally constructed. It is much longer than most academic journal articles because it presents autoethnographic reflections on the three films, by all four of the OWFG members. These reflections are followed by autoethnographic reflections on their involvement in the project written by the two academics. The next section comprises an analysis by the two academics of the themes that emerged in the autoethnographic readings, focusing on the emergent concepts of "reading with age," "reading with care," and "boundaries of care." The conclusion consists of an account of the group's discussion of the themes that were then shared and of the group's final reflections on the use of collaborative autoethnography as a research method.

The structure of this research, as outlined above, corresponds to Julie Stephens' (2010) experiences of doing feminist autoethnography and is an example of memory work that is "messy" (Denzin 1997). Certainly, it has been a challenge to adequately capture all the complexities of this collaboration for academic dissemination whilst attempting to remain ethically aware and respectful (Ellis 2007, 2009; Roth 2009) of the relationships and interactions that are manifest in it. The following section, written as a collaborative autoethnography by Jane and Rina, outlines the research process undertaken for this project, which evolved through face to face discussions and email exchanges with the other group members over several months.

Research process (Rina Rosselson & Jane Grant)

Two of us, Rina and Jane, were passionate about film and, increasingly, about the representation of ageing in films. In early 2016 the OWFG had viewed and discussed Amour (2013) *and later analysed* Chronic (2015), *as both films dealt with the subjects of "caring" and "end of life." Soon after this, we decided to include* A Woman's Tale (1991) *which dealt with the same subjects.*

Several weeks later we asked two other members of the group (Sylvia and Rita) to join us in the project, as each of them had a great deal of experience in caring. When they both expressed concern that they did not know enough about film criticism, they were reassured that what was important was their knowledge of caring.

The films were each viewed at home and then everyone met up to discuss them several weeks later. To facilitate the group's thinking, Jane and Rina drew up some initial questions to guide our thinking as we watched the films individually. We then met together, and Jane recorded and transcribed the discussions that took place. We had two discussions about the films, with an eight-week gap between discussions. Our meetings usually lasted approximately two hours. We shared transcripts of the recordings over email and another meeting was arranged to discuss where we were going with the project.

We chose to view the films at home separately because it enabled us to focus fully on the films and our gut reactions to them. We could make our own notes, using the guided questions, and reflect fully. This enabled our individual views to be articulated more clearly before meeting to discuss and debate our differing reactions. The four of us had very different experiences of seeing these three films. Rina had already seen all three films in a variety of settings, Amour *several times, and had written about them. Jane had seen two, and Sylvia and Rita had not seen any of them previously. In addition, it was hard enough setting times that the four of us could meet for the discussions—let alone viewing three films as well.*

In November/December 2016, there was an air of deep discouragement. The results of our discussions were very disappointing. We found that we had different understandings and major disagreements about how to frame our views. Were we to isolate the representation of caring in the light of our experience, ignoring its function in the film, or apply our experience to explore the role of caring in the film as a whole? This led to chaotic disagreements, often reacting to each other in ways that barred any real discussion about our respective views. How did each of us understand our intentions and aims in the project? Revisiting the transcripts, what were the main themes, agreements and disagreements? We asked: What can we do with anything we produce—who might be interested? Did we have different assumptions about this?

Over this period, Jane and Rina attended the conference "Discourses of Care" *in Glasgow in September 2016, where they met Hannah and Ros, who were interested in our project. Rina kept in touch with them about our progress, and when it was clear that we had reached a stand-still they offered to meet up to discuss the possibility of our taking an auto-ethnographic approach to the subject. Hannah and Ros joined our project in December 2016, and our first meeting took place in February 2017.*

At our first meeting with Ros and Hannah, we explained the history of the project and our ambitions for it, and Hannah and Ros in turn explained how we might use autoethnography to produce a paper for publication in an academic journal. Once we had decided, an autoethnographic approach would help us to move the project forward, Hannah and Ros set an April 2017 deadline to complete a draft of our autoethnographies. We then shared discussions via email about our work and agreed that Ros and Hannah would explore our autoethnographies for themes and create a draft structure for this paper. In the following weeks, we each wrote back with comments and corrections via email. In November 2017, we met in person and discussed the need to shorten our autoethnographies in order to submit to a journal, and decided to allow Ros and Hannah to edit as necessary. We shared drafts via email and agreed corrections and suggested changes. In December 2017, sixteen months after beginning the project, our paper was complete and submitted to the editors for their consideration.

Using ageing, feminism and autoethnography as an exploratory framework

The arrival of cultural gerontology in the last decade has signalled a shift in the way ageing is studied and conceptualised. Where research on older age was once dominated by biomedical models which grouped ageing bodies into categories of "success" or "decline" (Dolan and Tincknell 2012), cultural gerontologists and ageing studies scholars recognise that "people don't line up neatly with either positive ageing or biodecline—although the assaults certainly do make life nastier and, sometimes, shorter" (Gullette 2017, xvi).

The reconstitution of ageing thesis suggests that late modernity has fundamentally changed the experience of ageing and that it has become heavily influenced by cultural phenomena (Twigg and Martin 2015, 2). Margaret Morganroth Gullette's seminal work *Aged by Culture* (2004) argues that, like gender and race, age is a social construct intimately tied to neoliberal narratives of decline, which fuel negative personal narratives and perpetuate ageist discourses (cf. Gullette 2017). To examine how these dominant cultural narratives impact on our understandings of age and ageing, "Gullette's age critical perspective emphasises the power of autobiography and storytelling" (Jennings and Grist 2017, 196), an approach which fits well with the autoethnographic research method employed in this project. Moreover, cultural gerontological and ageing studies perspectives eschew biomedical approaches which tend to carry out research "on" older people, and instead adopt a collaborative perspective where "older people themselves are at the centre of debates to discuss their own identities, their own lives and the policies governing them" (WAM Manifesto 2012).

As we will outline below in more detail, this research project adopts a collaborative autoethnographic approach (Chang, Ngunjiri, and Hernandez 2013), which is intergenerational in nature, to examine personal responses to cultural products which narrate both older age and care/care giving in later life. The relationship between ageing and care has traditionally been tied to biomedical models of ageing as decline, often mobilising the "dementia trope" in the popular cultural imaginary (Chivers 2011; Gravagne 2013; Gullette 2017). In response, ageing studies approaches have facilitated work which positions dementia as a cultural phenomenon, offering a voice to those affected, challenging banal and harmful depictions and highlighting new representational possibilities (Chivers and Kriebernegg 2017; Swinnen and Schweda 2015).

Thinking through the representational possibilities connected to care and care giving, new research (Jennings and Grist Forthcoming) has shown that the providers of care to those with dementia, those who work within the nursing home space, remain both invisible and hyper-visible (Woodward 1999). The films examined through this project thus represent a few notable exceptions in the representation of carers on screen and therefore highlight the importance of collaborative methodological approaches informed by ageing studies concepts.

Autoethnography is an approach to writing and research that "foregrounds the researcher's personal experience (*auto*) as it is embedded within, and informed by, cultural identities and contexts (*ethno*) and as it is expressed through writing, performance, or other creative means (*graphy*)" (Manning and Adams 2015, 188–189). Both process and product, autoethnography connects the personal to the cultural and "allows us to examine how the private troubles of individuals are connected to public issues and to public responses to these troubles" (Denzin 1997, 5–6).

Approaches to autoethnography are commonly divided between two camps: evocative autoethnography and analytic autoethnography (Denshire 2013). The evocative approach focuses on producing "research grounded in personal experience" to "sensitise readers to issues of identity politics, to experiences shrouded in silence, and to forms of representation that deepen our capacity to empathise with people who are different from us" (Ellis and Bochner 2000, online), which repositions "readers and subjects as coparticipants in dialogue" (Ellis 1999, 669). The analytic approach focuses on using empirical data, including and beyond the self, to theorise a set of broader social phenomena, an approach that is consistent with qualitative inquiry rooted in traditional symbolic interactionism (Anderson 2006).

A third approach has emerged as a way through the seemingly oppositional construction of evocative versus analytic approaches to autoethnography. Whilst autoethnography usually has a focus on the self (*auto*), the method has also evolved to include community, co-constructed and collaborative autoethnographies (Chang, Ngunjiri, and Hernandez 2013). These approaches view experiences and relationships as "jointly-authored, incomplete, and historically situated affairs" (Ellis and Bochner 2000, online) and focus on "the personal experience of researchers-in-collaboration" to explore broader social phenomena (Bochner and Ellis 2000, online). These kinds of layered autoethnographies bring together multiple voices to reflect on the "emergent experience" of doing and writing research (Ronai 1992, 123, cited in Bochner and Ellis 2000, online).

This research project offers readings of films about older people which are rarely heard; readings by older women themselves. A feminist project from its inception, this research utilises the power of collaborative feminist autoethnography (Ettore 2017). Feminist autoethnography is "a method of being, knowing and doing that combines two concerns: telling the stories of those who are marginalized and making good use of our experience" (Allen and Piercy 2005, 156). In this project, "our experience" straddles both academic and non-academic approaches to the films and to autoethnography as a method. Leni Marshall (2006) notes: "As feminists and scholars, we write what we know—what we learn from our lives, the lives of those around us, and the texts we encounter" (xii). This project represents a process of feminist collaboration, drawing upon our individual experiences and our reactions to the texts, using autoethnography as process and product to "say something" as women about the representation of ageing and care on screen.

Autoethnography has a complex history and multiple applications. Jimmie Manning and Tony E. Adams (2015) draw attention to the ways in which autoethnography is increasingly drawn upon by scholars in multiple disciplines to explore questions of race, ethnicity, and gender (see Boylorn and Orbe 2013; Pelias 2014), and to examine personal and interpersonal understandings of popular culture (see Bochner 2012; Drew 2001; Herrmann 2012; Leavy 2013). Like those who brought autoethnography to popular cultural studies, this paper adopts the method of feminist collaborative autoethnography (Chang, Ngunjiri, and Hernandez 2013) to bring together the voices of four older women and two academics reflecting on films about older age and care. As Manning and Adams (2015) assert, "popular culture texts can bring us together, make us reflect on our own lives, and encourage us to think about the values we hold dear" (198).

With our shared motivation to work against endemic cultural ageism and to challenge representations of older age and care, the following sections present four autoethnographies which explore each member of the OWFG's reading of the three films. All the autoethnographic elements have been italicised, though the style of each autoethnography is unique to its writer—for example, some of the autoethnographies are titled and contain subtitles; others contain bullet points, the use of bold, and one contains academic references. These differences in approach to the autoethnographic writing and differences in style have been retained for this article as evidence of "aesthetic and evocative thick descriptions of personal and interpersonal experience" (Ellis, Adams, and Bochner 2011), which is characteristic of co-constructed autoethnographic narratives (Bochner and Ellis 1995).

Autoethnography—Writing Project re. End of Life Films/Films Portraying Older People (Rita Ferris-Taylor)

With all three films, I felt hesitant about viewing them, knowing the content may be upsetting or grim and having been forewarned of this by other members of the group.

It's not because I can't face such subject matter, but due to multiple illness and bereavement in my own family, I have to be feeling strong to do so and sometimes need instead to watch something completely vacuous!! I am a 60-year-old woman, and although in some groups of older people that I attend, I am regarded as a "younger" older woman, many recent deaths of family members and friends, sometimes at a relatively young age, have made me acutely aware of my own mortality and never knowing what is around the corner. I'm not so much fearful about death as worried about what the process of getting there may be like! I have experience of supporting family members and friends in hospices and care homes. I have worked variously as a day and residential worker, a speech and language therapist, an adult and further education teacher with disabled adults and on health and social care courses.

***All three films were unflinching and graphic in their unusual portrayal of the physicality of caring and ageing**, e.g. very prolonged intimate care scenes in* Chronic, *with the camera lingering long enough in some scenes to hint that in this unusual relationship, there can hang some sensuality in the air even if there is no actual wrongdoing. By contrast, in* A Woman's Tale, *Martha bathes herself—her body is bold, unadorned, gaunt and still beautiful in her old age. However, she is shown later on starting to struggle, e.g. tripping on the stairwell, leaving things on the stove, being in pain. Throughout the film there is the caged bird image of Jesus, her pet, linking to how she herself is gradually being caged in and having fewer choices.*

In Amour, *the successive indignities are portrayed, i.e. the incontinence and the infantilising tendencies of the nurse, who is helpful and knowledgeable but still calls the pads "diapers" or "nappies."*

***How older people can become seen as less of a person**, e.g. increasing dependency may mean the older person cannot take on the same role in the family anymore/ are almost absent/overlooked in what is happening to them. In* A Woman's Tale, *Martha shows her horror at the thought of being in a home or going on an outing with other older people. At one point, she talks angrily about not wanting to be one of the "prisoners" like those in the old people's home. A horror I share too!! In* Amour, *Anne's spiritedness is portrayed at the beginning, as well as throughout her successive strokes. She is still clearly her same self, however, in one scene, her daughter becomes upset that Anne is now "talking gibberish" although, if she had listened more carefully, she may have been able to catch what her mother was saying. In* Chronic, *which focuses more on the paid carer's experience, Dave tries to relate to the people he is caring for, but the tasks can make things seem like a conveyor belt.*

***The sadness and tedium of caring and being cared for is well portrayed**. In* Chronic, *static clips gave the sense of the repetitiveness of caring. These clips are interspersed by scenes of Dave running on a treadmill, which made me feel that this is what his caring role is like.*

In Amour, *I think the changes, as Anne's strokes progressed, were portrayed realistically and unsentimentally. It conveyed the time consuming-ness of doing everyday things, e.g. the slow movements as Georges tries to physically care for Anne, holding each other a bit like a shuffling dance, to get to the loo. This film shows the changing roles as Georges becomes "the carer" while Anne becomes the "cared for."*

I have personally hated it when people refer to me as a relation's "carer" or indeed my husband's "carer" (he is blind, and I am his wife, not his carer)—I feel this distorts what the relationship essentially is. It doesn't mean that defines the whole of the relationship—it just sounds like government speak for ways of offloading responsibilities onto families and saying certain needs are taken care of. I think it is important to preserve the original relationship as far as possible.

***Dilemmas about how paid carers and family members relate** e.g. in* Chronic, *Dave is shown as a professional nurse who knows what he is doing, completing caring tasks more easily and calmly than the family members. Initially, they are glad someone else can do the tasks they cannot cope with. Marta's family are portrayed as only too glad when they don't need to come over. Dave is expected to dutifully do the donkey work yet at the* *same time, due to the intimacy of it, he establishes close relationships with his patients, which the families come to resent or just don't recognise. He is expected to be anonymous and dispensable, despite such an intimate role. However, the shots near the beginning of the film which show Dave in an ambiguous, potentially stalkerish, and over-identified manner with his clients, highlight the potential risks that we take when having a paid carer in our home—we don't really know who they are and what motivations they have.*

Thinking of my own experiences, I never felt I wanted to care in a personal way for my father, as it would have been an intimacy that challenged/transgressed my relationship as his daughter (fortunately it did not become necessary). I was more easily able to provide intimate care for a male neighbour when needed, in unexpected ways. However, I found that when paid carers care for your relations and friends, they can sometimes very quickly establish a close relationship, which could make me feel usurped as a family member. Or, feeling that they are not caring in a sufficient or competent enough way, or that they are doing things that are undignified or potentially abusive, and then feeling the need to be vigilant. All of which came out in the films, e.g. Chronic, *where Dave was probably falsely accused;* Amour, *where Georges challenges the sadistic female carer who brushes his wife's hair in such a humiliating way.* A Woman's Tale *had a different take when the paid carer, Anna, is groped by Martha's male neighbour. This scene felt all too realistic, as did Martha, asking Anna why she didn't let him do it, as he didn't have long to live!! I felt appalled by this, as it mirrors some situations I have been involved with in everyday life, where groping by an older and/or disabled man is felt to be somehow less serious (perhaps because due to age or disability, he is seen as being less of a man/not a threat). It's often seen as something to be expected/something the carer should put up with and not complain about. Martha suggests it can be seen as life affirming, but also condones his actions in a way that my feminist principles would not accept for any carer.*

What is and isn't "appropriate"? Things can be over professional and cold/over boundaried, rather than genuine and warm but where do the dividing lines lie? Some of what was shown in the physical and emotional closeness of the relationship would be frowned upon now and probably a cause for disciplinary action, as paid caring is now a much more professionalised activity with national occupational standards, stressing boundaries. But should it be such a professionalised, impersonal relationship, or more close and genuine, as portrayed in A Woman's Tale*?*

All three films highlight the need to re-think ways to approach end of life*. The need for better, high quality care and more options, sadly difficult in these straightened financial times, where there is a lot of government rhetoric about choice in social care but maybe the reality sadly lacking, e.g. many old people end up in care homes against their will/choice.*

In Chronic, *the scene with Martha dying was very unsentimental, functional, calm and felt slow, like real time, with no dramatic deathbed revelations.*

In Amour, *although Anne wishes to stay out of hospital when she realises the significance of her illness, to end it early on, there is no straightforward legal way to accomplish this. Later, at the end, maybe Georges would have acceded to her request early on if he had really known what lay in wait!!*

Martha gets her wish to be at home and die there through Anna's support, but I found this final scene a bit hackneyed, i.e. that her dying words are about life being beautiful rather than, as often in my own experience, something fairly mundane, or to do with pain or discomfort.

Autoethnography (Jane Grant)

I'm 73 and came to the UK from the States to study film when I was 20. I was involved in political activism and film in the 1960s and woke up to feminism in 1970.

I joined the Old Women's Film Group (OWFG) when I was 61–62. I had a year off work following an accident and went to the group because I love films, felt the representation of old women was important, and had the time. I didn't particularly see myself as old—although the accident certainly made me feel I'd been kicked into old age prematurely. It didn't take long to realise that I was getting old and that acknowledging this was a good thing as well as an act of solidarity. My own experiences of disability have taught me that life can change in a second and that there is a difficult (if healthy) tension between stretching myself and accepting limiting changes and adapting.

I retired from part time work as a midwife researcher in 2013 when my daughter went back to work and needed help with childcare. I do a lot to stay as fit as I can and to prevent respiratory infections I'm prone to get. I love films and see a lot of them, being with friends, and reading.

Caring

I've been a midwife most of my working life and before that I was an ambulance driver and so my perspective on caring is very much influenced by my experience and identity in these jobs.

I haven't had much experience with end of life care apart from spending a lot of time with one friend in her last year of chemo. During that period, I was able to observe a professional carer, and that made big impressions on me.

My own experience of being cared for has also influenced my ideas about caring. After losing my leg in a motorbike accident, I learned a lot about what I liked and what worked for me in terms of care, and how to discuss this with professionals.

I have always been fascinated by illness narratives and introduced the medical humanities into my midwifery teaching—using literature, poetry, and films. I think my exposure to this body of work helped me in recovering from the acute trauma of my accident.

Amour

I thought it was a very cerebral and cold film and if I had to say one sentence about Amour *I would say* "It's a cautionary tale on how not to care or provide care for a loved one." I kept thinking, "I wouldn't like this," *or* "I wouldn't like that," "that's not right," "that's not fair." *I felt angry with Georges for failing to help Anne die when she wanted and for slapping her. I felt manipulated by the director in making me care more about the fate of a pigeon than any of the people.*

I appreciated the film showing Anne returning to the flat in a chair, followed by a succession of medical equipment to support her in her new ill role. For me, the offer of a wheelchair and handrails was both exciting and welcome as they provided mobility and safety. I'm aware that someone with a chronic and progressive condition might have very different feelings about being offered such "aids." I also appreciated the film showing what are usually regarded as the indignities of illness and/or ageing—needing assistance to get up, sit down, walk, eat, to dress, and to use the toilet.

The representation of professional carers was chilling. The care was infantilising, humiliating, cruel and violent. When I trained as a midwife in the 1970s many obstetricians and sometimes midwives behaved like this. Woman or patient centred care was a long way off. There is no interaction between Georges and the carers—apart from a scene in which he angrily dismisses one of them for being uncaring. The professionals offer no support to Georges, much less to his daughter—either practical or emotional.

Amour *was for me a call to "be prepared." It encouraged discussing things that are very important—e.g. illness and decrepitude and the kind of support you'd like and who's best to provide it if and when you need it. I loved Atul Gawande's "Being Mortal."*

After seeing Amour, *I told my daughter that I thought it might be a good idea if she watched it and she said: "What's it about?" I could see the blood draining from her face when I told her. I think if those in our friendship network organised a showing that we didn't attend, but all of our children attended, that could be useful because then they wouldn't feel so isolated and they could share their concerns, gallows humour, and fears about the future.*

The film really brought home, in its absence, the importance of having both professional and family support in such an acute and terminal situation with negotiated boundaries and effective communication between everyone.

Chronic

I found Chronic *interesting but unsettling the first time I saw it, so I was pleased we included it in our project about the representation of caring. Suddenly the film became more interesting than unsettling. The film is a portrait of a carer, a man with a mysterious and troubling back-story. Like* Amour, *I found it cerebral and cold.*

Initially I thought the shot of David washing Sara's emaciated body was cruel and cold. But I also saw a tenderness in David's slow movements. I imagined he'd had a long carer relationship with Sara in which both felt comfortable. The lingering gaze documented a kind and normal event. Midwife friends and I used to discuss how care in childbirth and at the end of life are similar. Trust between the carer and the cared for is central in both, and I think we are so predisposed to trust in these situations that it takes a lot to "blow it," making tales of cruelty in childbirth or end of life care so disturbing. In all David's interactions with Sara I recognised this trust.

In another scene, David washes a woman's bottom. She's been having chemo and couldn't make it to a toilet. This too seemed normal and kind. Shit has a place in the narrative of childbirth. Telling women what the need to push might feel like, telling them they might pass a bit of poo, and that we might get excited because that meant the baby was coming soon—always seemed to help diffuse worries about "soiling," "being unclean," and "concerns" about what others might think of them. The scene in the film gently documents a common end of life activity.

I didn't like that David did almost all his talking with the patient and no talking with the family. It's really important, whatever the caring situation, that you establish some kind of "how're we going to do this?" with the family and friends. This may be hard to do if the family is difficult, put out by the carer's skill or close relationship with a loved one. But not doing so can lead to wild accusations by the family against the carer, carer burnout, and most importantly the needs of the loved one being ignored.

David clearly had little appreciation of boundaries and was very damaged. He helped his son to die. Was he seeking absolution in his work as a carer? Was a woman's request for help to die distressing because he never had wanted to do it again? "That's the worst thing you could ask me," he said. I found the mystery aspect tedious but thought it was useful to show how carers may be "wounded" and this needn't make them bad carers. Indeed, if they have insight into their suffering they may be very empathic. Unfortunately, David did not, and he was killed in what I took to be suicide.

A Woman's Tale

In the opening shot a multitude of themes central to A Woman's Tale, *are introduced before the opening credits finish: ageing, illness and facing death, isolation, friendship, defiance and love. Her opening lines establish Martha as judgemental about anyone who rolls over, doesn't fight for life. "I'm still here eyes wide open looking straight at the world. They'll have to drag me out of here."*

In contrast to the other two films, the characters are well drawn and developed, especially that of Martha. Where the other films felt cold, this one felt warm. In Anna, caring is represented as professional, personal and very positive.

- *She develops caring appropriate to each person she's looking after.*
- *She encourages independence where necessary (Billy).*
- *She advocates strongly for patients in her care.*
- *She can assert personal boundaries not to be crossed—Billy groping her.*
- *She knows when to tell the truth—at the end with Martha.*
- *She cares* ***about*** *not just* ***for*** *someone.*
- *Anna crosses boundaries by current criteria in many ways, as David did, but not so weirdly.*
- *In the way she occasionally spoke to Martha's son.*
- *Going swimming with Martha.*
- *Accompanying Martha on a social outing that would be banned on safety grounds.*
- *Seeing an estate agent with a view to renting a flat she and Martha can share if Martha is locked out of her own.*
- *Meeting her lover in Martha's flat.*
- *Speaking about another patient with Martha.*

From my own experience, I identified with some of these things (swimming with a woman to encourage her contractions) and got in trouble for working longer than my shift or coming in on days off. I identified with Anna advocating more for the patient, when it came to it, than supporting her son. I also worried that she was going to burn out.

Martha is represented as carer in a number of ways:

- *In her support for her ill neighbour and another friend.*
- *In her support for Anna and Peter.*
- *As mother to her son and in the haunting memories of her daughters.*
- *In her attempt to help a suicidal teenager on a phone-in radio show.*

There was reciprocity in caring (between the carer and the cared for) to a greater or lesser degree in these instances.

John (Martha's son) as carer:

He does (like Anne and George's daughter) care, but unlike her is at great pains to work out how to best do this. The image of his and Peter's faces staring through the frosted glass of Martha's flat as she lay inside dying in Anna arms is desolate.

I identified with Martha as a patient—attempting to develop reciprocity in my relationships with carers was a way of maintaining my independence, as well as demonstrating respect and sometimes establishing the space for affection.

If I need end of life care, I would want to have a human relationship with my professional carer—to be cared about as well as cared for. Equally, I would want someone who knew what they were doing, knew how to take care of themselves in their professional role, encouraged, and supported my autonomy and the informed involvement of friends and family. These films made me think about all this and I imagine would make anyone else do the same. That has to be a good thing.

Autoethnography (Rina Rosselson)

On my retirement aged 60, fresh from a self-affirming "Growing Old Disgracefully" residential week, I attended the course "Ageing and the Media" at the City Literary Institute (1995). We were shown Brief Encounter *(1945). I still remember how furious I was. We were offered nostalgia instead of a demonstration of the sexism/ageism of the film industry or a screening of a film about ageing characters. I enrolled for an MA course in Film and TV Studies so that I could comment knowledgeably on the representation of old women in films.*

The responses to my dissertation and further experiences of witnessing the ageism at every stage of the film industry, a certain internalised ageism in women audiences, the lack of research on the subject, determined me to carry on my research (See Rosselson, online). *Occasionally a review, an academic paper, or the poor distribution of some interesting film made me so angry that I needed to make ordinary women's voices heard. The Older Women in Film Group gave space for discussion and successful projects.*

It is Chronic's *Cannes award and Anna Harpin's talk about Amour at "Ageing Embodiment and the Self," a Symposium held at Warwick University (2016), that stimulated me to explore the themes of love and care. Harpin asks: Do questions of authenticity, appropriation, and ethics, for example, apply in related manners to the portrait of physical decline in late life? What are the politics of performing care?*

Chronic *(2015): or "terminal pain but Tim Roth is a pleasure" (Bradshaw 2015, online)*

Its strong young male point of view annoyed me intensely. This film is about a professional home carer, Tim Roth as David, who has helped his terminally ill son to die. Its realist style mixed with a thriller keeps the carer's psychology a mystery. The many ambiguities about his behaviour and motivations culminate in his death—accident or suicide?—as shocking as it is gratuitous.

For the first 50 min, the viewer is presented with a man who may be a stalker, a morose inscrutable man who works as a palliative carer, a man who does not or cannot relate to people. Voyeuristic long takes of a young woman who is dying of AIDS being washed are followed with washing of her dead body. He helps his next patient John to watch porn and excludes other carers and family members from his care. He invents relationships and identities for himself and is finally dismissed, accused of the sexual abuse of his patient. Is his behaviour care or abuse? In both cases, he arranges to be the exclusive carer.

Short scenes show him with his ex-wife, his daughter and an old friend. It is then that it is revealed that he helped his terminally ill son to die. The only time he shows any feelings are the few seconds where he seeks his daughter's forgiveness. We are no more informed about his odd behaviour: was he a carer then or did he become a carer as a consequence of this trauma?

He is then employed by determined Martha. She knows his background. She wants to be helped to die. Long takes of over a minute show her vomiting, soiling herself. Close-ups of her soiled backside are offensive and dehumanising. Martha is determined to end her life and rejects David's care when he refuses. But his refusal does not last. The fatal injection is deliberately executed and takes 3 min of screen time.

There is no doubt that Roth has researched the role of carer. He performs the physical care of patients extremely well. The washing, the carrying, the supporting. But the many scenes of washing equate terminal illness with dirt. The Spartan mise-en-scene and soundtrack, the still camera, the bare interiors convey no warmth, or empathy. In its ambiguities, its suspense style, its voyeuristic shots, the film shows neither sensitivity to nor respect about end of life issues. I see in this film the exploitation of these subjects to show the director's and actor's proficiency to shock the audience.

A Woman's Tale *(1991) or "care and friendship"*

The film is based on the last days of the actor Sheila Florence, aged 75, a friend of director Cox. He transforms her real personality and experience into a fiction film and uses visual metaphors to express inner-feelings.

In a very straight narrative we are presented with two neighbours in a modest block of flats, Martha and Billy, who share a young, energetic, empathetic carer, Anna. The end of life of the two characters contrasts the sad isolation of Billy with Martha's full social life. Martha's naked body is seen in all its deterioration but does not elicit disgust. She is overtly cheerful, optimistic and sometimes acerbic. She expresses that life must be lived and enjoyed. Her inner life and her traumatised past that she cannot share with anybody are expressed in her dreams and when she is on her own. The sound track and images of the nightmare contrast with the daytime zest for life.

Anna and Martha develop a friendship and the two roles of friend and carer become merged. Anna understands her friend's needs and is the link between mother and concerned but overprotective son. Anna's care for Billy remains professional and cannot alleviate his isolation. When Martha is diagnosed with terminal cancer she decides, supported by Anna, not to have any more treatment. Anna helps the son to understand his mother's choice. Martha's fall, stay in hospital, her death, follow a trajectory all too familiar. She dies in Anna's arms.

Amour (2012) *or "it does not have to be like that"*

The film is about a husband caring for his severely handicapped wife at home and fulfilling her wish to die and dies himself.

Haneke forces the viewer to consider a loving couple's terminal moments. The decision to have a male carer focuses the attention on the carer's functions. We know nothing about

Georges. It is Anne who is the professional person in the household, and the couple are isolated. A role reversal without appropriation. Their relationship seems to be loving but formal. The initiating event is the promise that Anne forces Georges into making: do not send me back to hospital. It is also very early in the film that there is a cut from the daughter's recollection of her parents' love making to a specially adapted bed that separates them. There are other important mise-en-scene and editing details worth examining: the flat with its window open, the front door that is often banged shut and locked against the outside world, the sound track with the music stopping. There are powerful images: the disembodied hand on Georges' mouth in his nightmare, the body of Anne on the floor at the bottom of the open window, the flowers heads cut from the stems. Without any sentimentality, from wellbeing to the death of the couple, we encounter the many facets of an end of life, euthanasia and suicide.

We are not spared the details of a carer's functions of cleaning a disabled, incontinent body but they are shown with no loss of dignity of the patient. The numerous issues are dealt with a light touch: the risks and failure of surgical intervention, the deterioration of the body, depression, the inadequacy of care professionals, the physical toll of 24 hours caring, the powerlessness of well-meaning people, the breakup of the family, the different expressions of grief, and the repeated scenes where Anne expresses her wish to die and Georges compliance to this demand.

The power of this film has reduced many audiences to prolonged silences. In the words of one woman in the film group: I am awed into quietness, as though having contemplated something holy.

I wrote: It does not ask me to identify with the couple. It is a thought experiment. It asks me to consider how I would react, where I stand, how I feel in relation to all these issues.

I found in Amour *the burden of being the sole carer of a dying loved one, at home.*

I found in *Amour* a political film abo*ut end of life and care needs.*

I found in Amour *the tragedy of the change from "love" to "care."*

Autoethnography—Thoughts on Three Films (Sylvia Wiseman)

Perhaps this is the wrong name; perhaps it should be reactions to these three films: Amour, Chronic, and A Woman's Tale *because I reacted more than rationally thought. My reactions were those of a woman of 84 years old, probably entering the last decade of my life and feeling vulnerable about possible needs for care.*

My background is of a social worker who mainly worked with people with disabilities. I was a medical Social Worker in a hospital department, later a Chief Officer for a Disability agency, then a Carers Counsellor for a project at the Kings Fund. In my private life, I was carer for my mother, who was elderly and partially sighted, and then for my husband, who had cancer and cardiac disease.

I was very pleased to be invited to join Rina's Older Women in Film group and to write about these three films. I am learning how to analyse films. Previously my experience was with art and books. My thoughts are still more emotional than analytical but I am eager to learn.

Death and dying are inevitable parts of life but it is unusual to view three films, in rapid succession, that treat these taboos in such depth: a challenging time for an elderly viewer.

Amour *tells the story of Anne and Georges living a comfortable, well-ordered life within a loving relationship but there is a sense of foreboding, something bad is going to disrupt this.*

Anne has a series of strokes that gradually transforms their lives. She is partially paralysed in a wheelchair. She loses her dignity, is dependent on Georges and wishes to die.

Their only daughter pays a fleeting visit from abroad and offers unwanted advice to Georges that he should put Anne in a home, but he has promised Anne previously that he would never do that. Georges shows his fear and frustration by hitting Anne when she refuses to eat. The film illustrates how both carer and cared for suffer in their own way, isolated from others.

Chronic *shows a very different pattern of caring. What seems to be the perfect professional care, David is a highly competent, compassionate home carer of the terminally ill, excellent at his job. In an early scene, he is shown bathing very carefully the body of a young woman, very sick and silent. Is she alive or is he preparing her dead body for her last rites? I found this scene very uncomfortable, rather creepy. The Director seemed obsessed with this helpless, female body. I felt it was close to soft porn.*

David makes very close friends of his patients to the extent that they turn to him for everything, both physical and companionable. This affects the family members, first delighted with such care but later feeling isolated, left out from any relationship with the patient. Many carers express this struggle between relief at having good care offered, to feeling helpless to be close to their relative in the last days or weeks of their life. It is hard to accept David's stretching the boundaries of professional behaviour—or does he? This is very subtly played.

A Woman's Tale *is about Martha, a 78-year-old woman living out her final weeks with great vitality. Her carer is a young nurse, Anna. Their relationship is that of close friends to the extent that Martha encourages Ann to use her bed for romantic trysts with her married lover. This is clearly beyond the boundaries of professional working life but neither of them are concerned about this. Martha says, "I am going to die in this bed. You are going to love in it." Now, in my old age, I understand that she wants life to be more important than convention or professional ethics. What would I have thought as a young professional woman? Rather differently I expect.*

Another scene in which I felt differently as an older woman was when Anna visits Martha's senile and lonely neighbour Billy. Billy fondles Anna's breast and she allows him. I understand this as an act of kindness on her part. As a young woman, I would probably have found it sleazy and abusive. I found this film the most touching and challenging of the three. I identified with Martha's defiant wish to retain her independence. She prefers to focus on helping others, Anna, Billy, an older friend and a young suicidal girl on the telephone, rather than thinking about her own vulnerability.

This causes considerable anxiety and frustration to Martha's busy son who would like to move her to a home where she would have full-time care. I have to face how frustrating I may become to my own loving family. This has been a valuable process in using past experience as a carer, and of working with carers.

Academic reflections on sharing the readings

Ros Jennings

When Hannah and I met with the OWFG to discuss autoethnography as a possible method for their project, we were welcomed into their group and made privy to their real frustrations in not being able to come to a unified position on the films. They agreed to explore using autoethnography to produce a piece of research that was collective but individual; to situate their analyses from the perspective of being older women. At the end of that meeting, they agreed to produce their individual analyses that embraced the possibilities of autoethnography.

Once the film readings had been produced, they were shared amongst the six research participants by email and then Hannah and I visited the authors at Sylvia's house in London. Jane, Rita and Rina had arrived before me and discussions about the individual pieces had already been taking place. Jane related to us that she and Rina had been talking about remembering and misremembering, which was to filter into our discussions when we went on to think through the film readings and the next steps of the project together. In a room where there were three women of the pre-baby boomer generation (born before 1946) and two (one of them being me) firmly in that chronologically demarcated age category (1946–1962), memory and recall was commonly being called into question and an empathetic understanding of this underpinned our interactions. For instance, there was a conversation about A Woman's Tale *and how Sylvia had wrongly remembered that Anna had allowed the older man she was caring for to fondle her breast. In the meeting, it was decided that this should be changed in Sylvia's account, but when I came to reflect on it afterwards the discussion that Sylvia produces on the boundaries of intimate care* (Twigg et al. 2011) *adds depth to this as an important theme that emerges across the readings. We therefore put it to the group that it remains as it is, although factually inaccurate.*

As I have found in my many years of teaching autoethnography as a research method, and equally when supervising students using it for their PhDs, it seems that anyone encountering autoethnography for the first time seems to disbelieve that it is academically valid. After agreeing to explore autoethnography, my feeling was not that there was disbelief amongst the group in its validity, but rather some concern about the extent to which each person was willing, or able, to ground their readings in their personal life experiences. This is a personal decision as, by making the autoethnographic-self public, it is both an act of vulnerability and power for each person to negotiate (Ellis, Adams, and Bochner 2011). *In Rina's case, her commitment to her practice of textual analysis and talking about films about old women with old women that had been developed over many years, led her to produce a reading that evoked strong critiques of the representations of caring and old age that were portrayed in the films. We discussed the fact that other readings were more personal, and it was clear that the personal perspectives on care that were incorporated in Rita and Sylvia's reflections on the films reinforced Jane and Rina's original idea that it would be beneficial to the project if they were invited to join the group. Perhaps less skilled in the academic methods of reading film, their readings were underpinned by their professional and personal experiences of caring. One of the strengths of autoethnography is that it recognises that emotions are often not only a valid part of the research process* (Brannan 2011; Ellis, Adams, and Bochner 2011; Jewkes 2011) *but they can add to the depth and power to analyses.*

When I first looked at the film readings, it was Jane's that resonated with me most powerfully. During this meeting at Sylvia's house, the emotional power of the autoethnographic process for Jane was clear, when tears welled up as she recounted how engaging with the process had put her back in touch with what mattered most to her as a midwife—supporting women. Although she continued working as a research midwife, her accident had abruptly ended the role she most cared about and identified with. Quite unexpectedly, this project stimulated an acute sense of loss that she had not previously acknowledged, much less addressed.

Hannah Grist

Born in 1987, I was the youngest member of the group, which structured my thinking and approach to the films and sharing the reflections, and my own process of thinking through this research project. I quickly realised that although the other members of the group were representatives of boomer and pre-boomer generations, as well as being lovers of film, and feminists, we each shared a history of professional and personal/private care-giving, though separated by several decades.

I was responsible for mining the autoethnographic reflections produced by the four members of the OWFG for themes and for articulating to the group the structure we felt might work best for this publication. This meant I often adopted an organisational position within the group, outlining a direction for our discussions at meetings, documenting our thought process, co-ordinating responses, scoping publication possibilities, and structuring the final paper.

When I began this project, I brought with me reflections on professional care-giving, having worked as a care assistant and activities coordinator in large residential and nursing homes for several years whilst I completed my master's and doctorate. My experiences of professional care-giving and my knowledge of frameworks which might help unpack some of the disagreements between Jane, Sylvia, Rita, and Rina simmered as I took part in discussions and listened to the women discuss their thoughts on the films, and as I eagerly read through each email and autoethnography as it arrived. That Jane, Sylvia, Rita, and Rina did not, at first, appear to agree on their readings of the films presented an opportunity to adopt a non-traditional approach to autoethnography. Reflecting on each autoethnography and on the conversations we shared at meetings, it seems the OWFG do share many understandings of the films, but it was that their different reading positions and articulations of their readings that caused the most disagreement.

Intergenerational thinking and working has been a feature of my academic career. My experience in using autoethnography as a method, my experience of care work and my own thoughts on the films added the voice of a Millennial to this project and furthered the intergenerational composition of the group. In my position as co-director of the Centre for Women, Ageing and Media, and often as the youngest member in research projects we undertake, for me, intergenerationality forms one of the main ways in which scholarship like this might make a political and cultural intervention against endemic cultural ageism. Media representations of what it is to care and be cared for, and what it is to grow older, structure the way older people are viewed and construct for older and younger people alike an expectation of what life should be like, is like, or will soon be like. This project allowed an intergenerational exploration of the meanings of three films which presented three different imaginaries of later life and, through our reflections and co-construction of this paper, offered six different readings of those possibilities.

Emergent themes: Older age and representations of caring in the three films

In the spirit of feminist autoethnography, the process of analysis is more visible than is usual in academic papers and consequently also more open to scrutiny. This, of course, makes all six co-authors vulnerable but collectively we regard this as a strength of the method and the project. It is possible to analyse the contents of the four autoethnographically inflected readings of *Amour*, *Chronic*, and *A Woman's Tale* for many more themes than we choose to highlight, but what follows in this section are the key themes that we feel collectively express our engagement with the films in terms of older people and notions of care and caring.

When examining the film readings altogether, some of the differences produced in the readings which emerged as tensions amongst the group prior to adopting an autoethnographic approach are still there, but we can now see that they amount to matters of interpretation rather than fundamental disagreement. The earlier tensions were in many ways trapped by the method that required consensus about meanings. Once autoethnography was adopted, however, the differences became a collective strength of the process of interpretation, which enriched understandings of the ways that the films engage with representations of older age and care through their differences and their complementarity.

The concept of care in its many dimensions is what is dominant in the themes that are drawn out below. In the interaction between the textual construction of the films and the viewers' themselves (Morley 1992), understandings of the ways that end of life and care are represented filmically prompted a range of interpretations. Some of the readings are based closely on filmic textual evidence and some, inspired by their viewings, move away into the realm of personal experience.

Reading with age

The mining of the intergenerational reflections for themes on the films for this paper results in a grouping of individual experiences into a collective "we," or what Margaret Morganroth Gullette might think of as a "utopian solidarity of those who are here and now ageing-beyond youth" (2017). Indeed, for Jane, recognising her own ageing formed an "*an act of solidarity*." For Gullette, those who are "ageing beyond youth" are also those who are "ready to treat the politics of age with defiance" (2017).

This paper works as an act of defiance, an intervention that we might think of as "reading with age"—a mode of viewing mediated representations of ageing that is both purposeful and political by illuminating ways that culture affects age and ageing. We might define reading with age as an oppositional or counter-hegemonic moment of decoding (Hall 1980) in which the viewer uses their own age as the lens through which to read film, and remains vigilant for instances of ageism within texts. Reading with age is akin to Frank's (1995, 2001) notion of reading about/with illness and suffering and to feminist approaches to ageing in film studies where issues of spectatorship and representation are central, where binary understandings of ageing as either success or decline (Dolan and Tincknell 2012) are instead replaced with "multiple perspectives, identities and possible spectatorships" (Smelik 2007, 491).

Reading films about care with age, for Sylvia, produced the following reflection: "It is unusual to view three films, in rapid succession, that treat these taboos in such depth: a challenging time for an elderly viewer." Whilst this was not a requirement, each writer framed their autoethnography with an opening reference to the writer's own position within the lifecourse (Katz 2005). Sylvia, at 84, is the oldest autoethnographer, with Rita at 60 being the youngest, and Jane and Rina positioned in-between at 73 and 82, respectively. For Rita, who is sometimes "regarded as a 'younger' older woman," reading with age has been informed by "many recent deaths of family members and friends, sometimes at a relatively young age, have made me acutely aware of my own mortality." Margaret Cruikshank (2009) cautions that whilst "some have suggested seeing ageing as part of the lifecourse rather than as a unique time [...] saying "old" is a stage in human development obscures the fact that youth is favoured, while age is not" (6). In the readings of *Amour*, *Chronic*, and *A Woman's Tale* and in the adoption of an intergenerational autoethnographic approach, however, the concept of lifecourse is brought to the fore, and mediated constructions of age (and care) are troubled. When reading with age, the results answer Cruikshank's challenge: "to see the politics of ageing and personal/individual ageing simultaneously" (6).

For Rina, reading with age was undoubtedly informed by her exposure to critical textual analysis methods and film studies concepts through her Master's in Film and TV Studies. In her autoethnography Rina recalls "*how furious*" she was having been shown "*nostalgic*" representations of ageing in film by the City Literary Institute, an encounter which propelled her to undertake the Master's. Just as Rina's academic training is prevalent in her autoethnography, where she writes knowledgably about cinematic apparatus, so is Rina's age as her reading position, when she writes: "I found in *Amour* the burden of being the sole carer of a dying loved one, at home. I found in *Amour* a political film about end of life and care needs. I found in *Amour* the tragedy of the change from 'love' to 'care'". Moreover, in a further reflection on the intersections between her academic training and her being 'an old woman' Rina noted:

> My experience is not only textual analysis but my strong feelings as an old woman about filmic representations of women and age. I have, at 82 years, witnessed the dying days of many relatives and friends but have no direct experience of being a carer, of being cared for. My experience of the subject is second-hand accumulated knowledge.

Reading with care

The readings of the films were nuanced by experiential, personal, and cultural understandings of age that were intersectional in nature and reinforced by other experiences and identifications (e.g. as a carer, a social worker, a midwife, a student, a wife). For the participants, autoethnographically inflected film analysis provided a valuable but differentiated engagement with the representations of care in the three films. For Ros, developing her own autoethnographic approaches to film studies has been important to her own scholarship (e.g. see Jennings 2005); using it as a means to make the interpretative practices involved more transparent. This is not, however, the dominant approach in the discipline and Rina's insistence on the importance of separating form from content when analysing a film, is nearer to the traditional view. By engaging with readings of care but not being able to draw on any "direct experience of being a carer, or being cared for" she is the exception to the group. In terms of film analysis, however, she nevertheless makes a powerful political bid for the recognition of the older woman's voice in film scholarship. By contrast, Sylvia's analysis is imbued with the emotions and self-reflexivity of caring and the prospect of her changing relationship to caring and being cared for as she considers her future.

Each of the films provoked participants to contemplate their futures and possible care needs (and more specifically how they might plan for them). There is a special poignancy for Sylvia, who was candid about the precarity of her current independence and autonomy as she writes: "probably entering the last decade of my life and feeling vulnerable about possible needs for care." Jane, from the experience of a life changing accident eleven years ago, also reads the films with understanding that "life can change in a second and that there is a difficult (if healthy) tension between stretching myself and accepting limiting changes and adapting." Although what is commonly referred to as the fourth age is understood as the time where the independence and autonomy of the third age transitions to that of dependence on full-time care (Gilleard and Higgs 2010; Woodward 1999), Jane's autoethnographic reflections on her own need for care when she was 11 years younger than she is now does much to disrupt the direct connection of old age with illness, disability and the need for care that is circulated in the media (Cruikshank 2009; Dolan and Tincknell 2012; Gullette 2004; Kriebernegg and Chivers 2017).

In her reading of the relationships that home caregiver David develops with his terminally ill patients in *Chronic*, Rita notes that "Some of what was shown in the physical and emotional closeness of the relationship would be frowned upon now and probably a cause for disciplinary action, as paid caring is now a much more professionalised activity with national occupational standards." Rina asks: "Is his behaviour care or abuse?" and Sylvia writes: "It is hard to accept David's stretching the boundaries of professional behaviour—or does he?" Whilst these readings differ slightly on how far David oversteps his position, both readings are framed by ideas of professionalism in paid care. Carers are frequently represented in the UK media as cruel and abusive (see Lawrence 2017), through regular news media coverage of abuse in residential nursing and home-care settings, and through documentary film exposés such as the BBC's *Panorama: Under-cover Elderly Care* (2013). The readings of the films are infused with and informed by a knowledge of these instances of abuse and malpractice and by an understanding (some through direct personal experience) of the caregiving policy frameworks which seek to govern the behaviour of carers.

The carers and care represented in *Chronic*, *Amour* and *A Woman's Tale*, like those who are cared for, are not homogenous. The representation of the isolation and bleakness of giving and receiving long-term care was referenced by Sylvia who writes that *Amour* "illustrates how both carer and cared for suffer in their own way, isolated from others," which is echoed by Rina, who writes of Anna and Billy's relationship in *Amour*, noting: "Anna's care for Billy in *A Woman's Tale* remains professional and cannot alleviate his isolation." Rita notes that in *Chronic*, "The sadness and tedium of caring and being cared for is well portrayed," which is found also in Rina's reflection on the same film, when she suggests: "He [David] performs the physical care of patients extremely well." Where, at times, the readings of the films appear to draw upon dominant cultural anxieties about care as cruelty and the over-stepping of professional boundaries, at other times the films are celebrated for their verisimilitude in representing the realities of care. This is perhaps evidence of the intricacy of what it means to care and be cared for, and that in responding to popular cultural texts on ageing the "negotiation process is nothing if not complex" (Lövgren 2013, 51).

Questions about the intersections between gender, sexuality, older age, and caring are found nuanced in the films. Care work is traditionally conceived of as "woman's work" (Cameron and Moss 2007; Innes 2009) which is supported by the fact that 80% of the UK's paid care work force is made up of women (Bowlby et al. 2010, 130). Five of the six women involved in this research project also have experiences of caregiving, both paid and unpaid, and as such their experiences and their gender informed their readings of the film. The groping incident in *A Woman's Tale*, where a female carer was touched inappropriately by an elderly man, was cause for reflection in both Rita and Sylvia's autoethnographies. Rita wrote: "I felt appalled by this, as it mirrors some situations I have been involved with in everyday life, where groping by an older and/or disabled man is felt to be somehow less serious (perhaps because due to age or disability, he is seen as being less of a man/not a threat)." Whilst we outlined in Section 5.1 that Sylvia's memory of the groping incident was factually inaccurate, her autoethnographic reflection on this scene inflects a reading position informed by both her age and her gender. Sylvia wrote: "Billy fondles Anna's breast and she allows him. I understand this as an act of kindness on her part. As a young woman, I would probably have found it sleazy and abusive." In her reflection Sylvia positions her initial reaction as one informed by her age and her experiences of giving care, though she also suggests that her younger self would have had a different, more negative reaction. Jo Krøjer, Lehn-Christiansen, and Nielsen (2014) estimated that in the Danish care context female care workers are three times more likely than their male counterparts to experience sexual harassment, and that "the group most at risk is women under 30" (84). Sylvia's suggestion that her younger self would have found the groping incident "sleazy and abusive" correlates with the experiences of many female care workers; whilst Sylvia's present self, in her current position on the life course, allows her to reflect differently on the same event. This highlights the instructive possibilities (Jennings and Krainitzki 2015, 182) of non-chronological understandings of time which involve "an interrelation of the past, present and future" (Baars 2012, 151).

Where real-life care is dominated by women, *Chronic* offers the perspective of a male care assistant through protagonist David. For Rina, while *Chronic's* "strong young male point of view annoyed [her] intensely," the decision to have a male carer in *Amour* "challenges assumptions about the 'naturalness' of femininities and care skills" (Bowlby et al. 2010, 130). The representation of David is, however, not free of the problematic status attached to male carers, which "reflects a wider set of cultural assumptions about masculinity and, in particular, male sexuality that regard it as containing an essentially predatory quality" (Twigg 2004, 69). When David is accused of sexual abuse for assisting one of his patients to watch pornography, the audience is invited to confront both the gendered discourse surrounding male carers and the taboo of sex and sexuality in later life, something the health care sector is gradually coming to terms with. Thus, the films invite us to question our own understandings of acceptable levels and forms of intimacy between carer and cared for, as well as to pose questions about the perceived transgression of boundaries. When does a caring relationship cease to be beneficial and instead become a "stretching of the boundaries" which might necessitate "disciplinary action"?

Boundaries of care

The films offer representations of care which take place within three distinct geographic contexts—the USA (*Chronic*), France (*Amour*), and Australia (*A Woman's Tale*)—each of which has a set of different national standards and quality control measures for the governance of older age care. In France, long-term care for older people (both home care and nursing care) is regulated by the National Inspectorate for Social Affairs (IAGS) and the

National Agency for the Assessment of Nursing Home and Home Care Providers (ANSEM). Governed by the "Aged Care Act" (1997), the Aged Care Quality Agency is responsible for "managing the accreditation process and for the ongoing monitoring of residential care services" in Australia (OECD 2013, 3). In the UK, the independent regulator of health and social care provision is the Care Quality Commission (CQC). The CQC states that good care (whether home care or residential nursing care) must be safe, effective, caring, responsive, and well-led. Specifically, the guidelines state that staff must treat the person they care for with "dignity and respect," to spend time developing "trusting relationships" and to demonstrate concern for their wellbeing (CQC 2017). Whilst the CQC guidelines are the benchmark against which all care providers in the UK are measured, individual care homes and care agencies have their own specific policies regarding expectations for quality care.

In the nursing homes in the UK that one of the authors of this paper has worked in as a care assistant, maintaining a level of emotional distance between carer and cared for was embedded in policy and in informal interactions with home management. As Laurie Beed (2013) recalled, in the care home in which his wife spent her final years, staff were discouraged from "becoming too attached to family and resident, but since person centred care requires understanding the family background to give good care, feelings and attachment are unavoidable" (3–4). Paradoxically then, while the "family model," where paid care workers are encouraged to treat those they care for as if they were a member of their own family, is considered the "golden" standard of care (Dodson and Zincavage 2015, 190; Tuominen 2003), this model also expects carers to maintain distance and professionalism.

Evidence of the complexity surrounding the "commodification of intimacy" (Dodson and Zincavage 2015) can be found in the different representations of care work in *Chronic*, *Amour*, and *A Woman's Tale*. Rita notes that in *Chronic*, carer David "establishes close relationships with his patients, which the families come to resent or just don't recognise. He is expected to be anonymous and dispensable, despite such an intimate role." Whilst the films focus on care provided at home for people with a variety of complex needs, Rita's reflection on the representation of David as dispensable chimes with the findings of Timothy Diamond's (1992) covert study of a US nursing home. Diamond suggests that "the structure of labour creates a revolving door of workers, as though they were replaceable parts, while the interpersonal nature of caregiving gets systematically ignored" (187).

Depictions of interpersonal relationships and of the family model of care was cause for further reflection, especially in terms of the displacement of "real" family members when carers are brought in to tend to their loved one. Reflecting on *Chronic*, Rita writes: "I found that when paid carers care for your relations and friends they can sometimes very quickly establish a close relationship, which could make me feel a usurped as a family member." Similarly, Sylvia notes of *A Woman's Tale* that: "Many carers express this struggle between relief at having good care offered, to feeling helpless to be close to their relative in the last days or weeks of their life." Jane suggests that the absence of a positive family model of care represented in *Amour* "really brought home the importance of having both professional and family support in such an acute and terminal situation, with negotiated boundaries and effective communication between everyone."

Where David is deliberately constructed as a morally ambiguous character whose suitability for the care role is questioned by the audience throughout *Chronic*, Rina suggests that the relationship between Anna and Martha takes a very different form in *A Woman's Tale*. In this film, the carer and cared for are shown developing "a friendship and the two roles of friend and carer become merged." If the Australian Aged Care Quality Agency were to have evaluated Anna's care practice it is more than likely that concerns would have been raised, especially when Anna is encouraged by Martha to use her bed for sex with her lover. Of this encounter, Sylvia notes: "This is clearly beyond the boundaries of professional working life but neither of them are concerned about this." Arlie Hochschild's (1983) concept of emotional labour has been applied to care settings and whilst it is frequently connected to burnout in care workers (Gray 2009; James 2008; Rodriguez 2014; Smith 2011), it has also been suggested that the emotional labour of nurses and care assistants can often result in positive outcomes. If the emotional labour of care work involves, at various times, surface acting, deep acting and genuine emotion (Hochschild 1983), then might care work also result in authentic friendships which blur boundaried professionalism (da Silva Vilelas and Diogo 2014), as we see in the relationship between Anna and Martha?

Conclusion

In using personal experience and storytelling, this paper highlights the possibilities of a collaborative autoethnographic method. At our final meeting, the group reflected on the ways in which the method brought about an unexpected resolution to conflict over the readings of the films and enabled them to move forward. At the outset, the group faced the prospect of disbanding, as tensions surrounding differing readings of the films and divergent experiences of care giving in group members' personal lives caused deep tensions. Reflecting on the experience at our final meeting, the group suggested that their encounter with autoethnography was productive and worthwhile, reminding us of Tami Spry's (2001) assertion that the "transformative and efficacious potential for researcher, researched, and reader/audience is a primary goal of effective autoethnography in print and performance" (712). At this final meeting, the group shared that employing autoethnography had reawakened their own experiences of consciousness raising and the need for old feminists to reengage with that activity. The project had transformed an analytic process into action and they continue to meet as a consciousness raising group focused on ageing, called Tricks of the Mind.

Underpinned by the notion of "thinking with age" this project has, to paraphrase Frank (2000), challenged the methodological "line of fault" (357) between experiential and academic analyses. It has demonstrated the ways in which intergenerational, co-constructed autoethnographic research can bring together the voices, life stories and perspectives of women of different ages, nationalities and socio-economic backgrounds in order to "talk back to" filmic constructions and representations of old age and care that do not match our collective experiences or worse, "espouse harmful messages" (Manning and Adams 2015, 199). In this way, "thinking with age" provides reinforcement to the OWFG's feminist collaborative desire to produce older women's reading of films. It became the intellectual catalyst to prompt those involved to reflect autoethnographically on understandings and reactions to films; creating textual practices of "reading with age" and, in relation to the specificities of the three films, textual practices of "reading with age and care."

Disclosure Statement

No potential conflict of interest was reported by the authors.

References

Allen, Katherine R., and Fred P. Piercy. 2005. "Feminist Autoethnography." In *Research Methods in Family Therapy*, edited by Douglas H. Sprenkle and Fred P. Piercy, 155–169. New York: Guilford.

Anderson, Leon. 2006. "Analytic Autoethnography." *Journal of Contemporary Ethnography* 35 (4): 373–395. doi:10.1177/0891241605280449.

Baars, Jaan. 2012. "Critical Turns of Aging, Narrative and Time." *International Journal of Ageing and Later Life* 7 (2): 143–165. doi:10.3384/ijal.1652-8670.1272.

Beed, Laurie. 2013. "Experiences of Being a Carer: Thoughts, Reflections and Ideas." *Old Age Psychiatrist* 56: 1–6. https://www.rcpsych.ac.uk/pdf/Reflections%20of%20a%20Former%20Carer%20Final.pdf.

Bochner, Arthur P. 2012. "Bird on the Wire: Freeing the Father Within Me." *Qualitative Inquiry* 18 (2): 168–173. doi:10.1177/1077800411429094.

Bochner, Arthur P., and Carolyn Ellis. 1995. "Telling and Living: Narrative Co-construction and the Practices of Interpersonal Relationships." In *Social Approaches to Communication*, edited by Wendy Leeds-Hurwitz, 201–213. New York: Guilford.

Bowlby, Sophia, Linda McKie, Susan Gregory, and Isobel McPherson. 2010. *Interdependency and Care Over the Lifecourse*. London: Routledge.

Bradshaw, Peter. 2016. "Chronic review – a cool, calm look at death and the naked human body." In *The Guardian*. Accessed 6 September 2017. https://www.theguardian.com/film/2016/feb/18/chronic-review-tim-roth-michel-franco

Boylorn, Robin, and Mark P. Orbe, ed. 2013. *Critical Autoethnography: Intersecting Cultural Identities in Everyday Life. Walnut Creek*. CA: Left Coast Press.

Brannan, Matthew J. 2011. "Researching Emotions and the Emotions of Researching: The Strange Case of Alexithymia in Reflexive Research." *International Journal of Work Organisation and Emotion* 4 (3–4): 322–339. doi:10.1504/IJWOE.2011.045969.

British Film Institute & University of the Third Age. 2006. *Older Women in Feature Films: A Research Guide about Representations of Women Over 60*. Accessed August 24, 2017. https://oldwomaninfeaturefilms.files.wordpress.com/2010/08/bfi.pdf.

Cameron, Claire, and Peter Moss. 2007. *Care Work in Europe: Current Understandings and Future Directions*. London: Routledge.

Care Quality Commission. 2017. "The Five Key Questions We Ask." Accessed September 1, 2017. http://www.cqc.org.uk/what-we-do/how-we-do-our-job/five-key-questions-we-ask.

Centre for Women, Ageing and Media. 2012. "The WAM Manifesto." http://wamuog.co.uk/the-wam-manifesto.

Chang, Heewon, Faith Ngunjiri, and Kathy-Ann C Hernandez. 2013. *Collaborative Autoethnography*. Oxon: Routledge.

Chivers, Sally. 2011. *The Silvering Screen: Old Age and Disability in Cinema*. Toronto: University of Toronto Press.

Chivers, Sally and Ulla Kriebernegg, eds. 2017. *Care Home Stories: Aging, Disability, and Long-Term Residential Care*. Transcript: Verlag.

Cruikshank, Margaret. 2009. *Learning to be Old: Gender, Culture, and Aging*. New York: Rowman and Littlefield.

da Silva Vilelas, Jose, and Paula M.J. Diogo. 2014. "Emotional Labour in Nursing Praxis." *Revista Gaúcha de Enfermagem* 35 (3). doi:1983-1447.2014.03.45784, Accessed 3 September 2017.

Denshire, Sally. 2013. "Autoethnography." *Sociopedia.isa*, 1–12. doi:10.1177/205684601351.

Denzin, Norman. 1997. *Interpretive Ethnography*. Thousand Oaks, CA: Sage.

Diamond, Timothy. 1992. *Making Gray Gold: Narratives of Nursing Home Care*. Chicago and London: University of Chicago Press.

Dodson, Lisa, and Rebeka M. Zincavage. 2015. "'It's Like a Family': Caring Labour, Exploitation and Race in Nursing Homes." In *Caring on the Clock: The Complexities and Contradictions of Paid Care Work*, edited by Mignon Duffy, Amy Amenia, and Clare L. Stacey, 189–200. New Brunswick: Rutgers UP.

Dolan, Josephine, and Estella Tincknell, eds. 2012. *Aging Femininities: Troubling Representations*. Newcastle Upon Tyne: Cambridge Scholars Publishing.

Drew, Rob. 2001. *Karaoke Nights: An Ethnographic Rhapsody*. Walnut Creek, CA: AltaMira Press.

Ellis, Carolyn. 1999. "Heartful Autoethnography." *Qualitative Health Research* 9 (5): 669–683. doi:10.1177/104973299129122153.

Ellis, Carolyn. 2007. "Telling Secrets, Revealing Lives: Relational Ethics in Research with Intimate Others." *Qualitative Inquiry* 13 (1): 3–29. doi:10.1177/1077800406294947.

Ellis, Carolyn. 2009. "Telling Tales on Neighbours: Ethics in Two Voices." *International Review of Qualitative Research* 2 (1): 3–28. http://www.jstor.org/stable/10.1525/irqr.2009.2.1.3.

Ellis, Carolyn, Tony E. Adams, and Arthur P. Bochner. 2011. "Autoethnography: An Overview." *Forum: Qualitative Social Research* 12 (1) Online. http://nbn-resolving.de/urn:nbn:de:0114-fqs1101108.

Ellis, Carolyn, and Arthur P. Bochner. 2000. "Autoethnography, Personal Narrative, Reflexivity: Researcher as Subject." In *Handbook of Qualitative Research*, edited by Norman K. Denzin and Yvonne S. Lincoln, 733–768. Thousand Oaks, CA: Sage Publications.

Ettore, Elizabeth. 2017. *Autoethnography as Feminist Method: Sensitising the Feminist 'I'*. Oxon: Routledge.

Frank, Arthur W. 1995. *The Wounded Storyteller: Body, Illness, and Ethics*. Chicago: The University of Chicago Press.

Frank, Arthur W. 2000. "The Standpoint of Storyteller." *Qualitative Health Research* 10 (3): 354–365. doi:10.1177/104973200129118499.

Frank, Arthur W. 2001. "Can We Research Suffering?" *Qualitative Health Research* 11 (3): 353–362. doi:10.1177/104973201129119154.

Gilleard, Chris, and Paul Higgs. 2010. "Aging Without Agency: Theorising the Fourth Age." *Aging and Mental Health* 14 (2): 121–128. doi:10.1080/13607860903228762.

Gravagne, Pamela. 2013. *The Becoming of Age. Cinematic Visions of Mind, Body and Identity in Later Life*. Jefferson: MacFarland.

Gray, Benjamin. 2009. "The Emotional Labour of Nursing: Defining and Managing Emotions in Nursing Work." *Nurse Education Today* 29 (2): 168–175. doi10.1016/j.nedt.2008.08.003.

Gullette, Margaret Morganroth. 2004. *Aged by Culture*. Chicago: The University of Chicago Press.

Gullette, Margaret Morganroth. 2017. *Ending Ageism—Or How Not to Shoot Old People*. New Brunswick: Rutgers University Press.

Hall, Stuart. 1980. "Encoding/Decoding." In *Culture, Media, Language*, edited by Stuart Hall, Dorothy Hobson, Andrew Lowe, and Paul Willis, 128–138. London: Hutchinson.

Harpin, Anna. 2016. "'Imagination and Reality Have Little in Common: Anne in *Amour* by Michael Haneke." Paper presented at *ageing, embodiment and the self*, University of Warwick, 18 March 2016.

Herrmann, Andrew F. 2012. "'Never Mind the Scholar, Here's the Old Punk: Identity, Community, and the Aging Music Fan." In *Studies in Symbolic Interaction*, edited by Norman K. Denzin, 153–170. Bingley: Emerald Group.

Hochschild, Arlie. 1983. *The Managed Heart: Commercialisation of Human Feeling*. Berkley: University of California Press.

Innes, Anthea. 2009. *Dementia Studies: A Social Science Perspective*. London: Sage.

James, Nicky. 2008. "Care = Organisation + Physical Labour + Emotional Labour." *Sociology of Health & Illness* 14 (4): 488–509. doi:10.1111/1467-9566.ep10493127.

Jennings, Ros. 2005. "Beautiful Thing: British Queer Cinema, Positive Unoriginality and the Everyday." In *British Queer Cinema*, edited by Robin Griffiths, 183–195. London: Routledge.

Jennings, Ros, and Abigail Gardner. 2012. *Rock On!: Women, Ageing and Popular Music*. Farnham: Ashgate.

Jennings, Ros, and Hannah Grist. 2017. "Future and Present Imaginaries: The Politics of the Ageing Female Body in Lena Dunham's *Girls* (HB0, 2012–Present)." In *Ageing Women in Literature and Visual Culture: Reflections, Refractions, Reimaginings*, edited by Cathy McGlynn, Margaret O'Neill, and Michaela Schrage-Früh, 195–216. Basingstoke: Palgrave Macmillan.

Jennings, Ros, and Hannah Grist. Forthcoming. *Carers, Care Homes and the British Media: Caring for Older People*. Basingstoke: Palgrave Macmillan.

Jennings, Ros, and Eva Krainitzki. 2015. "'Call the Celebrity': Voicing the Experience of Women and Ageing Through the Distinctive Vocal Presence of Vanessa Redgrave." In *Women, Celebrity and Cultures of Ageing*, edited by Deborah Jermyn and Su Holmes, 178–196. London: Palgrave Macmillan.

Jewkes, Yvonne. 2011. "Autoethnography and Emotion as Intellectual Resources: Doing Prison Research Differently." *Qualitative Enquiry* 18 (1): 63–75. doi:10.1177/1077800411428942.

Katz, Stephen. 2005. *Aging: Life Course, Lifestyle, and Senior Worlds*. Peterborough: Broadview Press.

Kriebernegg, Ulla, and Sally Chivers. 2017. *Care Home Stories: Ageing, Disability, and Long-term Residential Care*. Bielefeld: Transcript.

Krøjer, Jo, Sine Lehn-Christiansen, and Mette Lykee Nielsen. 2014. "Sexual Harassment of Newcomers in Elder Care: An Institutional Practice?" *Nordic Journal of Working Life Studies* 4 (1): 81–98. doi:10.19154/njwls.v4i1.3553.

Lawrence, Bill. 2017. *When the Unacceptable Becomes the Norm: Choosing a Care Home in the 21st Century*. Kibworth Beauchamp: Matador.

Leavy, Patricia. 2013. *Fiction as Research Practice: Short Stories, Novellas, and Novels*. Walnut Creek, CA: Left Coast Press.

Lövgren, Karin. 2013. "Celebrating or Denying Age? On Cultural Studies as an Analytical Approach in Gerontology." In *The Ages of Life: Living and Aging in Conflict*, edited by Ulla Kriebernegg and Roberta Maierhofer, 37–56. Bielefeld: Transcript.

Manning, Jimmie, and Tony E. Adams. 2015. "Popular Culture Studies and Autoethnography: An Essay on Method." *The Popular Culture Studies Journal* 3 (1&2): 187–221. http://commons.lib.niu.edu/handle/10843/14754.

Marshall, Leni. 2006. "Aging: A Feminist Issue." *NWSA Journal* 18 (1): vii–xiii. doi:10.1353/nwsa.2006.0014.

Morley, David. 1992. *Television, Audiences and Cultural Studies*. London: Routledge.

Organisation for Economic Co-operation and Development. 2013. "Highlights from a Good Life in Old Age? Monitoring and Improving Quality in Long-term Care." Accessed 6 September 2017. https://www.oecd.org/els/health-systems/Australia-OECD-EC-Good-Time-in-Old-Age.pdf.

Pelias, Ronald J. 2014. *Performance: An Alphabet of Performative Writing*. Walnut Creek, CA: Left Coast Press.

Rodriguez, Jason. 2014. *Labour of Love: Nursing Homes and the Structures of Care Work*. New York and London: New York University Press.

Ronai, Carol R. 1992. "The Reflexive Self Through Narrative: A Night in the Life of an Erotic Dancer/Researcher." In *Investigating Subjectivity: Research on Lived Experience*, edited by Carolyn Ellis and Michael G. Flaherty, 102–124. Newbury Park, CA: Sage.

Rosselson, Rina. 2017. "Ageing, Ageism and Feature Films." https://oldwomaninfeaturefilms.wordpress.com/.

Roth, Wolff-Michael. 2009. "Auto/Ethnography and the Question of Ethics." *Forum: Qualitative Social Research* 10 (1). Accessed September 6, 2017. http://www.qualitative-research.net/index.php/fqs/article/view/1213/2645.

Smelik, Anne. 2007. "Feminist Film Theory." In *The Cinema Book*, edited by Pam Cook, 491–585. London: BFI.

Smith, Pam. 2011. *The Emotional Labour of Nursing Revisited: Can Nurses Still Care?* Basingstoke: Palgrave Macmillan.

Spry, Tami. 2001. "Performing autoethnography: An embodied methodological praxis." *Qualitative Inquiry* 7 (6): 706–732. doi:10.1177/107780040100700605

Stephens, Julie. 2010. "Our Remembered Selves." *Oral History* 38 (1): 81–90. http://www.jstor.org/stable/40650318.

Swinnen, Aagje, and Mark Schweda, eds. 2015. *Popularising Dementia: Public Expressions and Representations of Forgetfulness*. Bielefeld: Transcript Verlag.

Tuominen, Mary C. 2003. *We are Not Babysitters: Family Childcare Providers Redefine Work and Care*. New Brunswick: Rutgers UP.

Twigg, Julia. 2004. "The Body, Gender, and Age: Feminist Insights in Social Gerontology." *Journal of Aging Studies* 18: 59–73. doi:10.1016/j.jaging.2003.09.001.

Twigg, Julia, and Wendy Martin, eds. 2015. *Routledge Handbook of Cultural Gerontology*. Oxon: Routledge.

Twigg, Julia, Carol Wolowitz, Rachel L. Cohen, and Sarah Nettleton. 2011. "Conceptualising Body Work in Health and Social Care." *Sociology of Health and Illness* 33 (2): 171–188. doi:10.1111/j.1467-9566.2010.01323.x.

Woodward, Kathleen, ed. 1999. *Figuring Age: Women, Bodies, Generations*. Bloomington: Indiana University Press.

Filmography

A Woman's Tale. Film. Australia: Paul Cox, 1991.

Amour. Film. Austria/France: Michael Haneke, 2012.

Chronic. Film. Mexico/France: Michael Franco, 2015.

Grace and Grit: The Politics, Poetics and Performance of Ageing as a Woman

Ann Webster-Wright

ABSTRACT
The demographic shift to an ageing population in contemporary Western society offers a new cultural frontier, with rapidly shifting contours that demand creative and critical examination. Rather than take the predominant bio-medical perspective that views ageing in terms of decline and deficit, in this paper I emphasise the poetics and potential of ageing, within a framework of cultural gerontology. From an existential, phenomenological perspective, I weave together current socio-political and psycho-biological research into gendered ageing, with feminist literature on the topic and my own auto-ethnographic narrative as an ageing woman. Drawing on Simone de Beauvoir and Paul Ricoeur, I examine how narrative identity can shift in older age, particularly if a new sense of creative agency is developed that supports the re-storying of lives. I argue that the diverse group of "baby boomer" women currently in their 60s, who I focus on in this essay, will reinvent the face of ageing, as they once transformed the makeup of the workplace.

Standing in the shadows, we feel our hearts pound. We clutch each others' hands for courage. A sideways glance reveals us as a motley bunch of older women, all shapes and sizes, dressed in strange garb. But we're not waiting for a medical procedure. We're waiting for our first chance to perform on stage. My mouth is dry, but I can already taste delight. We take a collective breath as the music surges, lights go up and we stride on stage. As we sway to Edith Piaf's evocative voice, our costumes spangle in the shifting light, stretched across our well-used bodies. We own rather than camouflage our ageing shapes. The laid-back cabaret audience know who we are and cheer us on. The 12 of us are on stage for three minutes, though it only seems like three seconds. In that time, I feel I've learnt to fly.

Afterwards, I pinch myself with disbelief. Here I am, an ageing academic with stumpy legs, who walked into a lecture room at an Ideas Festival to hear a talk about the benefits of dancing for older women. Although it was only five years ago, what followed has changed the way I think of myself, inhabit my body, and view ageing. At the age of 60, I'd reached a turning point. My health was deteriorating; my mind was weary. I was tired of the treadmill; annoyed with administrative trivia. I was considering retirement, but the word stuck in my throat like a sharp fish bone. The prevailing social stereotypes of life as an ageing woman seemed unpalatable (Silver 2016).

How we "perform" ageing as women is influenced by our own, as well as society's expectations. In examining what it means to age in contemporary society, Lynne Segal (2013) highlights how sharing alternative stories is a radical act that challenges stereotypes of older women by creating new cultural images. Stories speak more loudly than statistics, when exploring the shifting landscape of ageing. Many of us currently in our 60s will be gifted with an extended lifespan. Yet there is still limited discussion of imaginative possibilities for older healthy women who will have the time, and experience, to contribute to a world sometimes inimical to their existence. This group of "baby boomer" women may reinvent the face of ageing as they once transformed the makeup of the workplace.

In this essay, I weave together current socio-political and psycho-biological research into ageing, with feminist literature on the topic and my own narrative as an ageing woman by way of auto-ethnographic example (Ellis 2009). Rather than take the predominant medical perspective that views ageing in terms of decline and deficit, I focus on the poetics and potential of ageing and, in particular, on how creative agency can shape narrative identity in re-storying lives in older age.

Whilst cognisant of the limits of life writing (McCooey 2017), in crafting this article, I wear many hats: as an academic researcher with a background in existential phenomenology, as a writer of creative non-fiction, as a creative performance artist, and as an older woman. The existential question at the heart of this paper, the one many women before me have posed, as I've also asked myself, is "How am I to live as an older woman?"

Socio-political landscape

Ageing offers a new cultural frontier in contemporary Western society, with rapidly shifting contours that make its pathways difficult to map using traditional research approaches. Over the past century, up to 30 years have been added to the life span (Schein and Haruvi 2015, 31). Established health and education systems, workplace organisations and general social mores have yet to adapt to the changes wrought by what can be described as a "longevity revolution" (Butler 2008).

The current brouhaha about the burden of an ageing society is based on narrow economic measurements of value. Concern has been founded on outmoded assumptions about age that are rapidly being confounded by research findings (Venne and Hannay 2017). The search for possible ways of dealing with this demographic shift is restricted by stale dichotomies and a dearth of creative ideas. As you age, you're classified as either working or retired, well or sick, an asset or a burden, a lifter or a leaner.

The media is hooked on a fear driven storyline that warns of impending disaster. Hordes of baby boomers clutching the life raft of their extended lifespan are seen as the forefront of a tidal wave of geriatrics who threaten to swamp the overburdened ship of health care. Many younger generation, understandably, feel the boomers have had their day in the sun and wish they could be denied boarding rights—or even thrown overboard. But the boomers will be around for a while yet. The sheer numbers of women, and men, entering their 60s cannot help but influence the way society deals with ageing. Such changes should not be framed as an intergenerational battleground. Ways of productively managing a longer lifespan will benefit future generations. Living longer is their probable destiny as well.

Although valid concerns exist about the health care needs of people in later life, neurobiomedical evidence suggests that continuing active engagement offers physical and mental benefits, delaying illness and dependence (Boudiny 2013; Menichetti et al. 2016). Rates of chronic diseases affected by lifestyle choices are already decreasing in this 60s age group (Costa 2000). Even the age-specific risk of Alzheimer's seems to be in decline, though the number of people with this disease will increase due to growth in the overall number of older people (Langa 2015). Nor is Alzheimer's a definite destination of old age; it currently affects only 1 in 3 people over 90 (Hebert et al. 2001). Neuroscientific research demonstrates that the brain continues to develop new neurones and synapses as we age, providing people stay actively engaged, particularly in ventures that require new learning (Cozolino 2008).

Despite increasing health costs, the universally negative spectre of an ageing society is oversimplified. Economic and health concerns are interlinked. Evidence is growing that those aged between 60 and 80 are net contributors to communities (Schein and Haruvi 2015). Even if they are not working in some capacity, they contribute benefits through their unpaid work and spending patterns. Because people currently in their 60s are generally healthier and better educated than previous generations of older people (32), this cohort could become a valuable resource for society. Little consideration has been given to the support that capable, experienced older people may offer to individuals and communities struggling with current social and environmental crises.

Recent expansion of the transdisciplinary field of cultural gerontology has broadened research into the experience of ageing in contemporary society by considering ageing as an evolving process rather than a state. As defined by Twigg and Martin (2015), such an approach takes into account the subjective, embodied nature of ageing as well as the way experience is shaped by environmental and cultural contexts. This rich source of research is yet to impact on policy decisions to do with ageing, however.

There are currently two foci to the political concerns about an ageing population (Börsch-Supan 2013). The first considers the role of older workers, the second the problems of the "frail" elderly. Little thought has been given to the 20 or more years of the so-called third age, between full time conventional work and a possibly dependant "fourth age" (Gilleard and Higgs 2005). There has been limited investigation of policies beyond these two options: encouraging people to work for longer and improving aged care facilities. It seems as if we are expected to work till we drop, then rapidly swap briefcases for wheelchairs while we wait to die. Despite the benefit of these programmes, they ignore a verdant field of possibility within the shifting landscape of ageing.

Socially gendered ageing

Although men are also living longer, the fastest growing demographic group today is still women over 60 (United Nations 2013, 33). Ageing is socially gendered, with some challenges unique to women (Carney 2018). Susan Sontag wrote about the "double standard of ageing", in that society's depictions of older women were more negative than for men, especially with respect to physical and sexual appearances (Deutsch, Zalenski, and Clark 1986). Anecdotally, old age is said to enhance a man but diminish a woman (Hilário 2016). Although such differences in perspectives cannot always be empirically verified (Narayan 2008), women do face a markedly more delineated physical onset to ageing because of menopause (Chrisler 2011).

With an increase in awareness of the importance of lifestyle choices on health, there is a risk that a woman's performance of ageing can be judged as good or bad (Segal 2013, 18). This simplistic notion classifies those who are productive and successful as ageing well, against those with chronic illness or depression, financial struggles or even homelessness, as ageing poorly (Higgs and Gilleard 2015, 117). For women who have already been disadvantaged by minority status, interrupted careers, low pay and unemployment, the difficulties of ageing can be magnified (Hartmann and English 2009; Muhlbauer 2015).

Apart from the fact that women can have a number of chronic illnesses and feel relatively well, or have limited financial means but be rich with social connections, such dichotomies lack what Segal calls "radical ambiguity" (2013, 32). Ageing is experienced as fluid and changing. An individual woman may experience situations within a single day where she registers fear, doubt, contentment or joy. Sometimes, ageing is accompanied by a feeling of shame, other times it's felt as a liberation from the constraints of society (Isopahkala-Bouret 2017; Liechty 2012).

A particular challenge for older women is coming to terms with our changing bodies (Hofmeier et al. 2017). Our life is written on our bodies, the vessel that has carried us through time and place. Despite the emphasis in second-wave feminism of accepting our bodies as they are, in professional working lives, bodies are still effectively ignored (Scott 2011). We expect them to perform on cue and actively camouflage the messiness of essential female bodily functions at work, such as menstruation, breast feeding and menopause (Funnell 2013). Although there are many ways to deny, defy or distance ourselves from growing older, our bodies continue to age and demand attention. They protest against neglect, sending insistent messages. Even in jobs that require little manual effort, joints seize from static postures, discs crumble from sustained sitting, and arteries clog from chronic underuse.

Few researchers consider the realities of the lived body on women's identity and well-being, particularly in ageing, with the exception of feminist researchers such as phenomenologist Elizabeth Grosz and sociologist Julia Twigg. Grosz's comment that "the body has remained a conceptual blind spot in both mainstream Western philosophical thought and contemporary feminist theory" remains relevant (1994, 3). Twigg notes the "problematic revival of Cartesian dualism" in some accounts of the ageing body where it is seen as separate from an older person's identity (2013, 63).

Sexuality and body image can alter dramatically with menopause. Older women may feel invisible or fear their bodies become "hyper-visible" and stigmatised as objects of disgust (Kuhlmann and Babitsch 2002; Woodward 1991). Participating in groups where similar experiences are shared can help women to neutralise such stigma and develop resilience to resist negative stereotypes (Chrisler 2011; Wilinska 2016). From personal observation, it seems that even with lumps and lines, wrinkles and wobbles, older women may find a form of freedom through embracing creative embodied experiences such as dance.

Professional suffragettes

While statements about demographic groupings are dangerous because they ignore diversity, the experience of ageing is generally different for the group of women currently in their60s than for those who have gone before. These baby boomer women were the first generation for whom having a professional career as well as a family was the norm rather than the exception. They have been in the vanguard of social change during their adult lives, partly due to the rise of contraception and second-wave feminism as they were coming of age. In many ways, they could be described as "professional suffragettes".

Many of these women were the first in their families to be well-educated, and the first to have a lifetime career instead of a job that was given up when children came. They were the first to choose when and if to have children, then to manage care of their children with full time work. Without older role models, they launched headlong into breaking down barriers to workplace equality, seeking to "have it all" with no expectations of the "double shift" they were to encounter (Hochschild and Machung 2003; Pocock 2006). Their life experiences were vastly different from their mothers, yet many felt stretched between proving they were as good as their mothers at home, and as good as a man at work (Isopahkala-Bouret 2017, 268).

Germaine Greer has always argued for women's liberation to decide their own destiny, rather than settle for equality with the hierarchical and "tyrannical" male status quo (2000, 384). She describes how the rhetoric of equality is used as a smokescreen "to mask the hammering that women are taking" from all sides (3). Nearly 50 years after the push for equal rights at work, the gender gap still exists, not only in pay, but increasingly in well-being (Offer and Schneider 2011). In an uncertain contemporary work environment, women are under increasing stress and are at higher risk of illness (OECD 2013). Even though men die earlier, rates of depression and anxiety are higher for older women (O'Brien and Whitbourne 2015, 163).

Many women have arrived at the precipice of ageing, shaken and exhausted. In just a single generation, an extra decade or two of life has been found. It's as if additional years have turned up unannounced; were hidden under a pile of folders. For the past 40 years, my generation have been head down, often fumbling the balls rather than juggling them. In many cases we were struggling to survive, far too busy to contemplate, let alone plan for, life beyond work.

Even for those fortunate enough to have choices in their 60s, deciding to "retire" from a lifetime's career can be confronting (Loe and Johnston 2016). Despite being weary of long hours, seemingly pointless outcome measures or office politics, there are issues beyond finances and health to consider in making decisions about retirement (Sherry et al. 2017). Our society values paid work, equating such work with personal status. These days, the potential loss of a woman's identity with age could be framed around an empty briefcase rather than an empty nest.

When seeking direction for the uncertain terrain ahead, few roadmaps exist. Standard markers of a woman's progress through a lifetime have been passed by now: education, career, relationships, reproduction. After 60, often the only signpost up ahead points towards death.

Existential questions of ageing

Half a century ago, Simone de Beauvoir struggled with her own ageing, as she struggled in many ways with Sartre. In her final existential phenomenological treatise, *The Coming of Age* (1973), she expressed, perhaps more clearly than Sartre did, the temporal finitude that lies at the heart of existentialism. Facing our finitude, knowing that death is the only certainty in life, is a profound way to reflect on what really matters —at any age. It has particular poignancy as we feel the weight of our mortality.

From an existentialist perspective, within the socio-cultural context into which we are thrown, we have freedom to choose. What we choose to do in our daily lives, and how we live our lives, shapes who we become. Within a lifetime there are a multitude of choices, but fewer as we age. As de Beauvoir noted, the older person is inside us always; she is who we are becoming, through our ways of being-in-the-world (Bair 1991, 540).

In a similar way to her earlier exposition of women as "the other" in *The Second Sex* (1949/1997), de Beauvoir demonstrated how the elderly are objectified in relation to youth. She speaks of postmenopausal women as being no longer sexualised, and therefore embodying a "third sex" (Bergoffen 2012, 367). Through her analysis, she also mourns the losses that accompany ageing: the way our bodies can become a hindrance to our engagement with the world. Despite such changes, de Beauvoir stresses that we remain free, even in older age, to define ourselves.

Twenty-five years ago, Betty Friedan also wrote about her own ageing in *The Fountain of Age*. She described drawing together the triumphs and despair of her life experiences into a whole—a story of being a social activist and political organiser, a mother and lover, a writer and teacher—to enable her continuing engagement with life. She cautioned against wasting energy on trivialities, "killing time" while waiting for death, for in doing so we miss the possibility of drawing on whatever skills we have developed, to help address problems facing society (1993, 615). A feeling of integrity and of contributing to something worthwhile, is what many of us seek. Ageing adds urgency.

De Beauvoir noted that a particular existential dimension to the lived experience of ageing was an altered relationship to time and to one's own history, the narrative of one's life (1973, 15). Age allows us to take a distant view, as opposed to the close rendering of minutia in day-to-day life. Reviewing our lives as Friedan did can foster an awareness of this self-narrative, which we carry with us and share with the world. In undertaking a contemporary analysis of ageing, Segal (2013) stresses the importance to our shared well-being of the varied stories of ageing we tell ourselves and each other.

Narrative identity

These stories of our lives hold meaning for us. In *Time and Narrative* (1984), phenomenological philosopher Paul Ricoeur describes how we construct meaning through our being enmeshed in the discursive processes of the lifeworld: in actions, conversations and texts. He posits the notion of "narrative identity" to describe how, in our construction of meaning from lived experience, we instinctively draw on cultural narratives from history as well as fiction.

Ricoeur's concept, as re-articulated in his essay *Narrative Identity*, holds in tension the postmodern idea of the self as hybrid and amorphous, and the realist notion of the self as having a stable core identity (1991, 77). Our narrative identity is in constant flux, yet coheres around a core thread of remembered and narrated time. Ricoeur notes, from a hermeneutic standpoint, that "our knowledge of the self is always an interpretation" (73). Yet an awareness of an inner self, who has changed yet remains the same in essential ways, is an experience many older people share (Segal 2013, 5). This self is glimpsed and continually reshaped through the stories we tell, both in our imaginations as well as in social settings. Our narrative identity remains open to the possibility of change, even in much older age.

Having a good strong narrative may be as important as having a good strong body in dealing with the challenges that old age presents (Randall 2012, 174). In the arts strand of a recent interdisciplinary research project called "The New Dynamics of Ageing", the most extensive ever established in the UK, older people have been supported to re-story their lives and identities, through theatre, drama, music and writing, in creative ways that broaden or deepen the meaning they gain from their life experiences (2018).

Developing robust, resilient and sometimes radical stories of their lives and relationships can sustain people as they age, so that they can live "off" rather than "in" the past (Randall 2012, 175). Narratives that view life as an evolving story, rather than one that is prematurely foreclosed, can hold a future open, right to the end. By connecting memory with meaning, stories can also reveal the beauty, the "poetics", of ageing (Randall and McKim 2004). As threads of experience are drawn together, they can be braided into narratives of purpose.

But as we age, our evolving stories also need to factor in loss. As Ricoeur noted in an interview shortly before his death at aged 92, losses, large and small, accumulate in ageing and each loss calls to be mourned by being incorporated into our life story. He states, "to mourn is to learn to narrate otherwise" (Ricoeur and Antohi 2005, 23). The remedy to the sadness of such losses, according to Ricoeur, is "the pleasure of always seeing something new, [...] continu[ing] to be astonished" (21). Sociologist Sara Lawrence-Lightfoot (2012, 2) muses in a similar vein in describing how we need to pay attention to the way we take leave of situations as we age, so they can become "endings that set us free".

Creative agency

Researchers are realising that ageing offers its own possibilities for development. Indeed, an additional stage has been added to Erikson's well-established psycho-social developmental theory, a theory that presents individual growth as a process that involves resolving stages of internal conflict. The additional stage is about dealing with a tension between involvement and resignation in continuing to engage with life (Bugajska 2016). Involvement in new creative ventures, from art to writing, drama to poetry, can enhance health and wellbeing in older people as past research (Becker 2002; Cohen 2000; Perlstein 2010) and current projects affirm (New Dynamics 2018). Creativity may blossom in transformative ways (Lear 2016). Development of a sense of creative agency can help women reframe their identity as ageing women; help them rethink what it means to be older (Searles 1990).

As I was turning 60, mortality looked me squarely in the eye. Friends of mine, still in their 50s, had died. I felt a need for change but was uncertain about what to do. With no real conception of what a possible future as an older woman might look like, I was prompted by an acute awareness of a finite life to take a leap. I took a gap year, following the examples of my children and their young friends.

In deciding a course of action, I turned to my lifelong companions and guides—books. James Hollis's Jung-inspired *What Matters Most* (2010) and Andrew Sayer's phenomenologically-based *Why Things Matter* (2011) helped me reflect on what I stood for in life and the values that underpinned that stance. In addition to wanting to be involved in something of benefit to society, my neglected health had to be taken into account. Howard Thurman, a mentor of Martin Luther King, responded to the question of how best to contribute to the world in this way: "Don't ask what the world needs. Ask what makes you come alive, and go do it. Because what the world needs is people who have come alive" (Powery 2012). As a weary 60-year-old, the image of "coming alive" burned brightly for me.

At the age of 60, I learnt to dance. By joining WaW Dance, a dance ensemble for mature-aged women, I embarked on an unfulfilled childhood dream, buried long ago under a life crammed with family and career demands. That was five years ago. To eventually perform in public as a group has taken gritty determination and doughty practice. But we are graced with dedicated teachers, experienced artists of our own age, and with an eye for aesthetics, who choreograph in a way that celebrates rather than ridicules the caprices of ageing bodies.

As extensive literature reviews of dance research confirm, the combination of physical, cognitive and social engagement in dance has multiple objective and subjective benefits on health and well-being for older people, both men and women (CPA 2011; Kshtriya et al. 2015). Humanistic gerontologists, such as Glen Cohen (2010, 199), ascribe positive psychological benefits of creative experiences to a renewed sense of mastery. But there's also the transcendent delight in some forms of creative expression, such as the dance I'm describing, that feeds the soul in unquantifiable ways.

Like most of the women I dance with, I had not considered myself to be creative. Yet we are now involved in co-creating choreography, adding drama, poetry and voice to our public performances, trying out new ways of being. The joy of this unexpected creative agency is sublime. Such explorations draw on what Ricoeur describes as the dual functions of the imagination: to preserve the memory of the past as well as to "disrupt" such thinking, so we can understand situations and ourselves in new ways (1986, 266).

This experience of joy is intensified by being shared in a group with women of similar age. The energy in the room is positively charged. Several dance researchers refer to the notion of "communitas" (e.g. Cooper and Thomas 2002), originally introduced by cultural anthropologist Victor Turner in his work on tribal rituals. Turner describes communitas in terms of "shared flow—an holistic sensation when we act with total involvement, when action and awareness are one" (1983, 118).

It's a paradox that when I'm dancing, I'm unaware of how my ageing body looks, even though it's bared in loose dance attire. All thoughts disappear. I'm suspended in an eternity where my body, as a source of pleasure, merges into the music. My spirits are lifted and lulled as the music soars and dips. It's a profound experience with benefits that seep into the rest of our lives.

Transition to life-work

In a previous publication, I coined the term "life-work' as a way of describing the stage beyond conventional "work life", with a nod to the phenomenological concept of the "life-world" (Webster-Wright 2012, 85). Ideally, such life-work can draw on skills and experience gained throughout life so that the older person can continue to contribute to the world in ways that also sustain his or her well-being. My own transition from full time academia to life-work has been supported through involvement with a cohort of older academic colleagues. As part of a research project, we investigated the use of an adapted form of life review to support women in academia (Brown-Shaw, Westwood, and De Vries 1999). We called ourselves "Women in Transition" or WITs for short (Barker et al. 2018).

As part of a pilot programme, we used this group reflective process to explore our pasts in order to frame our futures. Since turning 60, I've ventured away from academia without giving it up completely. During this time, I've explored a variety of creative forms of life-work, although I focus on dancing in this paper. A facilitated structured process such as life review could offer invaluable support to a range of people considering transition from working life, who are not interested in "just' retiring. We are exploring the possibility of running such groups.

Almost a decade is spent in educating and inducting a person into a career following the end of compulsory schooling. Little thought or support is given to the transition to life beyond conventional work, apart from perhaps a retirement seminar on superannuation or advice on staying healthy. Although change can happen suddenly and dramatically, ideally retirement is not limited to a singular event or a point in time, but can be a process that involves a transitional period of up to ten years (Schein and Haruvi 2015, 38).

Even the word "retirement', with its implications of stepping back from the essential hubbub of life is inappropriate for today's group in their 60s. Other terms such as encore careers or third act are preferable, but the broad notion of moving from work life to "life-work" better captures the variability and possible vitality of this stage of life.

Most older people could be practically supported to explore their own viable forms of keeping actively engaged in meaningful life-work. Through a review of their lives, looking back on their life stories, skills and strengths, fears and resilience, causes and passions, they could be encouraged to craft creative ideas for their future. Active engagement increases wellbeing (Kulik 2015, 60). Volunteers or those involved in worthwhile causes report having better health (56).

Ageing activism

Beyond the benefits to physical and emotional wellbeing, what has fascinated me in taking this new step is the unexpected places to which it has led. As part of the WaW Dance group, we've performed in edgy pieces that subvert notions of what an older body can create. I've found myself dancing with younger women from Vulcana Women's Circus in collaboratively performing a history of women and work. Called "Small Change", this intergenerational creative development process took a group of 30 women aged 18 to 75, most without performance backgrounds, and developed a multimedia live performance of circus, dance, voice and text. In doing so, we shared women's experiences and political history across generations throughout a full performance season (Vulcana 2013).

Dance, indeed a variety of creative art forms, can be performed as protest. "One Billion Rising for Revolution" is a global action campaign, originally begun by Eve Ensler in 2012, demanding an end to violence against women. One billion is estimated to be the number of women and girls at risk of abuse. Its focus is on women (and men) rising to dance together in solidarity, to empower women and raise awareness for change. Events are organised locally to address local issues. In 2016, events took place in over two hundred countries. It may seem a simplistic way to address violence, but, anecdotally, survivors of abuse highlight the benefit of taking back ownership and enjoyment of their own bodies as a critical step in developing strength. Such outcomes lack supporting research, at this stage.

This year, I was involved in organising the protest in my local town, bringing together members of WaW and Vulcana with Domestic Violence Services. Older women can support younger women in the fight against injustice and violence in ways as diverse as our imagination allows. Younger women, especially working mothers, are still struggling. The pressure of the double shift, discrimination, intimidation and violence against women still pervade societies. The opportunity to support or mentor younger women is a privilege of ageing that brings benefits to both groups (Denmark and Williams 2012). Indeed, Bugajska claimed recently that "society needs the courage of older people and their involvement in the ethical preservation of the world" (2016, 1109).

My newly found creative agency has shifted my previous research in the area of women and work from the safe knowns of critique and rigour to the playing fields of performance. It has taken the philosophical idea of an embodied storied self to a new visible form. I"ve moved from theories and frameworks to action and protest, and in doing so, I've come alive again. I feel better than I have in decades, despite multiple chronic health issues, and am finding new connections and ways to live as I age, ways that draw on rather than dismiss my academic intellectual credentials.

Liberating older age

Greer muses that second-wave feminists learnt strategies to confront inequality from the Black Power movement. But instead of highlighting their difference through song and dance, as many black people did, women studied their difference. Instead of celebrating the beauty of womanhood, endowing it with its own unique dignity and prestige, they set up women's study centres (2000, 420). Greer has always argued for the liberation of women to own their differences and choose their directions. Claiming our bodies and stories is also important for older women. Perhaps we could celebrate the beauty of ageing—could liberate ageing—by singing and dancing about a life well lived. Margaret Cruikshank refers to the potential power within our emerging older generation: "Having few models at present, we improvise. Later, perhaps, we organise" (2013, 209).

Those of us who came of age in the 60s were a generation of idealists and protesters, from the women libbers and anti-war activists to the women for life on earth at Greenham Common. Apart from the committed few, life seemed to swallow up many of our youthful dreams as we were swept into the hard slog of work and family. As these responsibilities drop away, time opens up to devote to issues that matter for us and society. There's a simmering energy amongst older women I know, who want to take a stand in their encore stage of life against inequality, social injustice, climate degradation and other issues of importance. As Segal (2013, 210) points out, dissent and disobedience may flare up in old age. Many women with a lifetime of experience, garnered from knuckle-skinning gains and get-up-again failures, are determined to make the last part of their life count for something.

Creative ventures can often bring a renewed energy and a different voice to protests. In Australia, older women who feel an intergenerational responsibility to leave behind a better world, are forming environmental protest groups, such as the Knitting Nannas, who use ironic humour and handcrafts, or the Growling Grannies, indigenous elders passing on traditions about caring for country. Ireland's annual Bealtaine festival brings together older people, social researchers and creative artists to "Imagine a New Old". In America, an association called Encore offers fellowships for older people with the ideas and skills to make a difference in the world (Freedman 2011). Ventures like these illustrate the value of "life-work" that engages older people with their communities, supporting creative personal growth as well as civic activism.

To stay alive to life as we age, and to continue to act in the world, requires a certain resilience: it requires the grace of forgiveness in coming to terms with our lives and the grit of perseverance to keep going and make the most of life while we have it. Essentially, it's our "ethical imagination" that keeps us attached to others in the world (Segal 2013, 277). As de Beauvoir says about old age: "One's life has value as long as one attributes value to the life of others, by means of love, friendship, indignation and compassion" (1973, 601).

There are everyday stories of women (and men) in their 60s and beyond, with strong ethical imaginations, influencing the world in positive ways, yet most stories go unsung. A quick glance around women I know provides examples of involvement, from supporting refugees to mentoring teenage girls, from organising community gardens to advocating for people with dementia. Each woman has crafted an individual form of life-work, drawing on her experiences and strengths, enjoying the involvement and influencing the world in powerful ways. Some act as a grace note to a career, others because of a gritty determination to live later life differently.

Greer claims "adaptability as the insignia of the female, survival rather than victory her success" (2000, 419), continuing that "because we bend, we do not break" (421). Adaptability is a quality urgently required by our society for survival. Adaptable older women, acting with grace and grit, offer much to a society in crisis and in need of strong, stereotypically female strategies, such as care, conversation and collaboration.

In turning 65, I"ve crossed a divide. Like the extended dawn of early adulthood, reaching from teens through 20s, the 60s and 70s have become a drawn-out dusk. The outlook is hazy, but it's still light and the colours are intense. A slanting sun throws deep shadows, richly brown with experience rather than bleakly black. That final plunge off the horizon seems as far away as ever, though logic tells me this thought is an illusion, a trick of the light. Before that unknown end, a vast country opens. It is essentially unfenced, though it can be artificially hedged by society's expectations and narrowed for many by illness, poverty and chance. The view is both enticing and bewildering.

After a rule-bound working routine, it may be time for the madness of risks: to live life fully, to listen to unexplored whisperings of the heart, to consider what matters in the end. In considering our future as older women, drawing back the curtains to consider the night ahead, we can choose neither to rage against, nor to run from the dying of the light, but to reach out and explore it before that final light goes out.

Acknowledgements

I would like to thank the two reviewers of this paper for their useful suggestions that have helped enhance it. I also gratefully acknowledge the women with whom I've had the privilege of sharing ideas and opportunities over this past five years, all of which have contributed to this paper in different ways. This includes my WIT academic colleagues, my creative writing group, my fellow WaW dancers and my long-term friends. Thank you.

Disclosure statement

No potential conflict of interest was reported by the author.

References

Bair, Deidre. *Simone de Beauvoir: A Biography*. London: Vintage, 1991.

Barker, Michelle, Ann Webster-Wright, Deanne Gannaway, and Wendy Green. 2018. "You're Not Alone: Discovering the Power of Sharing Life Narratives as Academic Women." In *Women Activating Agency in Academia: Metaphors, Manifestos and Memoirs*, edited by Susanne Garvis and Ali Black, 11–22. London: Routledge.

de Beauvoir, Simone. 1949/1997. *The Second Sex*. Trans. H. Psarshley. London: Vintage Books.

de Beauvoir, Simone. 1973. *The Coming of Age*. Trans. Patrick O'Brian. New York: Warner.

Becker, Babette. 2002. "Stage Presence – Body Presence: Movement and Body Experience with the Elderly." *Care Management Journals* 3 (2): 99–106.

Bergoffen, Debra. 2012. "Simone de Beauvoir in Her Times and Ours: The Second Sex and Its Legacy in French Feminist Thought." In *Situating Existentialism: Key Texts in Context*, edited by Robert Bernasconi and Jonathan Judaken, 360–385. New York: Columbia University Press.

Börsch-Supan, Axel. 2013. "Myths, Scientific Evidence and Economic Policy in an Aging World." *The Journal of the Economics of Ageing* 1–2: 3–15.

Boudiny, Kim. 2013. "'Active Ageing': From Empty Rhetoric to Effective Policy Tool." *Ageing and Society* 33: 1077–1098.

Brown-Shaw, Muriel, Marv Westwood, and Brian De Vries. 1999. "Integrating Personal Reflection and Group-Based Enactments." *Journal of Aging Studies* 13 (1): 109–119.

Bugajska, Beata E. 2016. "The Ninth Stage in the Cycle of Life – Reflections on E. H. Erikson's Theory." *Ageing and Society* 37 (6): 1095–1110.

Butler, Robert. 2008. *The Longevity Revolution: The Benefits and Challenges of Living a Long Life*. New York: Perseus Publishing.

Carney, Gemma M. 2018. "Toward a Gender Politics of Aging." *Journal of Women & Aging* 30 (3): 242–258.

Chrisler, Joan C. 2011. "Leaks, Lumps, and Lines: Stigma and Women's Bodies." *Psychology of Women Quarterly* 35: 202–214.

Cohen, Gene. 2000. *The Creative Age: Awakening Human Potential in the Second Half of Life*. New York: HarperCollins.

Cohen, Gene. 2010. "Creativity and Aging: Psychological Growth, Health and Well-Being." In *A Guide to Humanistic Studies in Aging*, edited by Thomas R. Cole, Ruth E. Ray, and Robert Kastenbaum, 182–205. Baltimore: The John Hopkins University Press.

Cooper, Lesley, and Helen Thomas. 2002. "Growing Old Gracefully: Social Dance in the Third Age." *Ageing and Society* 22: 689–708.

Costa, Dora L. 2000. "Understanding the Twentieth-Century Decline in Chronic Conditions among Older Men." *Demography* 37 (1): 53–72.

Cozolino, Louis. 2008. *The Healthy Aging Brain: Sustaining Attachment, Attaining Wisdom*. New York: W. W. Norton & Co.

CPA (Centre for Policy on Ageing). 2011. *Keep Dancing: The Health and Well-being Benefits of Dance for Older People*. http://www.cpa.org.uk/information/reviews/shall-we-dance-report.pdf

Cruikshank, Margaret. 2013. *Learning to Be Old: Gender, Culture, and Aging*. 3rd ed. Lanham MD: Rowman & Littlefield.

Denmark, Florence, and Deborah A. Williams. 2012. "The Older Woman as Sage: The Satisfaction of Mentoring." *Women and Therapy* 35 (3): 261–278.

Deutsch, Francine M., Carla M. Zalenski, and Mary E. Clark. 1986. "Is There a Double Standard of Aging?" *Journal of Applied Social Psychology* 16 (9): 771–785.

Ellis, Carolyn. 2009. *Revision: Autoethnographic Reflections on Life and Work, Writing Lives: Ethnographic Narratives*. Walnut Creek, CA: Left Coast Press.

Freedman, Mark. 2011. *The Big Shift: Navigating the New Stage Beyond Midlife*. New York: Public Affairs Books.

Friedan, Betty. 1993. *The Fountain of Age*. New York: Simon & Schuster.

Funnell, Nina. 2013. "Leaky Ladies and Their Troublesome Wombs." In *Destroying the Joint: Why Women Have to Change the World*, edited by Jane Caro, 228–245. St Lucia: University of Queensland Press.

Gilleard, Chris, and Paul Higgs. 2005. *Contexts of Ageing: Class, Cohort and Community*. Cambridge: Polity Press.

Greer, Germaine. 2000. *The Whole Woman*. London and Sydney: Anchor and Random House.

Grosz, Elizabeth A. 1994. *Volatile Bodies: Toward a Corporeal Feminism*. St. Leonards: Allen and Unwin.

Hartmann, Heidi, and Ashley English. 2009. "Older Women's Retirement Security." *Journal of Women, Politics and Policy* 30 (2): 109–140.

Hebert, Liesi E., Paul A. Scherr, Judith J. McCann, Laurel A. Becket, and Denis A. Evans. 2001. "Is the Risk of Developing Alzheimer's Disease Greater for Women than for Men?" *American Journal of Epidemiology* 153 (2): 132–136.

Higgs, Paul, and Chris Gilleard. 2015. *Rethinking Old Age: Theorising the Fourth Age*. London: Palgrave Macmillan.

Hilário, Ana Patrícia. 2016. "Witnessing a Body in Decline: Men's and Women's Perceptions of an Altered Physical Appearance." *Journal of Women & Aging* 28 (6): 498–509.

Hochschild, Arlie Russell, and Anne Machung. 2003. *The Second Shift*. Updated ed., with a new introd. ed. New York: Penguin Books.

Hofmeier, Sara M., Cristin D. Runfola, Margarita Sala, Danielle A. Gagne, Kimberly A. Brownley, and Cynthia M. Bulik. 2017. "Body Image, Aging, and Identity in Women Over 50: The Gender and Body Image (GABI) Study." *Journal of Women & Aging* 29 (1): 3–14.

Hollis, James. 2010. *What Matters Most: Living a More Considered Life*. New York: Gotham Books.

Isopahkala-Bouret, Ulpukka. 2017. "'It's a Great Benefit to Have Gray Hair!' The Intersection of Gender, Aging, and Visibility in Midlife Professional Women's Narratives." *Journal of Women & Aging* 29 (3): 267–277.

Kshtriya, Sowmya, Rebecca Barnstaple, Débora B. Rabinovich, and Joseph F. X. DeSouza. 2015. "Dance and Aging: A Critical Review of Findings in Neuroscience." *American Journal of Dance Therapy* 37 (2): 81–112.

Kuhlmann, Ellen, and Birgit Babitsch. 2002. "Bodies, Health and Gender: Bridging Feminist Theories and Women's Health." *Women's Studies International Forum* 25 (4): 433–442.

Kulik, Liat. 2015. "The Impact of Multiple Roles on the Well-being of Older Women: Strain or Enrichment?" In *Women and Aging: An International, Intersectional Power Perspective*, edited by Varda Muhlbauer, Joan C. Chrisler and Florence Denmark, 51–69. New York: Springer.

Langa, Kenneth. 2015. "Is the Risk of Alzheimer's Disease and Dementia Declining?" *Alzheimer's Research and Therapy* 7 (34): 1–4.

Lawrence-Lightfoot, Sara. 2012. "Endings That Set Us Free." *The Chronicle of Higher Education* 58 (40): 2.

Lear, Glenna. 2016. "Midlife Awakening." *Journal of Transformative Education* 15 (4): 277–295. doi:10.1177/1541344616670264.

Liechty, Toni. 2012. "'Yes I Worry About my Weight … but for the Most Part I'm Content with my Body': Older Women's Body Dissatisfaction Alongside Contentment." *Journal of Women and Aging* 24 (1): 70–88.

Loe, Meika, and Kay D. Johnston. 2016. "Professional Women 'Rebalancing' in Retirement: Time, Relationships, and Body." *Journal of Women and Aging* 28 (5): 418–430.

McCooey, David. 2017. "The Limits of Life Writing." *Life Writing* 14 (3): 277–280.

Menichetti, Julia, Pietro Cipresso, Dario Bussolin, and Guendalina Graffigna. 2016. "Engaging Older People in Healthy and Active Lifestyles: A Systematic Review." *Ageing and Society* 39 (10): 2036–2060.

Muhlbauer, Varda. 2015. "Introduction." In *Women and Aging: An International, Intersectional Power Perspective*, edited by Varda Muhlbauer, Joan C. Chrisler, and Florence L. Denmark, 1–7. New York: Springer.

Narayan, Chetna. 2008. "Is There a Double Standard of Aging? Older Men and Women and Ageism." *Educational Gerontology* 34: 782–787.

New Dynamics of Ageing. 2018. http://www.newdynamics.group.shef.ac.uk/ageingresearchprojects.html.

O'Brien, Jennifer L., and Susan Krauss Whitbourne. 2015. "Clinical Interventions to Empower Older Women." In *Women and Aging: An International, Intersectional Power Perspective*, edited by Varda Muhlbauer, Joan C. Chrisler and Florence Denmark, 147-167. New York: Springer.

OECD. 2013. Gender Differences in Well-being: Can Women and Men Have It All? doi:10.1787/9789264201392-en.

Offer, Shira, and Barbara Schneider. 2011. "Revisiting the Gender Gap in Time-use Patterns: Multitasking and Well-being among Mothers and Fathers in Dual-earner Families." *American Sociological Review* 76 (6): 809–833.

Perlstein, Susan. 2010. ""A Visionary Investigation and Dynamic Exchange between Science and Artistic Practice." *Journal of Aging, Humanities, and the Arts* 4 (4): 251–261.

Pocock, Barbara. 2006. *The Labour Market Ate my Babies: Work, Children and a Sustainable Future*. Annandale: The Federation Press.

Powery, Luke. 2012. "The Living Wisdom of Howard Thurman: A Visionary for Our Time." *Black Theology* 10 (1): 122–123.

Randall, William. 2012. "Positive Aging Through Reading our Lives." *Psychological Studies* 57 (2): 172–178.

Randall, William, and Elizabeth McKim. 2004. ""Towards a Poetics of Aging: The Links between Literature and Life."." *Narrative Inquiry* 14 (2): 235–260.

Ricoeur, Paul. 1984. *Time and Narrative*. Pbk. ed. Chicago: University of Chicago Press.

Ricoeur, Paul. 1986. *Lectures on Ideology and Utopia*. New York: Columbia University Press.

Ricoeur, Paul. 1991. "Narrative Identity." *Philosophy Today* 35 (1): 73–81.

Ricoeur, Paul, and Sorin Antohi. 2005. "Memory, History, Forgiveness: A Dialogue Between Paul Ricoeur and Sorin Antohi." *Janus Head* 8 (1): 14–25.

Sayer, Andrew. 2011. *Why Things Matter to People: Social Science, Values and Ethical Life*. Cambridge: Cambridge University Press.

Schein, Andrew J., and Nava Haruvi. 2015. "Older Women, Economic Power, and Consumerism." In *Women and Aging: An International, Intersectional Power Perspective*, edited by Varda Muhlbauer, Joan C. Chrisler, and Florence L. Denmark, 31–49. New York: Springer.

Scott, Julie-Ann. 2011. "Attending to the Disembodied Character in Research on Professional Narratives." *Narrative Inquiry* 21 (2): 238–257.

Searles, John E. 1990. "Inventing Freedom." *Journal of Women & Aging* 2 (2): 153–160.

Segal, Lynne. 2013. *Out of Time: The Pleasures and Perils of Ageing*. London: Verso.

Sherry, Ariel, Jennifer M. Tomlinson, Meika Loe, Kay Johnston, and Brooke C. Feeney. 2017. "Apprehensive About Retirement: Women, Life Transitions, and Relationships." *Journal of Women & Aging* 29 (2): 173–184.

Silver, Michelle Pannor. 2016. "An Inquiry into Self-identification with Retirement." *Journal of Women & Aging* 28 (6): 477–488.

Turner, Victor. 1983. "Carnival in Rio: Dionysian Drama in an Industrializing Society." In *The Celebration of Society: Perspectives on Contemporary Cultural Performance*, edited by Frank Manning, 103–124. Bowling Green, OH: Bowling Green University Popular Press.

Twigg, Julia. 2013. "The Body, Gender, and Age: Feminist Insights in Social Gerontology." *Journal of Aging Studies* 18: 59–73.

Twigg, Julia, and Wendy Martin. 2015. "The Challenge of Cultural Gerontology." *The Gerontologist* 55 (3): 353–359.

United Nations, Department of Economic, Social Affairs, and Population Division. 2013. 'World Population Ageing.' United Nations publication. http://www.un.org/en/development/desa/population/publications/pdf/ageing/WorldPopulationAgeing2013.pdf.

Venne, Rosemary A., and Maureen Hannay. 2017. "Demographics, the Third Age and Partial Retirement: Policy Proposals to Accommodate the Changing Picture of Female Retirement in Canada." *Journal of Women & Aging* 29 (6): 475–493.

Vulcana Women's Circus. 2013. http://www.vulcana.org.au/z/small-change/ https://www.youtube.com/watch?v=S4HQt_uqT0s&t=802s.

Webster-Wright, Ann. 2012. "Performing in the Afternoon: Narrative Identity and Ageing." *Literature in North Queensland: Life Writing* 39 (December): 76–87.

Wilinska, Monika. 2016. "Proud to Be a Woman: Womanhood, Old Age, and Emotions." *Journal of Women and Aging* 28 (4): 334–345.

Woodward, Kathleen. 1991. *Aging and Its Discontents: Freud and Other Fictions*. Bloomington: Indiana University Press.

Writing Life and Death Online: "I'm Not Sure How Many More Days I'll Have on the Computer"

Cathy Fowley

ABSTRACT
The narrative on digital spaces and online experience is one dominated by youth, from the so-called digital natives first heralded by Prensky to digital entrepreneurs and influencers. However, there has recently been a significant growth in the numbers of older people going online. Often forgotten, "digital settlers", many of them women, went online when the World Wide Web came to life in the 1990s, creating communities and networks of affinity, writing online journals and weblogs. They have stayed ever since, sometimes at the heart of digital spaces, sometimes hidden in the fringes. One of these spaces was home to a community of older women; from 1997 to 2012 we wrote our lives online, in daily conversations and stories. In this autoethnographical paper, through a multivoiced narrative, I explore concepts of death and mourning online and offline, and I celebrate my mentors in ageing. I draw on literary theory to relate these themes to time and space online through the concept of the Bakhtinian chronotope.

Internet research has often been linked to youth research – youth online, cyberbullying, how young people navigate a new landscape which seems to belong to them exclusively. The oft-maligned term of digital natives is still bandied about. Yet the fastest-growing internet population is people over 50, grandparents often to those who used social media first. Before social media, at the dawn of web 2.0, there were some, older than others, who engaged with technology and with each other online. Some were also women.

When the World Wide Web came to our lives in the 1990s, a vast number of "digital settlers" created communities and networks of affinity; their textual and visual communications moved life writing from a private to a public area, with online journals and blogs. Some members of an older generation thus became online diarists, bloggers, or shared their life stories through discussion boards. Many have stayed online ever since; sometimes at the heart of digital spaces, sometimes hidden in the fringes.

Whereas online communities such as found in the Well (Rheingold 2000) have been researched and written about, there were other, smaller communities, sometimes hidden behind walls. One of those was women2women, a small community for women, where registration was needed to access any board or forum. In 1999, Eva Shaderowfsky and Sue Boettcher, the founders of the women2women community, wrote a case study outlining their experience. As this article is no longer available online, I quote from a personal copy:

> In late fall 1997, we decided to build our own women's community. We had worked together on AOL building their first women's forum, Women's Network. Eva had a couple of long-running women's issues chats on AOL as well. Aside from that, we each had worked with different web-based communities. We had the experience and the background, we knew, to build a top-notch women's area. Statistics were showing that women over 35 were the fastest-growing demographic group online. Yet the existing big women's sites were marketing to younger women, and there was almost no content on the net targeting "30-somethings" and up. We saw a huge hole, and we knew we had what it took to build a site to fill it.

The road would be long and difficult, but within two years the site had gained momentum. It became home to an international group of older women. The numbers varied throughout the life of the website, as did nationalities, with a core group of older women living in various states and cities of the United States. I registered with the site in 1999 and remained until the community ended in 2012. It is not always easy to see when and how an online community takes form; for us, at that time, in that place, the community formed through life writing; this writing took the form of diaries, journals, creative writing groups, and themed conversations.

While the website, through its threaded discussions, was the heart of the community, other forms of writing occurred for one-to-one communication: this was done through email, MSN chats, even telephone calls. If this writing from our lives, about our lives, formed the basis of our community, it also became a space of learning: learning about different cultures, different generations, different outlooks. For me, it became a way of learning about ageing, from ageing mentors. In time, writing about life also involved writing about ill health, and writing about impending death.

The site was a place outside our usual places. It was an "other" place, transitory yet always there, akin to a Foucauldian heterotopia, a space set apart from our usual spaces, and, although real, functioning outside our habitual social spaces (Foucault 1984). In our kitchens, studies, sitting rooms, through our computers, we entered what we felt were our "rooms". It was linked to a time outside our usual time; short-term and transitory during our exchanges, yet long-term and transformative (Lemke 2005). It was our own chronotope (Bakhtin 1981); a narrative time and place where writing and text enabled deep connections, emotions and learning.

This autoethnographic essay has been written in retrospect, using texts which were saved by various members of the community, as well as texts and notes which I wrote throughout the time of this community. As I decided to write this autoethnography, I was granted access to the site, which is no longer online, and I was allowed to wander alone in the empty rooms, reading our texts as if they had been written yesterday. The remaining members of the group, as well as family members of some now dead, are part of a Facebook group; they helped me remember events and times, provided their own memories and reflections, and supported me in writing this piece, which uses their words and their writing as well as mine, reproducing, in a way, the conversations and exchanges of our communal life writing. Literary theory becomes another voice in the autoethnography, amplifying and making meaning of our online lives and friendships.

Memories, time and place

When I remember Kate, or Maureen, the images that come to my mind are mostly words on a pink background. When I remember Kate and Maureen, I don't remember with my senses as I do my grandmother; not smells of a house with cats and dogs, not the wind blowing around a Canadian lake in winter, not the smell of summer in Australia. Those, I imagine from their words. When I remember them, I remember their faces smiling from scanned photographs, and the sound of their voice, once or twice, on a telephone line. And now, because I am renewing my research and writing on a long-defunct website, I have gained access to my memories, and I have gained access to my friends. I log in, my fingers remember a password, and here I am, with them. Within our shared home, we had rooms, different spaces with our names that we said were ours. I go to their place, and here they are, waiting for me, their words read and re-read, nothing changed, nothing out of place.

As it was in our place, this autoethnographic account will also be a multivoiced text, my narrative entwined with their voices. I take to heart the insight on autoethnography from Bochner and Ellis (2016),

> the practices of human communication – the ways in which human beings negotiate and perform meaning – ought to become the model for how we tell about the empirical world and how we deal with the human condition and make sense of our lived experiences. (loc. 560)

In 1998, when I bought my first desktop – we didn't call them desktops, just PCs – Annette Markham was publishing *Life Online: Researching Real Experience in Virtual Space*. From her long conversations with heavy Internet users, she identified the main metaphors that helped them to make sense of their experience: the internet was a tool, a place, and a way of being (Markham 1998). For us, it certainly was a place, a place with a name, "the pink place", which we often also called home, and which helped to create a strong community, a family of sorts.

We were an unusual bunch for an online community. Preece and Maloney-Krichmar (2005) highlight the broad range of definitions when it comes to online community, the "in-term" as they call it. These definitions take into account either the relationships between people or the platform they use. They quote Amy Bruckman in conversation on "fuzzy boundaries" of community and the importance of looking at membership to define a community.

There we were, members of this community, but maybe seeing it more as a group of friends connecting in a different space. Most of us were middle-aged or older, we were online when many women of our age weren't, writing and telling our lives in a bounded online space, words on pink. We were indeed a "community of choice," based on friendship (Friedman 1989). The support we found online, with our "pink ladies," was one that extended and sometimes superseded that of our local communities or families, allowing us to show fear, anger, doubt, regret, written emotions which were hidden from families and friends at home, but allowed in this other space. Mostly, it allowed us to play, with words, with ideas, acting sometimes nonsensical games and situations, creating stories of imaginary visits, cakes, broomsticks. Yarnal (2006) refers to play theorists in her study of the Red Hat Society, highlighting liminality and communitas to examine the role of play in their communities. She adds that "liminal or third places foster behaviour or conduct that might not be appropriate at work or home or in the company of other family members" (69).

The community

We are all in different places, behind our keyboards. First my keyboard was in Paris, on a white desk in a white apartment, far from our home in Dublin. Then, my keyboard was back in Ireland, on a different white desk, close to the window. Somehow most of us can't remember how we found our Pink Place. I remember the first days of dial-up connections, sifting through pages of blogs, always drawn to those written by women my age or older. I read but would never have thought of committing to writing – what would I write, and for whom? But one day, there was a purple link, and a peach-coloured page, which was the door to Women2Women. I pushed that door slowly and rather timidly, reading several threaded discussions before committing to registration. Most women used aliases, but I kept my name. I would be Cathy, and under that name, which was mine, I posted my first contribution. Nobody noticed.

When I arrived, some conversations seemed to be teeming with posts and participation from a lot of women – Choconancy, another Nancy, Zephyr, someone with the name of a flower, Tzales, KateDu. The two main hosts had already taken a back seat and would soon hand over the reins and the role of system operator to Katedu. As the site changed, so did the age of women involved; some grew older within the community, as I did over more than 10 years of participation. Many were already in their late fifties or sixties when they joined, which makes the pink place a very unusual place indeed, in a digital world of younger people.

My second contribution was a short post to introduce myself. Nationality, my children, where I lived – the skeleton of a self. It was the same for many of the women who joined after me, and who would remain as the core of the community. Most of us had reasons to look for a community, even though those reasons would only be revealed gradually, as our stories unfolded in conversations and in our private journals.

PJ remembers:

> H. was struggling w/Parkinson's, and our lives had become pretty centered on that struggle. I was 66 at the time, and he was 78. Caring for H.—he wouldn't put up w/any other caretaker except his son who lived in Texas--tied me to home, and I was craving social interaction. W2W came into my life at a time I most needed such a connection w/other women, and the "pink ladies" helped me through a difficult time.

Very soon, we had started calling our site "the pink place," and our friends "the pink ladies." Behind her keyboard, Katedu lived in Australia, as did one or two others at the time. Most were in the United States, scattered from Washington State to Texas and New Jersey. Circe was in Holland, Person in Pakistan, and I was in Ireland.

Jigsy remembers:

> When I tell people I have been in an online group for a million years they don't believe me. I say a million years because I can't remember when I joined this little group. But I know its at least half a million. lol But thats how I explain to them why I don't post private stuff more on my home page. I have a couple closed groups I am a part of and thats where I feel I can really say what is on my mind

Memories are hazy, but discussions revive in our Facebook group when we start remembering and telling the story of our place:

> (Wren) I think I discovered and started lurking as a voyeur pink somewhere around the end of 98/start of 99. Posting regularly probably mid 99.

> (Terri) … when I brought her out of obscurity.

Part of the appeal of the Pink Place was writing; most of us truly liked writing. Tzales was writing her memoir; KateDu was also writing stories from her life, and nonfiction essays; OldMD liked to tell her stories through photographs, and also through discussions on culture, craft, and spirituality. Katedu created journals for each of us, which would become private, to be read only by the core membership, and unavailable to visitors. Life stories developed, and through those, emotional support for each other.

> (Early) Tzales then Katedu helped me with the grief of mine with brother, and parents deaths in 4/97 and 9/97. Katedu used to say she could see me in the pit I had dug for myself and all she could see were my eyes peeking out until she could pull me out.

When loss happened in our lives, the stories of loss appeared in our online space. These narratives of grief became more common as all of the women of the group got older, lost friends and partners. Grief could be expressed fully, with no fear of hurting or worrying, and knowledge that support would come.

> (Betty) The pink site helped me through one of the most difficult times of my life, when my Del passed away, will always be dear to me.

Yet, very soon, grief would also be a feature of our community.

Katedu's journal became a daily read for most of us, all the more when she was diagnosed with lung cancer. The next few short months would see two narratives of illness and death appear in her and OldMD's journals. OldMD had been a lecturer and medical doctor until her retirement. She joined the site well into her seventies, already suffering from generalised cancer.

Both women wrote with honesty and sometimes brutal frankness of their lives, their thoughts and their family relationships through their illness. Those stories became distributed throughout different media; sometimes comfort had to come from personal conversations. Close to her death, Katedu couldn't sleep. She would stay up through the night, navigating her insomnia through our varying time zones to talk to Tzales, Circe and me; long and funny conversations about her life and her death. She bought a kimono and wore it constantly, posting smiling pictures of the moribund in her finery.

In our pink place, or in personal online communication, both KateDU and OldMD wrote what is seldom written, and taught us what is seldom shared. In these small bubbles of time, we, with them, talked and wrote through their approaching death, to what we knew would be the end of our time together. Time stretches online, or maybe collapses; in the non-space where our abandoned site is kept, I read back, I am there, in the past, and memory takes shape out of the pink place.

Vigil 1. It is a miliary tumour (Many little areas)

OldMD's formidable presence came through clearly on our screens. She had been a lecturer, a medical doctor, and was a lifelong student of philosophy and religions. She wrote about her life, her childhood, her beliefs, her philosophy of life. Bakhtin (1981, 130) refers to the Platonic type of autobiography in Ancient Greece, which embodies the chronotope of "the life course of one seeking true knowledge." If our time and space on the site was a chronotope of autobiographical lives, within this were smaller chronotopes, and OldMD echoes the autobiographical chronotopes of some of her favourite philosophers.

> I'm not sure I should be considered a woman of science ... medicine was also considered an "art"—once upon a time.

She might have been seen as eccentric, but to me she was a shining beacon, a proof that you can grow old with the beautiful gift of intellectual rigour mixed with whimsy and fun. May Sarton (1984, 11) writes: "I have always longed to be old, and that is because all my life I have had such great exemplars of old age." My years online have given me examplars who would have been difficult to find in other places, where talk about ageing is not encouraged.

Ageing for OldMD could sometimes be embodied by her memories of her own grandmother:

> At age 3 I "helped out" my grandmother by dusting the spindles on the staircase "you are the only one whose hands will fit in between and do the best job". I also weeded the upper levels of her terraced herb garden "you are the only one small enough to fit". I worked HARD in hopes that the fairies would reward me by showing themselves as they really looked, instead of as butterflies. The story I got from Mom and the aunts was that Gran could always see the fairies. Indoors or out, she was one of the greatest con artists that ever lived. Her whole life was FUN—for her and everybody around her.

She was not alone in this approach to ageing. Tzales often echoed those sentiments:

> I've decided 79 is the age of doing and saying what I want [...] I will quit feeling guilty for sitting here at the computer too long, knowing my feet will swell ... they swell anyway, I might as well be doing something I enjoy. I am, after all, 79 years old. It is my time to wear purple and do and say what I want. Would you believe my doctor agreed with me? (grinning emoticon) He's SUCH a GOOD doctor!

In March 2009, OldMD talked more about ageing and dying on her own terms:

> Once the decision was made that "fighting" wasn't going to change anything and getting rid of the stress might make things go more naturally, I just started making the list of things about my life that were satisfying ...

She had known for a time that her cancer would not go into remission, and the clarity of her training and of her spirit converged, enlightening us all. The cancer was named: a miliary tumour. While we were learning medical terms, we were also learning OldMD's way of meeting terminal illness. She made lists, she knitted when she could, and studied religions and philosophy. Her list of things that were satisfying included her online life with us, and communication with many of us either on the site, by email, or sometimes by post. In March 2009, her writings were less about memories or political analysis, and more about death, and the end of her own life. Sometimes her contributions were humorous about what could help at the end:

> Believing I've been here before and will probably come around again to annoy people (this list isn't NEARLY meriting nirvana ☺ helps too.

Learning never ended for her, after long studies in her youth, she kept learning and researching as a third level lecturer and educator, and in older age became fascinated by ancient or eastern philosophies and religions.

> If I can remember enough from these courses and stay calm during what Johnny calls "the transition", maybe I'll be fortunate enough to be a teaching human—rather than a mosquito!

Later in the month, her body started giving signs which she rightly interpreted as impending death:

> It's been over a week since I had a symptom-free day SO … I'm getting used to the idea that I may be getting what I wished—a FAST course.

OldMD would come to the pink place to live and write her death on her own terms, in her own time. In her geographical place, people came and visited *trying to take my mind off things*, she smiled emoticonally. *Blast ALL visitors*. In the pink place, she visited when she wanted to, and we knew that minds cannot be taken off death. She wrote her dying body too, as it was and felt:

> Right after she left, the stomach cramped up (worst to date) and I started vomiting. Three bouts later, pills all messed up because of recurrent bouts of vomiting, belly still rock hard - it's going to be an interesting night …

Eventually, time and space online, in our chronotope, came to an end. OldMD said her goodbyes, and together, yet not together, we held vigil and waited for word from her husband.

> (March 29, 2009) Sorry this is so depressing, dears. Wanted to get on a time or two while I'm still up to it—I'm not sure how many more days I'll have on the computer, even for short spells.
>
> Love you all—John has your e mails so you'll be hearing from one or other of us.
>
> (Kate) I know you don't want sympathy, but you have all mine whether you want it or not. I do wish I could be with you at this time, to hold your head and hand, not to talk and wear us both out, but just to be close to you.
>
> Know I am there in spirit, and love you greatly.
>
> (Tzales) Yours has been one of the strongest, most respected voices to ever come from my computer. Please know I stand by you in spirit sending you peace and tranquility.

This was indeed one of OldMD's last postings. We held vigil for our friend in our space, while her body was dying in her space. We wrote to her words she wouldn't read, yet we felt they belonged to her and needed writing. Her presence in many little areas of the site, her lasting words in our discussions, were to be treasured and still are.

Vigil 2. A lot of living

In the same place, at the same time, at the other end of the world, KateDU had a lot of living to do. She was the sysop of the site, but also the den mother, the writing prompt specialist, the heart of the community. In her geographical space, she was a mother, grandmother, daughter, crafter, and spent many holidays driving around Australia in a caravan with her husband. Her life was lived offline and narrated online for her readers, her friends and her network. Eakin (2004, 122) writes: "autobiography is not merely something we read in a book; rather, as a discourse of identity, delivered bit by bit in the stories we tell about ourselves day in and day out, autobiography structures our living." At the end of the day in Australia, Kate would go to her online space to narrate her life. Bakhtin (1981, 131), on autobiographical chronotopes in Ancient Greece, valid now in our virtual forums, states: "This real-life chronotope is constituted by the public square (the agora). In ancient times the autobiographical and biographical self-consciousness of an individual and his life was first laid bare and shaped in the public square."

She posted many photographs, at a time when posting photographs on a website involved creating accounts with different hosting sites and embedding pictures with HTML commands. When others, less digitally able, wanted to share photos with the group, Kate always helped. Gradually, photographs became part of our daily life on the site, linking our offline lives to our precious place and time online.

KateDu was much younger than OldMD. She was in her sixties when health problems started to become prominent in her daily life. As with a diary, Kate shared her daily problems on the site, as well as by email, chat, and telephone calls – mostly to her best friend of all, Tzales.

> (Tzales) Once, long before either of us knew she was ill, I told her I'd always thought I would die when I was young and my prayer had been to live long enough to raise my child. Kate said, "Don't be silly, God knew you would be needed here to help me." I think I did help her pass some rough nights when Australia was asleep and Texas was just starting the day they'd already finished.

It soon became obvious to us all that Kate was seriously ill. She would write humorous posts, but in her personal diary, shared with us, she would also write of her illness and her worries. Soon, her doctor sent her for tests and she shared the diagnosis: lung cancer at an advanced stage. She talked then about palliative care, and one of the community's members, a hospice nurse, responded to her.

> (Andre, March 27th) Palliative care may be the best words of all … because that concept is totally aligned with your goals of quality of life and comfort. Except for the diagnosis (which as you say, not unexpected), all good news ☺.

> You have been such a rock for so many of us. Hoping that you know you can say anything here in your place and be supported in return. I hope you have a good nap ☺

As the illness progressed and personal communications increased through Instant Messaging, KateDU's narrative echoed OldMD's; she was enjoying her life, riding a mechanical rodeo bull at a wedding, going on a cruise to an island when she had always dreaded boats, buying silk kimonos to display and to wear. Yet, like OldMD, she did not shirk from narratives of the dying body. On the same day, we read and wrote our goodbyes to OldMD and read about KateDU's failing body.

> (March 29) Woke up thinking I would probably choke to death with the coughing, but last night I took my first dose of the liquid morphine. Peggy tells me that it might be loosening up the congestion and helping me clear the breathing a bit, but my mouth is so dry, aaack, 4 cuppas later and my tongue is no longer sticking to my teeth lol So I'll still stay on it, for some reason I have been afraid to take it until now. You hear so many stories about morphine … .and I am a big yellow feathered, lily livered chicken as you all know.
>
> I have also learned not to read the 3 massive sheets of info that come with medication, I think they have too much information lol
>
> From today I am on 2 oxycontin a day, pain level is increasing and I seem to need more pain control during the day now, and oxycontin are only 12 hour control.

Time was shared online when it couldn't be shared at home, sheltering loved ones and yet needing to give voice to an identity of fear, grief, and insomnia. Kate fell back on humour as a way of relating to death, and telling the end of her story, as she had done with her narratives of life. With these narratives, at times, came clarity and focus:

> (April 2, 2009) For some weird reason, I find myself unafraid of everything I have been wary about in the past, I have a lot of living to do here my friends.

On April 6th, Tzales sent me an email to ask for a chat in IM. There, she told me that Kate was in hospital, not expected to live the night. We stayed online, long typing silences were the rhythm of our tears.

We were all in different places, in spirit, as we used to say, even though we would find our way back to the place where our vigil was held, and where mourning would soon reign. Here I was, in Ireland, and there was Tzales, in Texas, our hearts and thoughts in Australia, but we went back to our place.

> (Cathy, April 6) I can't settle much on anything this morning. I came to the campus library, intending to write my introduction, but I find myself drifting back here, a little aimlessly. I hope Peggy is still asleep, and so do not expect any news, and yet here I am.

Online wake

Online, the narrative of dying and death moved to a narrative of grief. We kept coming back, every hour, connecting with a communal grief in our communal place. Offline, our grief was not always understood; we didn't know these people, we were told. Some implied that it was like grieving for a fictional character. Yet, if it was, then we too were fictional characters in our shared story. Online, others mirrored our feelings, echoed our words, and online was the only place where we could get some comfort. Online, in our pink place, that was our other home, our other family.

> (Betty, April 9) I know we are all in shock, you just go along, and it pops back into your head , it is like losing part of a family , which we have become over these years. When I first retired, this filled part of the void.[…] But I know I can always come back to my second home here where all of you are.

Place and time were always in our words, unexpressed longing for our chronotope, unexplained anchoring to physical and virtual places.

> (Tzales, April 10) I'm doing better. My eyes don't drip tears all the time now, just when I happen to wonder what on earth I will do with all those hours Kate and I spent sitting here typing silly thoughts to each other.

Those who couldn't be online at the time, who were away from their computers, felt pain and guilt at their perceived absence:

> (Tink) Had I posted here last week that we were leaving very early 4/4 and not returning until late 4/7 you all would have known why I hadn't posted. I received an email from Cathy earlier tonight (Thursday 4/9). When we did get home we were both very tired and had to run errands yesterday and today we were just relaxing and trying to catch up on some rest. I'm sorry I wasn't here.
>
> I know Kate would not have judged me for not being here, but there isn't any feeling better than hugging a friend, even if it has to be a cyber hug.

Already, the absence was felt in our discussions, names were missing from the message boards.

> (PJ, April 10) We're all hurting. […] I'll do my best to post often with the hope of hitting on something that will spark interest. We need to grieve honestly and openly while keeping sight of how fortunate we all are that we knew Kate: a beloved, compassionate, helpful, highly amusing and entertaining sister/friend who was a keenly intelligent, multi-faceted and talented individual who could, occasionally, be downright confounding. We humans don't come any better than that!
>
> "We gotta love each other and stay together!" Yes, TZ.

Mourning

Time passed online, as it did offline, and although the site remained open, we came less often, read a little, did not post as much as we used to. We felt a loss of place even as the place became gradually more silent. Our chronotope had ended, the place coming to a halt as time had stopped for two of us. The only narratives we cared for were narratives about our friends, their lives, and our place as it used to be. In these last life writings, we talk of place, of course, and some may contrast the digital and physical, but mostly the words are of absence and silence.

Remember

Mourning started early, and it lasted for a long time. Mourning was made of silences, of the absences of words and names on the site, but it was also made of postings, messages which brought mourning responses. A lot of our time on the site was a time for remembering.

> (Wren, Sept 2009) It amazes me how much of a daily impact MD and Kate had in my life. It is seems out of wack to me. My relationship with them was not as defined as the ones they had with many of the other women here, we didn't write, talk on the phone, or even IM very much … but … well, I don't let very many people past the surface of my life and losing

> them still hurts alot. Just their presence kept me grounded and challenged me to open myself up to new ways of thinking.
>
> (Rose, April 2011) You know this is actually the first time since MsDu left us that I've been able to read something about her and not ball my eyes out. I did think about and her family a lot the week that Oprah was in the Down Under. Maybe things are getting just a bit better.
>
> Its kind of weird actually to realize it took longer to get over the loss of her than it did on the loss of some family members and friends that I really knew. Life's strange some times, but it is what it is.
>
> (Cathy April 2011) I agree with you Rose, Kate's death—and MD's affected me much more powerfully and for longer than I would have thought. Their unseen presence on the site, and in my imaginary world map, was so strong that their departure left me bereft and lonely. I still think of them nearly daily, fleeting thoughts of what I would have said to them. I wonder did that actually stop me from posting as much as I used to.
>
> (Person, April 2011) this site did lose a lot with those two gone, cathy … and then all of us reacted to that loss by virtual silence … or less talk, anyway …
>
> (Circe, May 2011) I've been dreaming about Kate and OldMD—they counsel me in my dreams.
>
> (Early, August 2011) Since we can no longer talk on the phone, and the Im on this site is silent from you, When I think of you and are missing you so much, I come here, hoping you are looking down, or up as the case may be … a little joke … and reading what I/we write.

Later again, the site closed, and a core community moved to a private Facebook group. There, like friends grown apart yet still very fond of each other, we send occasional news, like the Christmas letters people used to send to catch up on a year's worth of news. We still gather for difficult times of loss, for times of celebration. Tzales and Rose died one after the other. In an online space where the visual has assumed a growing importance, the pictures of OldMD and KateDU I posted recently managed to revive conversations in the Facebook group.

When I think back now, I recall the time and place which have become bounded by death of four women and the death (disappearance) of the place. It strikes me how the narratives—which were flagging after the women's death—have never reappeared in a different space. Sometimes, algorithms play games with us. "It is Rose's birthday, write on her wall." "A year ago, J. posted this picture." OldMD smiles at me. I search for a term in my emails, and there on my screen, familiar words, usually in green and in italics, "love, Kate."

Disclosure statement

No potential conflict of interest was reported by the author.

References

Bakhtin, M. 1981. *Dialogic Imagination: Four Essays.* Austin: University of Texas Press. Print.

Bochner, A. P., and C. Ellis. 2016. *Evocative Autoethnography: Writing Lives and Telling Stories.* New York: Routledge. Print.

Eakin, P. J. 2004. "What Are We Reading When We Read Autobiography?" *Narrative* 12 (2): 121–132. Print.

Foucault, M. 1984. Des espaces autres (conférence au Cercle d'études architecturales, 14 mars 1967) Architecture, Mouvement, Continuité, no. 5, 46–49. Print.

Friedman, M. 1989. "Feminism and Modern Friendship: Dislocating the Community." *Ethics* 99 (2): 275–290. Stable URL: http://www.jstor.org/stable/2381435Frie.

Lemke, J. 2005. "Place, Pace and Meaning: Multimedia Chronotopes." In *Discourse in Action: Introducing Mediated Discourse Analysis*, edited by S. Norris and R. Jones, 110–122. New York: Routledge. Print.

Markham, A. 1998. *Life Online: Researching Real Experiences in Virtual Space.* Walnut Creek, CA: AltaMira Press.

Preece, J., and D. Maloney-Krichmar. 2005. "Online Communities: Design, Theory, and Practice." *Journal of Computer-Mediated Communication* 10 (4). doi:10.1111/j.1083-6101.2005.tb00264.x

Rheingold, H. 2000. *The Virtual Community: Homesteading on the Electronic Frontier.* 2nd ed. Cambridge, MA: MIT Press.

Sarton, M. 1984. *At Seventy: A Journal.* New York: Norton.

Yarnal, C. M. 2006. "The Red Hat Society: Exploring the Role of Play, Liminality, and Communitas in Older Women's Lives." *Journal of Women and Aging* 18 (1): 51–73.

Now that I'm Old: Life Writing, Women and Ageing

Elisabeth Hanscombe

ABSTRACT
Life writing can provide a chronicle of experiences, but for many women as they age, it also presents an opportunity to find meaning. My written story began in my mid-forties, in contrast to my mother who wrote her autobiography during her mid-seventies. In this essay, I explore how my mother's inability to give voice to certain memories impacted on my own ability to write my life. Her efforts to stay on the surface drove me deeper. Our writing becomes a way of holding onto earlier versions of ourselves, however much these versions might contradict later perspectives. The process of life writing interacts with the experience of ageing in a way that can reinvigorate the writer, and the reader by association. We can achieve so much more on the page than our ageing bodies will allow in the physical world. This includes an overview of our lives and a way of making meaning out of the patterns we perceive with each passing year. Such patterns become more apparent with age. Secrets can reach the surface, particularly events such as incest, a central factor in my family story. Or they can remain hidden, as in my mother's attempts to sanitise the past.

The art of disappearing

In the year my mother turned seventy-five, when I was forty-two years old, I first began work on my autobiographical writing. I had written as a child, bad poetry and the like, but from the time I left school until my late thirties I concentrated on my career, first as a social worker and later a psychologist, determined throughout to help people who grew up in families like mine. That was my conscious intention at the time, though I now consider that most people who enter the psychology profession do so to get a better understanding of themselves. This is also one of the recognised motivators for life writing. Autobiographies "are doubly constructed," as Paul John Eakin (1999, ix) argues, not only in our efforts to write our life story but also as part of "a lifelong process of identity formation of which the writing is usually a comparatively late phase."

Over the years, I moved up the ranks of the psychology world into the silent chambers of the psychoanalytic, where I found a society dominated by secrecy and concealment. Like my father and the priests at church, the psychoanalysts commanded respect, even as they sometimes behaved in ways that made little sense to me. There were unspoken rules of behaviour, formality in our exchanges, never on first name terms, and a tendency to follow the psychoanalytic stance maintained for work with patients. We were encouraged to give the impression of our therapist-selves as a *tabula rasa*, a blank screen, in line with Freud's dictum that the therapist remains opaque in all their dealings with patients. This extended to our dealings with supervisors and mentors, again with an unspoken sense that it was best to keep your feelings to yourself. Be quiet and strong, and keep your vulnerabilities hidden.

Just as I had doubts about the analysts, they also had doubts about me. They considered that I was not circumspect enough, too anxious in my dealings with them, not psychoanalyst material, and so they dismissed me from their training course. At least this is my understanding now, in retrospect, though at the time the analysts offered no explanation of their decision, other than some suggestion that I was unsuitable. My dismissal proved traumatic for me, an event that precipitated a resurgence of my need to write, not in later, but mid-life. Even so, life events sent us both, my mother and me, into writing as a means of reordering our thinking about our lives, though we both had different approaches.

Initially, I grieved for my lost life as a psychoanalyst, despite continuing to practise as a therapist. During this time, during the mid-1990s, I hatched a plan whereby I would produce a book in which each of my eight siblings and I could write a chapter. I wanted to capture what life was like for each of us children from a large Catholic and troubled family, who had migrated to Australia from Holland in the post-war exodus from Europe.

Although my siblings agreed to cooperate in the writing of this book, I came to understand that this was not feasible. Some of my five brothers, especially those who saw themselves as writers, did not want to give over editorial control to me—sixth born and second girl—and I realised I needed to write my own story and leave them to theirs. It took me another twenty plus years, including the completion of a doctorate on "Life Writing and the Desire for Revenge," a full working life as a psychotherapist, raising four daughters, along with many other efforts at life writing in between, to get to the stage where my memoir, *The Art of Disappearing*, was finally accepted for publication in 2017. The title of the book comes from my narrator self's central preoccupation with trying to hide in order to avoid my father's sexual advances, given his frequent visits to my older sister at night, and my belief that my turn was next. The irony is that in my childhood, I sought to hide myself, whereas in my writing I seek to reveal.

My mother's writing contrasts with my memoir, in which I focus on my remembered childhood. I do not idealise this childhood but reflect on it as a painful time, fraught with family violence. I write about a world that is different from my mother's, not only in its traumatic aspects, but also in its unflattering portrayal of my father.

My mother wrote her memoir during the course of her second marriage, which took place two years after my father's death in 1984. She and her second husband revisited Holland twice together; for all that her new husband was Australian born. They kept house together, grew older together, and for the next seventeen years my mother claimed to be happy, unlike during her marriage to my alcoholic and sexually abusive father. She wrote her story from the framework of this happy state, whereas I worked on mine, at least in the initial phases, from a distressed state, given my dismissal from the analytic training.

Many years later, grieving her second husband's death in 2001 and moving into a retirement village, my mother claimed again to be happy in her ageing, just as she had been happy throughout her childhood. Yet those forty years in the middle of her life when she was married to my father were a dark stain on her memory, one she wanted to expunge from her 1995 memoir.

As I have aged, I have developed more confidence as a writer, the impulse to write emerging from (what was for me) the cataclysmic event of my dismissal from analytic training, which initiated my wish to crack open my understanding of my life on the page. In writing her life story, however, it is as if my mother wanted to draw her life to a close. My mother finishes a number of chapters with the words, "And that was that," as if she is telling her reader, no further enquiry here, please. This is the final word. Whereas I have a tendency to leave things hanging, unfinished, in doubt.

Why write and why later?

From the moment we're born, we start to age. But it is only once we get beyond the seemingly slow-moving days of childhood, past our twenties and into levels of maturity that bespeak adulthood, that ageing takes on a new dimension. My first real sense of ageing hit me when I turned forty—midlife, I thought then—and a time of reckoning, as I went through the throes of a miscarriage soon after my dismissal from the analytic training, and for several months feared an early menopause and the end of the possibility of more children.

My mother's last child was stillborn when she was 43 years old and I was ten, a memory that stays with me and with my mother, though she told me she felt she should not grieve for this lost child too much, given that she then had nine healthy live children in her care.

I had three children at the time of my miscarriage and with it came a sharp reminder that life was finite. Several months later, when I was pregnant with my fourth and youngest daughter, my mother said, "No more babies for you now. You're getting too old." Her stillborn baby, she was told, had died because the placenta in her ageing body could not sustain the baby long enough.

At the time of my own miscarriage, I wrote out of loss, this lost-dreamed-for- baby and the end of my analytic dream. Along with this understanding came other understandings about the impermanence of life and of dreams, about the ways in which we are not simply on a trajectory to better things. Not as my mother liked to believe, with her sights aimed towards a place in heaven.

Life begins its slow decline and one way to help deal with that decline is to find something meaningful and manageable. For my mother, religion offered a strong belief in right and wrong, with little room for doubt. For me, meaning came with my writing, an opportunity to put my thoughts and experience down on the page, to tell the story of my life as I remember it and as it impacted upon me.

My mother wrote, she told me, to leave a record for her children so that they could know something of the life she had lived. Not so much to set the record straight, given that for my mother there was no record to set straight. She saw herself, and hoped others might see her, too, as a good woman who had led a good life. I, on the either hand, began to write out of a sense that I had failed. I was anything but a good woman.

My mother might have felt a failure in her first marriage, but she never said as much. Her greatest achievement rested in the fact of her children, their achievements and the sheer number of them. Others might disparage her, given overpopulation, but to my mother she had done a good thing. A few weeks before she died, she asked me yet again to remind her of the number of her great grandchildren. She never forgot the number of her children and her 23 grandchildren, to which she added an extra number to accommodate her second husband's grandchildren, whom she claimed as her own. Including both her biological and stepfamily, my mother was a grandmother some forty times over, and for her this was the best. "It is so good to think that none of these people would be here today without me."

One of my aims in conveying the struggle of my child-self was to write from a distance and let the reader make up their own mind, whereas mother's writing tends to "tell" the reader what to think. This is a sign of inexperience as a writer, but also a sign of my mother's desire to create an image consistent with her wishes to present well for future readers. And this wish to give a good impression increased as she aged, while my wish to subvert that impression has also increased as I age.

Some context

As I write, I find myself pulled towards a deeper compassion towards my mother and her struggle, even as I rail against what I experience as her narrowness. I check my thoughts.

Is my mother's approach part of a migrant's story? A wish to make good in a new land? A wish to convince herself and others that it was all worth it? Problematic past events must be glossed over to reveal a better life in her new home. And yet links slip out in places, of which I suspect my mother was unaware.

Throughout her story, my mother makes no mention whatsoever of my father's sexual abuse of my older sister. Early in her story, however, she refers to a period during the Second World War in Haarlem, Holland, when her "Papa [who] had been a member of the St Vincent de Paul organisation [...] one day [...] told [her] the tragic story of a young girl only 13 years old who had fallen pregnant as a result of incest" (Bury 1995, 46).

At this stage in the story, my mother, a young mother herself, offers some clothes to the baby's mother. My mother writes, "Later I became the baby's godmother." She slides this short paragraph in among all the difficulties she recounts of her life during the war. However, she fails to make any connection with the fact that her own daughter, born fifteen years after these events in Holland, was forced into a sexual relationship with her father, my mother's husband, before she had turned thirteen, though she never fell pregnant. It is as if in writing during her seventies, my mother whitewashes the past.

My mother states, "There was no TV. I often think that today's freedom of the press has done a lot of harm to many unstable people whose numbers are increasing" (Bury 1995, 46). In this way, my mother distances herself from her reader. At the time, however, she was aware of my father's abuse and claimed to believe it had happened. Yet, after my father's death, when my mother remarried, she refused to revisit the past of her former marriage, except cursorily. Her age and religious convictions encouraged her to distance herself from such events. She may have reframed her life story to absolve herself of her guilt given that she was unable to protect her children. This coheres with the notion that we tell our stories in order to present our best selves. As Eakin (1999, xi) writes: "our narrative self-fashioning, oriented as much to the present and future as to the past, may even possess an evolutionary, adaptive value, helping to anchor our shifting identities in time." I would add that our shifting identities increase in number as we age.

My mother did not want her new husband to know about her previous one, at least not in detail. She may have needed to obliterate any awareness of the connection between these events, as such knowledge might have unsettled her mind, even more so given her tendency towards extreme guilt for any wrong-doing. How else could she live with the knowledge that her husband had sexually abused her daughter? Whether my mother's airbrushing of aspects of the past that may have been too difficult for her to process is a feature of her age or of her personality, I cannot say. Most likely it was a combination of both.

Digging deeper

Unless we work on ourselves through therapeutic interventions or other efforts at self-understanding, our most significant personality traits can persevere and magnify in our final years. To make sense of my childhood, I spent twelve years driving from Hawthorn to Beaumaris once a day for an hour each week, except during holidays, to undergo an analysis with a woman whom I refer to as Mrs Milanova. During my analysis, I explored in intricate detail the struggles of my internal world, my memories, and my experience both of childhood and of everyday conflicts and issues with my current life. By comparison, my mother tried to get help for my father by visiting doctors and agencies throughout Melbourne. None were able to help, as my father refused to join her. Not until she joined Al-Anon, a self-help organisation for the families of alcoholics, did my mother find some way of managing her difficulties with my father. Certainly, she became more black and white in her thinking as she aged. Her tendency to idealise the past and to imagine that the world we occupy in the present is far worse than the one we left behind is evident throughout her memoir. Most often she blames it on the media:

> Now there are many more suicides and rape for instance was not heard of in the past in my neck of the woods. On the other hand, there was hypocrisy: we had to pay for our seats in the church and that meant that poor people could only sit in the back where it was free and never in their lifetime could they sit close to the altar [...] I blame the media. In Holland when crime was reported names were never mentioned. (Bury 1995, 118)

This section from my mother's "Final Thoughts" exemplifies a pull towards nostalgia. My mother also wears the blinkers of generalisation, as if her understanding of the world in which she lived is limited only to what she sees, experiences and remembers, despite her reference to those "poor people" who, unlike her, could never sit near the altar.

An empty pram

In some analytic circles we talk about developing a capacity to strengthen your internal mother, the one who lives in your head, a maternal voice shaped from your experience, in part, of your actual mother, but one who over time might be more helpful, more nurturing, less critical. As I age, the voice in my head, no longer the voice of my actual mother, takes on a different tone. It softens. My internal mother's voice, my internal critic, is less inclined to be censorious, less inclined to urge me to present only a good image.

My internal voice is more inclined to tell me to follow my thoughts wherever they lead, to follow the images in my head when I am telling the story of my life based on my memory and imagination, as if I am a small child again threading coloured beads onto a string. I pick up one bead after the other, one bead at a time, and the quiet thinking that goes on as the words fall onto the page involves the decision of which bead to select and then the slow threading on to form a pattern that represents my experience. Later, in the editing and reviewing phases, there are other issues with which I must contend.

My mother's internal process I cannot know, only that for some time during her seventy-fifth year she spent a few hours every day writing about her life from birth onwards. Each piece she wrote by hand she passed onto a beloved daughter-in-law, who worked as an editor and took my mother's partial manuscript as it evolved, moulding it into the final form. My mother needed to approve any changes but essentially her words remained, without typed or grammatical errors, given English was her second language, and she has some unusual expressions, most of which do not feature in her book.

In my memoir, I devoted a chapter to a story my mother told me repeatedly when I was young about the time during the Hunger Winter of 1945 when she travelled from Haarlem to Heilo beyond Castricum to stay with her cousins on a farm. There was not enough food left in the city to nourish a baby who was seriously unwell. So my mother left her then small son in the care of another cousin, while my father was trying to avoid the German work camps, and she walked the thirty kilometres back to Haarlem with her baby in her pram. My mother wrote about this story in her memoir and to this day it is the one section that reverberates for me, especially given my sense that when I was a child my mother had slid over her grief at losing this child, my older sister, who died soon after reaching Heilo. I borrowed the image my mother uses in her story when she conveys her grief, without whitewashing, more than fifty years after the event: "We walked all the way home to Haarlem with an empty pram and an empty place in my heart" (Bury 1995, 45) (Hanscombe 2017, 56). In my life story, this image becomes a symbol for the ways in which our writing reverberates.

Older age and identity formation

In later years, when I visited my mother in her retirement village, she told me repeatedly about how pleased she was to be able to have all her things around her, all her memories of the good things about her life, celebratory photos, ornaments and mementos, reminders of her wonderful childhood. My mother did not dwell on the awful aspects of the past and nor should I, she told me. After all, there was nothing she could do about it. It had happened, and it was awful, but it was over now, and her life was good. But she wondered from time to time how much longer she could go on like this [sitting day after day in her retirement home], doing nothing. I asked her if she felt guilty.

"No," she said. "What else can I do? I'm old. I don't feel old but I recognise I'm old. At 93 what else can I do but sit and read? At least I have my reading." My mother folded her hands in her lap and looked down at them with a sigh.

"Did you have a hard childhood?" she asked me then out of the blue as if it was a new idea. I sensed she wanted me to tell her that I had enjoyed a good childhood like hers, despite the hardships, but I reversed the order and told her that my childhood was indeed difficult, though not in everything.

I tried to explain to my mother that although she had hoped to block out the forty years of her life when she was married to my father, at least nineteen of them encapsulated my childhood from birth until the day I left home. I could not look upon our family years together with such ease of forgetfulness.

"But I tried to help you all leave home," my mother said.

> I was stuck there, I knew, but for you children I could see what a bad effect it had on you all and so I tried to get you the things you would need, the pots and pans, to move out and start your own lives. It was all I could do for you.

Whenever my mother presented her thoughts in this way, especially in her writing, I felt compelled to try to turn them on their head by paraphrasing these words, setting them out on the page so that a reader might re-think those notions with which I struggle. The pull to put on rose coloured glasses. Thereby my mother becomes an unreliable narrator. At the same time, I recognise myself, and my wish to reframe the past by way of turning my character too into that of an unreliable narrator.

As she grew older, my mother's memory of events moved further back into her childhood. It is not uncommon as we age that our short-term memory fades and our memory of past events become sharpened into a detailed and rich clarity. However, as Douwe Draaisma (2004, 1–2) explores regarding the "tricks" and patterns of memory, memory is both necessary and prone to distortion because memories do not stand alone. Memories jostle against other memories and "interfere" with one another (2004, 47). As Timothy Garton Ash writes "Memory is a rewritable CD that is constantly being rewritten. And rewritten in a particular way: one that both makes sense of the story to us and makes it more comfortable for us" (2002, 4–6). This jostling is reflected in my mother's writing as well as my own. It is as if my mother sealed off events from the most critical time of her children's life, her middle life, and held them in a drawer, one she only revisited under pressure from her children, especially from me in my determination to get to a deeper understanding of what happened during my childhood and why.

Incest introduces a "maelstrom of intense confusion and contradiction felt by children and their families" (Sheinberg and Fraenkel 2001, ix). My father's behaviour undermined the basis of our familial relationships. As Sheinberg and Fraenkel argue (2001, ix),

> Abused children and other non-offending family members often feel torn between love and hate, self-blame versus blame of the offending member, the wish to restore family unity versus the need to prevent further abuse, and the desire to go on as if nothing happened versus the need to face the awful truth.

My mother met this confusion in her desire "to do as if nothing had happened," her frequent mantra, which is reflected in her writing. It seems it was the only way she could go on being.

Not long before my mother wrote her memoir I had sent her a piece of my writing, which I called "Night Terrors." I wanted her to know what it was like to share a room with my older sister during my father's visits at night. My mother read my story and then hid it in a drawer. She did not want her second husband to read it, she told me. Later, when we talked, my mother told me how she found herself walking past that set of drawers and thinking about my story nestled there. "It makes me feel terrible. I want to avoid it," she said, and then told me how it had made her sad to read what I wrote and that she had tried to put a stop to my father's night-time visits to my sister all those years ago. She told me she had not realised until it was too late that despite telling my father she would kill him if he did not stop visiting my sister in this way, he did not stop until my sister was sixteen years old.

Writing to understand the compost of our past

Barbara Turner Vesselago (2017, 13) argues that in writing about our lives it is helpful to go back to experiences that have happened at least ten years ago or earlier. This gives our perceptions time to percolate and to help us "gain distance" from our material. Such writing tends to have a beginning, middle, and end. When we write about events that are still occurring it is harder to construct a natural story arc. We are caught in the middle of proceedings and it is more difficult to make sense of the issues.

It may be that given her tendency toward denial, my mother was not able to reflect in this way. However, even in my childhood I felt an intense need to understand things of which I only grasped snippets. Then in later years I learned that my father's childhood was also riddled with trauma. His father, my *Opa*, was imprisoned in Holland in 1942 on charges of *Ontucht,* which is Dutch for incestuous or licentious behaviour. My *Opa*'s then nineteen-year-old daughter, my aunt, brought these charges. I came to know this only in adulthood. My mother knew about it at the time she married my father, but she makes no mention of it in her memoir.

Our stories are not only about us, our stories become us, and they therefore change over time. This is most apparent as we grow old and slow down and have so much lived time behind us that we cannot hope to encapsulate it all in our writing. Instead, we must dig deep and sense patterns of meaning in our writing to help us understand and share our notions of the person we once were and the person we have become. As Eakin (2008, 2) argues,

> Talking [and writing] about ourselves involves a lot more than self-indulgence; when we do it, we perform a work of self-construction [...] There is a mutually enhancing interplay between what we are and what we say we are [...] [and] an extremely close and dynamic relation between narrative and identity, for narrative is not only a literary form but part of the fabric of our lived experience, [...] not merely about self but a constituent part of self.

In my writing, I am compelled to revisit my childhood in detail, turning my memories over and over, in a bid to help me to deal with the difficulties of my past, in conjunction with several years in therapy and psychoanalysis. In contrast, beyond her writing, my mother's resort to help came in the form of her religious connections and through her time at Al Anon, an organisation set up to help the families of alcoholics. Through Al Anon, my mother found "serenity," a state of mind that fostered distancing herself from painful events. This state of mind was one against which I rebelled, which I even came to despise. It is a state of mind reflected in my mother's writing.

Instead of finding serenity, I wanted to immerse myself in my life experiences, not simply in my mind but on the page. On the page, my childhood experiences could come to life, and in writing about them there was an opportunity for me to share the pain with my readers. This is a feature of life writing, one David Parker (2002, 493) refers to as "countertransference," the tendency of readers to resonate with writing, based on their own experiences in life, as they fire off what they read. As Nancy K

Miller (2000, 76) argues, "We read for what we need to find." For the writer, this wish to record one's life, and in so doing see patterns and make sense of past events, is also a feature of ageing. I, too, want to refashion my sense of myself against the relentless crush of the years. I want to do so in a different way from my mother, perhaps, but nevertheless this pull to create order out of the disorder of my life is compelling.

Ageing and life writing

As Joyce Carol Oates (2003, 64) writes, there is "a very literal advantage, now and then, to failure—a way of turning even the most melancholy of experiences inside out, until they resemble experiences of value, of growth, of profound significance." Ageing can lead us into a state, as Oates suggests, of not simply suffering but of being able "to negotiate with suffering, to choose or invent forms to accommodate it." Life writing provides one such means of "negotiation."

In her exploration of the genesis of art, Oates (2003, 39–41) lists four points of origin: art evolves in the play of childhood; in the later "rebellion [...] of youthful revolt" with its need to break away from the past and redefine oneself; in contrast to and as well as the "memorialisation of the past"; and finally, in later years, out of "a desire for redemption." According to Oates, "A sense of one's incompleteness or inadequacy fuels the instinct for ceaseless invention, as in an extension of the very self's perimeters" (Oates 2003, 67).

So, too, in life writing, there is an urge within the writer to play around with ideas, to revisit, remember and to redefine the past, to recreate oneself in aesthetic terms and thereby gain ascendancy on the page. There is an urge to make yourself the hero of your story. However, when children read their parent's story they are often troubled by the degree to which they feature very little, or if they feature in detail this can give a sense of being taken over. It is one thing to write about our parents' lives and our experience of them and another thing altogether to have a parent write about you.

Throughout my childhood, my mother, despite her efforts at optimism, seemed unhappy and filled with longing. Her longing infiltrated my sense of my place in the world as one of inferiority because I sensed my mother did not want to be with me and my sisters and brothers here in Australia. My mother wanted to be back home in Holland where life had been happier. Her migrant lament may be read in the below excerpt:

> Every Saturday morning the parish priest, Father Ashe, would visit the Hickling house to bring Holy Communion to Josie's sick mother who lived with her. And every Saturday morning I would get up early to make sure that our little cabin was clean and tidy and then I stood at the door waiting for him to come over and say hello but he never did and I felt terrible because I realised that in Australia I was a nobody while back home I was a member of a respected family. (Bury 1995, 79)

My mother's words reflect her experience as a newcomer to a strange country. Although by then an adult, my mother's sadness in her isolation at this time reflects a view, as Carolyn Steedman (1986, 6) writes in her *Landscape for a Good Woman*, that every child experiences a first loss, which then repeats itself again and again. "Lives shape themselves around this sense of being cut off and denied" (Steedman 1986, 6). Likewise, when I first read my mother's book I flicked through the pages to the time when I was born. My mother devotes a short paragraph to the event: "On top of that we had a new baby! Elisabeth was born on the 5th of November, 1952 in a small private hospital in Greensborough. I was much happier there than in the Queen Vic 18 months earlier" (Bury 1995, 81).

I had hoped my mother might write more about my birth, but characteristically she glosses over the birth of each one of her children, like so many visits to the shops. The only birth that rates is that of her last child, a daughter who was stillborn when my mother was forty-three years old. In Steedman's view, "children are always episodes in someone else's narrative" (1986, 88). With eleven pregnancies behind her, my mother can scarcely be expected to remember the details of each one. But still it stings to feel my birth could seem so inconsequential within my mother's narrative. My mother ends her memoir with a reflection on her bright future ahead travelling with her second husband, little knowing he would be dead in five years, and leaving "the future in God's hands" (Bury 1995, 128).

When I was young, like my mother before me, I imagined there was no need to keep up appearances beyond a certain age. Marriage and parenthood would signal the end of any need to keep on looking respectable. But it did not happen that way. I had my mother as a model. When she was not at work, she sat around for the best part of the day reading the newspaper and then at five o'clock smeared a streak of red across her lips before my father came home. It was the same when she went down the street for shopping. A smear of lipstick and a quick brushing of her hair. It seemed to me then, and it seems to me now, futile, this turning herself back into the apparent beauty of her younger self. Even into her nineties, my mother cared about her appearance. And people reinforced this in their constant praise for the youthful quality of her skin. Whenever someone asked my mother's age, she repeated it with pride. This occurred more so once she had passed the eighty-year mark, and people told her she looked much younger. She refused to wear glasses because they made her look older. For her ninetieth birthday, my mother insisted on buying a dress with three quarter length sleeves because she wanted to hide her baggy upper arms.

As a schoolgirl, I remember thinking that when I reached sixty I'd like to die. To live to sixty would be good enough. By then I would be past the best of my life and ready to go. I imagined myself frail and tired. Now that I have reached beyond this age and find I am not so weary, I am far from ready to die. My memoir reflects this determination to immerse myself in life, as well as to find a readership able to resonate to my story but also to make up their own minds about it. This form of writing requires an engaged and questioning readership, whereas my mother's memoir passes judgement on her experience, leaving readers less able to judge for themselves. This could well reflect the changing nature of narrative over time.

My mother wrote her memoir, she told me, to leave a legacy for her family, and though much as it caused ructions among her siblings, who reckoned she had so much of it wrong, still it provided solace to her at the end of her days. Writing as a maturing woman, here was an account of her life that suited my mother's sense of herself as a younger woman. She did not write directly about the ravages of old age, which she kept to herself. Nor could she write about her last three weeks alive. During this time, she was caught up in a hospital bed following an acute bout of pancreatitis that the doctors managed to control, but not before my mother began to refuse to eat, and gradually each of her organs failed.

Writing to show what is otherwise invisible, or seeking to hide it from view

My father stitched our mother's dresses from material they chose together at the fabric shop. He fashioned the bright floral patterns into tight waisted and low-cut frocks my mother wore most days in the summer. Perhaps the fact that my father had fashioned those dresses gave him licence to rip them off her in moments of rage. My mother, who was like a servant in the kitchen preparing the family meal, became a woman undressed, her face flushed, her eyes ablaze with fear as she grabbed at the scraps of fabric left hanging around her hips while my father glowered with indignation.

My mother wrote none of this in her memoir. But in mine, I pore over the visible and invisible. My father collected art books, which I pored through as a ten-year-old and there too I observed the same phenomena, the naked women sometimes with snippets of material draped around their shoulders or between their legs, exposed for all to see but behind their eyes, no one there. And I observed the men in robes, the fancy clothes of medieval times, dressed up like peacocks admiring the object of their desires. Is this what it means to be invisible, to be an object? I learned early to hide my body behind clothes while at the same time displaying myself as an object of desire once puberty hit and I discovered, like my mother before me, I had these things called breasts that were of me and not of me. They belonged to me but were also a source of desire for the other.

When my father visited my sister in bed at night even before she had reached the age of breasts and child bearing hips, even before she wore bras and stockings held up with suspender belts, I knew to keep myself invisible, to hide from him, to hide from men, or at least to hide my inside self from men. I could perform like the women I saw in the movies, the women on the billboards, my mother with her visitors. I could wear clothes that hugged my body once I had lost weight in an avalanche of starvation after I hit my late teens, but it was only the objective me, the displayed body open to view. In my writing, I can overcome the shame of this, by exposing it.

The rest I hid inside. I still hide her, and now it goes the other way. A woman over fifty ceases to be visible. Helen Garner sees it as a freeing time, no longer sexually available, no longer on the sexual market and therefore no longer needing to set ourselves the goal of external beauty for the camera. But a different kind of anxiety arises when you fear your image as an older woman marks you as one not to be taken seriously, as one to be ignored. Of course there's a flip side: "When I grow old I shall wear purple" (Joseph 1992). I shall say what I want, do as I please, without breaking the law, without revealing too much of the person inside who still fears visibility. It is a joy to hide, Donald Winnicott writes when describing the game of peek-a-boo as played by babies, of disappearing and then reappearing, but a tragedy never to be found (1971, 1–17). Life writing gives us an opportunity to get hold of these internal observations and turn them into something else, into some outer description of an inner state that might also look different for the reader. Life writing provides a way of getting hold of and almost defying death and ageing.

My mother cannot question my experiences now. Not from her grave. Yet I can challenge her writing, through my own. Still, with every passing year, I see my world differently. My adolescent self-saw the world in a particular way that was different from the way my child self, and now adult self, view the world. My mother's words and mine form a contrast in sensibilities. They are worlds apart. Yet both are attempts at dealing with our mortality. Still it remains difficult to write about my own life when I have the model of my mother who writes before me. It is difficult to represent myself not simply in a bid to contradict or confirm my mother's version but also to see my life through my own eyes. Despite the struggle, I keep on trying.

Disclosure statement

No potential conflict of interest was reported by the author.

References

Ash, Timothy Garton. 2002. "Truth is Another Country." *The Guardian*. November 16, 4–6.
Bury, Elisabeth. 1995. *My Story 1919–1995: From the Netherlands to Australia*. Melbourne: Self-published.
Draaisma, Douwe. 2004. *Why Life Speeds up as You Get Older: How Memory Shapes Our Past*. Cambridge: Cambridge University Press.
Eakin, Paul J. 1999. *How Our Lives Become Stories: Making Selves*. New York: Cornell University Press.
Eakin, Paul J. 2008. *Living Autobiographically: How We Create Identity in Narrative*. New York: Cornell University Press.
Hanscombe, Elisabeth. 2017. *The Art of Disappearing*. Brisbane: Interactive Publications.
Joseph, Jenny. 1992. *Selected Poems*. London: Bloodaxe Books.
Miller, Nancy K. 2000. *Bequest and Betrayal: Memoirs of a Parent's Death*. Bloomington: Indiana University Press.
Oates, Joyce Carol. 2003. *The Faith of a Writer: Life, Craft, Art*. New York: Harper Collins.
Parker, David. 2002. "Countertransference: The Case of Kathryn Harrison's *The Kiss*." *Biography* 25 (3): 493–504.
Sheinberg, Marcia, and Peter Fraenkel. 2001. *The Relational Trauma of Incest: A Family Based Approach to Treatment*. New York: Guilford Press.
Steedman, Carolyn Kay. 1986. *Landscape for a Good Woman*. London: Virago.
Tuner Vesselago, Barbara. 2017. *Freefall into Fiction Finding Form*. London: Jessica Kingsley.
Winnicott, Donald W. 1971. *Playing and Reality*. London: Tavistock/Routledge.

Index

Note: Page numbers followed by 'n' refer to end notes.

For Product Safety Concerns and Information please contact our EU representative GPSR@taylorandfrancis.com
Taylor & Francis Verlag GmbH, Kaufingerstraße 24, 80331 München, Germany

www.ingramcontent.com/pod-product-compliance
Lightning Source LLC
Chambersburg PA
CBHW081357090726
47908CB00011B/2710

* 9 7 8 0 3 6 7 5 6 2 1 7 5 *